The Biblical Basis
for Tradition

Why Catholics Don't Rely
On Scripture Alone

John Salza

THE BIBLICAL BASIS FOR TRADITION

Library of Congress Cataloging-in-Publication Data
Salza, John
The Biblical Basis for Tradition:
Why Catholics Don't Rely on Tradition Alone

ISBN: 978-0-615-41794-3 (paperback)

PRINTED AND PUBLISHED
IN THE UNITED STATES OF AMERICA

First Edition
First Printing

ACLA Press
P.O. Box 10092
Fairfield, NJ 07004

Unless stated otherwise, Scripture citations used in this work are from the *Second Catholic Edition of the Revised Standard Version of the Bible* (*RSV-CE*) © 1965, 1966, 2006 by the Division of Christian Education of the National Council of the Churches of Christ in the United States of America. Other Scripture citations are from the Douay-Rheims version of the Bible.

Cover Design: Tom Brannon

To Peter and Georgiana Salza

With blessings and gratitude

Love, your son

Remember that through your parents you were born;
and what can you give back to them that equals
their gift to you? (Sirach 7:28)

Table of Contents

III.
The Bible and the Church Fathers

Preface

Protestant Christianity is based upon the erroneous assumption that the Bible – as interpreted by the individual believer - is the sole, infallible rule of faith for Christians. This belief is called *sola Scriptura* which is Latin for "Scripture alone." The doctrine consequently holds that the oral teaching the apostles passed on to their successors, which Catholics call "Tradition," must be rejected as an authority. Because the Bible is their only rule of faith, Protestants also reject the divine authority of the 2,000 year-old Catholic Church.

If *sola Scriptura* were true, then we would expect it to be taught in Scripture. We would not only expect to find *sola Scriptura* in Scripture, but we would also expect to see the doctrine permeate the life of the early Church. We would expect to see it reflected in the Church's ancient liturgies. We would expect to see the early Church councils define its meaning and parameters. We would expect to see it in the writings of the early Church Fathers. We would expect to see it in the Church's creeds and catechisms. But we see nothing of the sort.

To the surprise of most Protestants, *sola Scriptura* was never heard of for the first 1500 years of Christianity. The doctrine was invented in the 16th century by Martin Luther, a Catholic priest, as he separated himself from the Catholic Church and ignited the so-called Protestant "Reformation." Before

Luther came along, Christians always believed the
Word of God has come to us both in written (Scripture)
and oral (Tradition) form, as authentically interpreted
by the teaching office (Magisterium)[1] of the Catholic
Church. Unlike their *sola Scriptura* counterparts,
Catholics believe in *sola verbum Dei* (the "Word of God"
alone).

Incredibly, Luther's revolt gained momentum and
has given birth to the truly scandalous divisions we see
in Christianity today. There are more than 30,000
different Protestant denominations all clinging to the
false and unworkable doctrine of *sola Scriptura* first
espoused by Luther less than five centuries years ago.[2]
These denominations not only disagree with Catholics
on major points of Christian doctrine, they also
disagree with each other. And they have no way to
resolve their disputes outside of Scripture because the
Bible is their only authority.

By eliminating the authority of Tradition and the
Church, Protestants have jettisoned their Christian
patrimony in favor of private judgment. They have
elevated their human intellects over the divine mind of
the Church. Ironically, as we will examine in detail, the
very Bible Protestants claim as their only authority *does
not teach sola Scriptura*. Instead, the Bible teaches that
we are to follow *both the written and oral Traditions* that
have come to us from the apostles (2 Thess 2:15).

---

[1] The word Magisterium describes the Church's divine teaching
office and comes from the Latin word *magistra* which means
"teacher."
[2] While Protestant apologists accuse Catholics of fabricating this
number, the evidence can be found in many *non-Catholic* scholarly
sources. For example, *The World Christian Encyclopedia* (Oxford
University Press 2001 edition), authored by David B. Barrett,
George T. Kurian and Todd M. Johnson, lists 33,820 Protestant
denominations.

When broaching the subject of extra-biblical Tradition, Catholics risk giving Protestants the impression that they have a diminished view of Scripture. Nothing could be further from the truth. In fact, I do not hesitate to say that Catholics have the most exalted view of Scripture of any Christian community. Why? Because of what the Catholic Church teaches about Scripture. The Church teaches that the Holy Spirit dictated the very books of Scripture to the authors of the Bible, all the while cooperating with their knowledge and intellectual abilities. This teaching has been reiterated by the popes throughout the ages.[3] This means that God is the *primary author* of Scripture, which makes the Scriptures inerrant and infallible on all that they teach (whether it's theology, history, geography, mathematics, science, etc).

Unfortunately, many Protestant denominations do not share the same esteemed view of Scripture held by Catholics. In fact, it was Protestant Bible scholars who first introduced the heresy that Scripture contains errors. This heretical view stemmed from a methodology that Protestant exegetes developed to interpret the Scriptures called "historical criticism."

Historical criticism seeks to uncover the deeper meanings of Scripture through a critical examination of history. Its techniques also include source, form, redaction and textual criticism, all intended to get the "real story" of Scripture. While historical critical techniques can be beneficial in understanding the sacred text and are also used by Catholic exegetes, they

---

[3] See, for example, Second Vatican Council, Dogmatic Constitution, *Dei Verbum*, No. 11; Pius XII, *Divino Afflante Spiritu* (1943); Benedict XV, *Spiritus Paraclitus* (1920); Pius X, *Lamentabili Sane* (1907); Leo XIII, *Providentissimus Deus* (1893); and Pius IX, *Syllabus of Errors* (1864).

can never be used to support interpretations that are contrary to the Tradition of the Church.[4]

Of course, it is impossible for Scripture to contain errors because God is the primary author of Scripture and God cannot lie.[5] Christ entrusted His revelation to the Church precisely to safeguard the integrity of the gospel against such novelties and attacks. Far from denigrating Scripture, this book, and any Catholic discussion of Tradition, seeks to exalt Scripture to its proper place in the economy of God's plan of salvation. As Catholics, we want to make sure that Scripture is interpreted the way in which God intended it to be interpreted – *in the light of the totality of His revelation*. In so doing, we emphasize that Christianity is not a religion of the book. It is a religion of the Word of God as revealed through Scripture and Tradition and interpreted by the Catholic Church.

Because God is the author of Sacred Scripture and cannot lie, Catholics have for 2,000 years taken His words at face value. For example, when Jesus said that we must be born of "water and the Spirit" to go to heaven, Catholics interpret Jesus' words literally to refer to the sacrament of Baptism (Jn 3:5). When Jesus said that the bread that He will give is His flesh for the life of the world, Catholics interpret His words literally to refer to the sacrament of the Eucharist (Jn 6:51).

When Jesus told His apostles "whose sins they forgive are forgiven," Catholics interpret His words literally to refer to the sacrament of Penance (Jn 20:23). When Jesus said that divorce and remarriage

---

[4] In his encyclical *Divino Afflante Spiritu* (1943), Pope Pius XII allowed Catholic scholars to use historical criticism in their study of Scripture, while upholding the Church's long-standing doctrine of biblical inerrancy.
[5] Heb 6:18; Tit 1:2.

constitutes the grave sin of adultery, Catholics condemn divorce and remarriage (Mt 19:9). Protestants, on the other hand, have many varied and diverse interpretations of these passages, all the while claiming that the Bible is their only authority.

Sacred Scripture also pervades Catholic worship. The prayers of the Holy Mass, which the Church has celebrated since the Last Supper, come almost exclusively from Sacred Scripture. These include readings from the Old and New Testaments, including the Psalms and Canticles. The daily prayers of the Church, called the Liturgy of the Hours or Divine Office, are also taken from Scripture. The prayers are recited in the morning, noon, evening and at night according to the Church's liturgical cycle. The Holy Rosary, which is the most popular Catholic devotion outside of praying the Mass, is also taken from the Word of God as recorded in Scripture. Faithful Catholics, who worship with the Church throughout the day, eat, sleep and breathe Scripture.

Don't get me wrong. I am not saying that Protestants don't claim to love Scripture and don't want to be faithful to its teachings. Quite the contrary, sincere Protestants want nothing more than to be obedient to Jesus Christ and His commandments as recorded in Scripture. Lukewarm Catholics can learn a lesson or two from their devotion to Holy Writ. But this is not a question of who is more devoted to Scripture or who loves Jesus more. It is a question of truth and error.

If *sola Scriptura* is a false doctrine, then it is leading many souls to ruin. Take, for example, Jesus' words in John 6. Catholics interpret Jesus' words literally and Protestants interpret them metaphorically. If the Catholic interpretation is correct, then Protestants, who don't believe in the Real Presence of Christ in the

Eucharist, "have no life" in them and are risking damnation (Jn 6:53). If the Protestant interpretation is correct, then Catholics are committing idolatry by worshiping a piece of bread and are risking damnation. There is no middle ground.

Since all theological errors stem from this question of authority and such errors have eternal consequences, the stakes have never been higher. Either *sola Scriptura* must be denounced as the grave theological error that it is and Protestants must become Catholics, or the thousands of competing factions of Protestantism triggered in the 16th century by Martin Luther is the unity that Christ desired when He prayed "that they may be perfectly one" (Jn 17:23). It is one or the other.

All of the disagreements between Catholics and Protestants – whether about the pope, the sacraments, Mary, or purgatory – stem from this single issue of authority. Is the Word of God found in Scripture alone? Or is it also found in the Apostolic Tradition as authentically interpreted by the Church? Indeed, this issue of authority is the principal reason why Protestants convert to the Catholic and Apostolic faith. Using Scripture and the early Church Fathers, this book reveals the monumental errors of *sola Scriptura* and sets forth the biblical basis for the Catholic Church's 2,000 year-old understanding of Tradition. The book also responds to the most frequent Protestant rebuttals of Catholic teaching based upon my experience in apologetics over the last ten years.

I hope this book helps Christians see that God has given us His Word, not through the written words of the apostles and evangelists only, but also through their oral teaching and example which they have entrusted to the Church under the guidance of the Holy Spirit. Both Scripture and Tradition must be accepted and honored by all Christians with equal reverence and devotion. By discovering the rich Tradition we have received from the apostles, I pray that Protestants will see, for the first time, Scripture *in the light of Tradition*. In so doing, they will, like the first century Christians, devote themselves "to the apostles' teaching and fellowship, to the breaking of bread and the prayers" (Acts 2:42).

> "But beyond these sayings, let us look at the very tradition, teaching and faith of the Catholic Church from the beginning, which was preached by the apostles and preserved by the Fathers. On this the Church was founded; and if anyone departs from this, he neither is nor any longer ought to be called a Christian." *Athanasius, Ad Serapion 1:28, A.D. 360.*

John Salza, J.D.
Saints Peter and Paul, Apostles
29 June, *Anno Domini* 2010

I.

The Bible and Tradition

Chapter 1

An Introduction to Tradition

The word "Tradition" comes from the Latin *tradere* which means "to hand on." Before Jesus ascended into heaven, He commanded His apostles to hand on the gospel by preaching it to all nations (Mt 28:19). The apostles obeyed Jesus' command by handing on His saving gospel *both orally and in writing*. Five of the apostles committed some of Christ's teaching to writing under the inspiration of the Holy Spirit.[6] All of the apostles handed on Christ's teaching by their preaching and example, either by what they heard or seen from Christ or by the prompting of the Holy Spirit.

The written transmission of the gospel is called Sacred Scripture. The oral transmission of the gospel which the apostles "handed on" to their successors is called Sacred Tradition. Together, Scripture and Tradition transmit the totality of the Word of God that Christ revealed to His apostles. They are the two lungs in the living body of Christ. This totality of God's revelation in Christ is often called the "Deposit of Faith" (Latin, *depositum fidei*).

---

[6] The five apostles who wrote Scripture are Peter, Matthew, John, James and Jude.

When we refer to Tradition (upper-case "T"), we are referring to divine revelation (e.g., the Blessed Trinity; the Divinity of Christ). This is to be distinguished from tradition (lower-case "t") which refers to practices developed by the Church which are not part of the Deposit of Faith (e.g., feast days; some liturgical rubrics).[7]

Even though lower-case "t" traditions are theoretically changeable because they are not part of divine revelation,[8] the Church doesn't change them haphazardly. Non-revelatory traditions develop over time under the guidance of the Holy Spirit and can evolve into what the Church calls "immemorial customs." The Church's canon law protects immemorial customs by giving them the force of law and preventing their abrogation without an explicit papal or Magisterial declaration.[9]

---

[7] While not the subject of this book, we note that the Church also has "ecclesiastical traditions" which refer to the manner in which the Deposit of Faith is taught, learned, expressed and lived in the Church. These traditions include venerating holy images, praying novenas, and certain elements of the Holy Mass (the priest facing the East to offer the sacrifice, the Roman canon, the use of Latin, communicants kneeling to receive Communion on the tongue, etc). The Second Council of Nicea (787) teaches that the Church's ecclesiastical tradition "comes from the Holy Spirit who dwells in her" and condemns anyone who would "deride the ecclesiastical traditions."

[8] There are some exceptions to this statement. For example, the Council of Trent teaches that the Roman canon of the Traditional Latin Mass "consists both of the words of God, and of the traditions of the apostles, and also of pious instructions of the holy Pontiffs." Session XXII, chapter 4 (1562).

[9] See canons 23-28, *Codex Iuris Canonici* (1983 Code of Canon Law). While the pope may have the legal authority to overturn immemorial customs, he would not have the moral authority to do so, since the positive law must be at the service of the Divine Law (which is why popes do not repeal immemorial customs).

Tradition and apostolic succession

While this book is about Tradition and not the Church per se, it is impossible to speak of one without the other. That is because we have received the Deposit of Faith (Scripture and Tradition) from St. Peter and the apostles *through the Catholic Church*. Just as the Catholic Church identified what writings are authentic Scripture, she also identifies what teachings are authentic Tradition. The apostolic Tradition has been preserved by the Church primarily in the writings of the early Church Fathers, the Church councils and the Church's liturgies.

Because Tradition is the orally inspired Word of God that the apostles handed on to their successors, the Church, in a sense, existed before Tradition. The apostles, who were the first members of the Church, had to appoint successors to "hand on" what they received from Christ. They did this by ordaining new bishops through the "laying on of hands," and entrusting them with the teachings of Jesus.[10] These new bishops ordained the next generation of bishops, and so forth and so on, throughout the Church age to the present day. This process is called "apostolic succession." Apostolic succession is the vehicle by which the Church preserves and transmits the Tradition from one generation to the next.

We see examples of apostolic succession in the accounts of the early Church. For example, in the Acts of the Apostles, we read:

---

[10] The ordination of men to the priesthood is called Holy Orders and is one of the seven sacraments instituted by Jesus Christ. The other six are Baptism, Confession, the Eucharist, Holy Matrimony and Anointing of the Sick (Extreme Unction).

- And what they said pleased the whole multitude, and they chose Stephen, a man full of faith and of the Holy Spirit, and Philip, and Prochorus, and Nicanor, and Timon, and Parmenas, and Nicolaus, a proselyte of Antioch. These they set before the apostles, and they prayed and *laid their hands upon them* (Acts 6:5-6).
- While they were worshiping the Lord and fasting, the Holy Spirit said, 'Set apart for me Barnabas and Saul for the work to which I have called them.' Then after fasting and praying they *laid their hands on them* and sent them off (Acts 13:2-3).
- And when they *had ordained to them priests* in every church, and had prayed with fasting, they commended them to the Lord, in whom they believed.[11]

St. Paul makes a clear connection between Tradition and apostolic succession in his letters to Timothy. Paul ordained Timothy as bishop of Ephesus around A.D. 65 and reminds him how he gained his apostolic office: "Hence I remind you to rekindle the gift of God that is within you through *the laying on of my hands*" (2 Tim 1:6).[12] Because Timothy is a successor to the apostles, Paul is able to charge him to guard the Tradition he received and to transmit it to future successors.

For example, in his first letter to Timothy, Paul writes, "O Timothy, *guard* what has been *entrusted* to

---

[11] Acts 14:22 (DR). The New Covenant process of investing a successor with apostolic authority follows the way in which Moses' leaders succeeded to their priestly offices in the Old Covenant. See, for example, Num 27:18,20,22-23; Dt 34:9.

[12] See also 1 Tim 4:14. Paul also warns Timothy: "Do not be hasty in the laying on of hands" (1 Tim 5:22).

you" (1 Tim 6:20). The Greek word for "entrusted" (*paratheke*) may also be translated as "deposit." Thus, Paul is telling Timothy to guard the Deposit of Faith which he has *already* received from Paul. Because this was Paul's *first* letter to Timothy, Timothy had not yet been "entrusted" with Scripture (as Paul had not written anything to him), but had been "entrusted" with the Tradition.

St. Paul is referring to the *oral Tradition* with which he had entrusted Timothy. According to Paul, this oral Tradition is guardable because it is objective, knowable revelation from God. If Timothy didn't know exactly what he received from Paul, he surely couldn't guard it. Nor would Paul exhort him to do the same. As the prophet Malachi revealed, "For the lips of a priest should *guard* knowledge, and men should seek instruction *from his mouth*, for he is the messenger of the LORD of hosts" (Mal 2:7).

In his second letter to Timothy, Paul similarly writes, "Follow the pattern of the sound words which you have *heard* from me, in the faith and love which are in Christ Jesus; *guard* the truth that has been *entrusted* (*paratheke*) to you by the Holy Spirit who dwells within us" (2 Tim 1:13-14). Again, Paul commands Timothy to guard the oral revelation he "heard" from Paul and not the written revelation only. Further, Paul calls this oral revelation "the truth."

Because this is Paul's second and final letter to Timothy means that Paul's written revelations do *not* override his previously entrusted oral revelations. Both contain divine truth and Paul commands Timothy to guard both of them. Because of the grace of his apostolic office, Timothy will be able to preserve and protect the oral Tradition by the power of the Holy Spirit. Of course, if the entirety of Paul's oral teaching would be eventually committed to Scripture, Paul's directive to Timothy to guard it would be superfluous and unnecessary.

Similarly, Paul tells Timothy, "Do your best to present yourself to God as one approved, a workman who has no need to be ashamed, rightly handling the *word of truth*" (2 Tim 2:15). The phrase "word of truth" refers to the *oral* revelation with which Paul has entrusted Timothy. Paul uses this same phrase in Ephesians 1:13 ("who have *heard* the word of truth") and Colossians 1:5 ("you have *heard* before in the word of truth") in regard to the oral apostolic Tradition. Because Timothy has the Tradition, Paul can command him to "remain at Ephesus that you may charge certain persons not to teach any different doctrine" (1 Tim 1:3).

Paul further instructs Timothy, "what you have *heard* from me before many witnesses entrust to faithful men who will be able to teach others also" (2 Tim 2:2). Not only is Timothy to guard the oral Tradition, he is to *hand it on to successors as well*. In this way, Timothy will "rightly handle" the Word of Truth (2 Tim 2:15). Thus, Paul views the oral Tradition as something capable of being preserved and transmitted beyond the first generation of the apostles. Peter does too, for he says that the "preached" oral apostolic Word "abides forever" (1 Pet 1:25).

The oral Tradition is safely guarded and faithfully handed on to apostolic successors because of the protection of the Holy Ghost "who dwells within us" (2 Tim 1:14). Jesus first sent the apostles the Holy Spirit on Pentecost Sunday and it is this same Spirit who calls men to succeed the apostles as bishops of the Church.[13] Through apostolic succession, the Deposit of Faith is passed on perpetually throughout the post-apostolic

---

[13] Acts 20:28; 2 Cor 1:22-23; 10:8.

age for the salvation of souls. If God intended to crystallize all oral Tradition into Scripture as many Protestants contend, it would be nonsensical for Him to command it to be guarded and passed on to future generations – especially through the very Scriptures that supposedly contain the Tradition!

St. Paul reveals his understanding of apostolic succession by referring to his position in the Church as an "office." St. Paul says, "I became a minister according to the divine *office* which was given to me for you" (Col 1:25). The word for "office" in Greek is *episkopee* which refers to the ecclesiastical office of bishop which has successors. Paul uses the same word to describe the office that Timothy holds (1 Tim 3:1). It is through the office of bishop that Tradition is "guarded" and "transmitted" to future generations.[14]

In addition to Timothy, Scripture reveals that Paul also ordained Titus as a bishop (of Crete). As with Timothy, Paul entrusted Titus with the apostolic Tradition and commanded him to appoint others in his diocese to receive and transmit it: "This is why I left you in Crete, that you might amend what was defective, and appoint elders in every town as I directed you" (Titus 1:5). After Paul writes about his commission of Titus, he describes the role of a bishop as one who "must hold firm to the sure word as taught, so that he may be able to give instruction in sound doctrine and also to confute those who contradict it" (v.9).

This "sure word" is the oral Tradition of the apostles, which is a divine body of knowledge that

---

[14] The New Testament Scriptures clearly show the hierarchical structure of the Church: there is a pope (Mt 16:18-19); bishops (Acts 20:28; Phil 1:1; Tit 1:7); priests (Acts 20:17; Tit 1:5; 1 Tim 5:17; Jas 5:14); and, deacons (Phil 1:1; 1 Tim 3:8).

forms truthful doctrine and confutes error. Thus, Paul commands Titus to "Declare these things; exhort and reprove with all authority. Let no one disregard you" (Titus 2:15). "These things" are both the oral and written revelations that Paul has transmitted to Titus. There is nothing in these directives about obeying Scripture alone.

Of course, if anyone could lay hands on anyone else, apostolic succession would be meaningless. If anyone could become a bishop without the proper ecclesiastical protocols, false teachers could easily infiltrate the Church, corrupt her Tradition, and destroy the Faith. St. Paul tells the bishops of the early Church, "Take heed to yourselves and to all the flock, in which the Holy Spirit has made you overseers (Greek, *episkopos*), to care for the church of God which he obtained with the blood of his own Son" (Acts 20:28). Then, in the next verse, St. Paul warns, "I know that after my departure fierce wolves will come in among you, not sparing the flock" (v.29). Similarly, after Paul commands Titus to "hold firm to the sure word as taught," he says that "there are many insubordinate men, empty talkers and deceivers…they must be silenced" (Titus 1:10-11).

To ensure the integrity of apostolic succession and the doctrinal purity of Tradition, Jesus promised that the Holy Spirit would be with the Church and guide her into all truth. Jesus said, "When the Spirit of truth comes, he will guide you into all the truth; for he will not speak on his own authority, but whatever he hears he will speak, and he will declare to you the things that are to come."[15] Because the Holy Ghost would lead the Church into understanding His revelation, Jesus said, "He who hears you, hears me" (Lk 10:16). Jesus also

---

[15] Jn 16:13; see also Jn 14:16-18.

told His apostles, "I am with you always, to the close of the age" (Mt 28:20). Because the apostles would eventually die, Jesus' promise to be present "to the close of the age" was for His apostles *and their successors.*

The papacy and apostolic succession

To guarantee the protection of His Church, Jesus established a supreme teaching office called the "papacy" for the apostle Peter and his successors.[16] After Simon Peter confessed Jesus' identity as Messiah and Son of God, Jesus identified Peter as the leader of the Church and changed his name to "rock": "you are Peter (Greek, *Petros* for "rock"), and on this rock I will build my church, and the powers of death shall not prevail against it" (Mt 16:18).

Further, to invest Peter with the authority to interpret Tradition and Scripture, as well as implement a plan for succession to his office, Jesus gave Peter "the keys to the kingdom of heaven" and told him, "whatever you bind on earth shall be bound in heaven, and whatever you loose on earth shall be loosed in heaven" (v.19).[17] Jesus also prayed specifically for Peter that his faith would not fail (Lk 22:32) and ordered Peter to strengthen the other apostles (v.32). Further, Jesus appointed Peter as the chief shepherd of the Church when He told him, "Feed my lambs...Tend my sheep...Feed my sheep" (Jn 21:15-17).

The authority that Christ gave St. Peter over the Church is truly incredible. As the rock and shepherd of

---

[16] The word "papacy" and its related word "pope" come from the Italian word "papa" which means "father." The "pope" is the spiritual father of the members of the Church.
[17] For a detailed treatment of the papacy, please see my book *The Biblical Basis for the Papacy* (Our Sunday Visitor).

the Church, Jesus would grant Peter the gift of infallibility through his "binding and loosing" authority. This means Peter would be safeguarded by the Holy Ghost from teaching error when proclaiming the gospel. Thus, whenever Peter intended to "bind" the Church to his teaching, Peter would be protected from error.[18] Because Jesus promised that heaven will confirm Peter's decisions, Peter's teachings *must be true*, for God cannot confirm error. The 2,000 year-old continuity in the Catholic Church's doctrine amidst a changing and divided world demonstrates that Jesus has kept His promise.

Although the Church's claim of infallibility is supported by strong biblical, patristic and historical evidence, Bible-only Protestants must resist it. But their resistance is without merit. If they can accept the infallible Scriptures, they can also accept an infallible Church. It takes no greater leap of faith to do so. Through God's power, just as sinful men can teach infallibly through the written Word (Scripture), sinful men can also teach infallibly through the oral Word (Tradition) as well.

Protestants often accuse Catholics of making a "fallible" choice to follow the "infallible" Church, as if that fact somehow undermines the Church's infallibility. It doesn't. The Protestant also makes a fallible choice to follow Christ, and that doesn't undermine Jesus' infallibility! Personal fallibility has

---

[18] The Holy Ghost protects the pope from error when the pope manifestly invokes his intention to promulgate an infallible teaching. The pope does this either through an *ex cathedra* ("from the chair") teaching or a council (a gathering of the world's bishops in union with the pope). The Church also teaches infallibly when she exercises her ordinary and universal Magisterium (which means a teaching has been taught "by all, always, and everywhere" and hence is part of the Deposit of Faith).

nothing to do with the infallible object of faith. Just as the Scriptures can be infallibly written by fallible men, they can also be interpreted infallibly by fallible men. The Protestant argument underscores the need to have an infallible interpreter of God's infallible Word. The interpretation is only as good as the interpreter.

Protestants like to point out that Catholics fallibly interpret the teachings of the infallible Church but, again, this doesn't prove the Church is fallible. It actually highlights that man needs an infallible guide to know infallible truths. If fallible Catholics have a dispute about an infallible teaching, the Church can resolve the dispute by issuing another infallible teaching that refines and clarifies the former teaching. Both teachings can be without error, but one teaching may be easier for the fallible intellect to understand than the other. The Protestant argument highlights that Catholics *have a place to go* for the resolution of doctrinal and disciplinary disputes through definitive, authoritative and infallible teaching, just as Jesus intended. Protestants do not.

Some Protestants retort by saying that Catholics cannot infallibly prove their position because they are not infallible. In other words, fallible beings can never prove anything beyond a shadow of a doubt (which means Protestants can't prove their case either). Not only does this argument have nothing to do with the existence of an infallible Church, but it is simply wrong. Proving something definitively does not require infallibility. For example, even though I am not infallible, I can prove things beyond a doubt by using the laws of reason and logic, such as the law of non-contradiction or the principle of causality. Moreover, if we take the Protestant's contention to its logical conclusion, we would doubt the existence of every Christian doctrine, even the existence of God Himself, since all infallible truths must pass through the fallible intellect.

By appointing one man over His Church, who would be divinely guided by the Spirit and protected from teaching error, Jesus established a definitive and objective means by which the faithful would receive the Word of God. Just as God would use men to transmit written revelation (Scripture), He would also use men to transmit His oral revelation (Tradition), and to interpret His revelation with divine authority, beginning with the pope.

Because the Church, not the Scriptures, is the God-appointed interpreter of revelation, St. Paul can say that she is the "pillar and bulwark of the truth" (1 Tim 3:15). The Church can only be the foundation and support of the truth if she can faithfully preserve and authentically interpret it. It takes a divine Church to protect, transmit and interpret divine revelation. Thus, St. Paul says that the wisdom of God is made known, not through Scripture, but "through the church" (Eph 3:10). Jesus also commands us to resolve doctrinal and disciplinary issues by bringing them "to the church" (Mt 18:17). The Catholic Church – not the individual believer – is the caretaker and interpreter of both Scripture and Tradition.

Revelation, inspiration and infallibility

This is a good place to point out the difference between revelation, inspiration and infallibility. Revelation refers to the supernatural truths that God has made known to us through Scripture and Tradition. Inspiration refers to the process by which God guided and controlled the apostles and evangelists to write (Scripture)[19] or speak (Tradition)[20] His revelation. Infallibility refers to the error-free interpretation of God's revelation in Scripture and Tradition.

Revelation ceased with the death of the last apostle, St. John. With his death, the Deposit of faith was sealed and "once for all delivered to the saints" (Jd 3). Thus, the Church does not receive new revelation or create new doctrines. She only safeguards, transmits and infallibly interprets what she has received from the apostles under the guidance of the Holy Ghost. In so doing, the Church clarifies and refines doctrines from time to time as exigencies dictate. She does so by analyzing, distilling and synthesizing all of the information gleaned from Scripture and Tradition. Theologians call this process the "development of doctrine" (more on this later).

The Deposit of Faith, then, has been entrusted by the apostles to the Catholic Church, preserved through apostolic succession, and protected by the Holy Ghost. Through the Church, to whom the transmission and interpretation of revelation has been entrusted, we have received the Word of God. The Deposit of Faith, whose source is the Triune God, has a triune character as well: (1) it is written (Scripture); (2) it is oral (Tradition); and, (3) it is authentically interpreted by the Church (Magisterium).

The Church first, then the Bible

In addition to existing before the implementation of apostolic succession and the transmission of Tradition, the Church also existed before the Scriptures. The Bible

---

[19] See, for example, 2 Tim 3:16.
[20] See, for example, 1 Thess 2:13.

did not drop down from heaven after Christ's ascension as some Protestants seem to imagine. Christ ascended into heaven in A.D. 33, but the first word of New Testament Scripture wasn't written until A.D. 45 or 50. The Apocalypse may not have been written until the end of the first century, leaving a 65-year gap between the Lord's ascension and the writing of the last book in the Bible. These are elementary historical facts which no reasonable person would deny.

In fact, the canon of Scripture – the books that belong in the Bible – wasn't determined until the end of the fourth century, leaving a 350-year gap between Christ's ascension and the official compilation of the Bible. During this period, Christianity thrived and souls were saved without a defined Bible. If the Bible is the sole infallible authority for Christians, who or what served as the final infallible authority during the gap between Christ' ascension and the completed Bible?

This question was of grave importance for the early Church who had to resolve some of the most critical doctrinal questions she ever faced (such as the divinity of Christ, His two natures and wills, His relation to the Father, etc.). False teachers had already entered the Church and she needed a definitive way to proclaim the truth and condemn heresy. If not, Christianity would have died in the womb. Moreover, the Church was being persecuted and the faithful were being martyred. Christians needed to know what they were living and dying for.

The Protestant will respond by saying that the apostles were the final authority until the Bible was completed. We have already demonstrated that Christ invested the apostles with His own authority, beginning with St. Peter. But since the Bible wasn't officially compiled until nearly 300 years after the death of the last apostle, St. John, the Protestant answer doesn't address who or what was the final authority during this 300-year period. Nevertheless, as we have seen, the Bible answers the question. It teaches that St. Peter and the apostles implemented a succession plan by ordaining bishops and authorizing them to preach the gospel and condemn error beyond the apostolic age.

In fact, implementing a plan of succession was the first thing St. Peter did as leader of the Church. In the first chapter of the Acts of the Apostles, Peter recognizes the vacancy in Judas Iscariot's apostolic office and enrolls Matthias as his successor (Acts 1:15-26). We also see the succession plan continue with the ordinations of Timothy and Titus - successors to the apostles but not apostles themselves.

The newly-ordained bishops had the *same* authority as the apostles, and were subject only to Peter, the rock of the Church. The apostles *consulted with the bishops they ordained* in resolving doctrinal questions.[21] This fact demonstrates that the "laying on of hands" confers real, apostolic authority to the recipient. In his letter to the Hebrews, St. Paul doesn't exhort the faithful to obey the apostles alone, but to "Obey your leaders and submit to them; for they are keeping watch over your souls as men who will have to give account" (Heb 13:17).

Protestants skirt the clear, biblical teaching on apostolic succession by arguing that the Holy Spirit guided the Church until the Bible was completed. Of course, Catholics agree. Jesus promised that He would send the Holy Spirit to guide the Church into all truth (Jn 16:13). The real question is: *What Church?* The Lutheran "church"? The Methodist "church"? The non-

---

[21] See Acts 15:2,4,6,22.

demoninational Evangelical "church"?[22] No, Jesus is referring to the Church He built upon the rock of the apostle Peter, to whom He gave the keys to the kingdom of heaven and the authority to bind and loose. This is the One, Holy, Catholic and Apostolic Church of the Bible. The Protestant's loose reference to the "Church" only begs the question, not answers it.

Further, the Protestant's admission that the Holy Spirit guided the Church undermines his Bible-only position. Why? Because the Holy Spirit *is an extra-biblical authority*. This would mean that Christians would have had two ultimate authorities: First, the Holy Spirit for the first 400 years; second, the Bible, which would replace the Holy Spirit for the rest of the Church age.

In other words, the Church would have followed *sola Spiritus* for the first four centuries, and *sola Scriptura* thereafter. Such a scenario completely refutes the doctrine of *sola Scriptura* which holds that the Scriptures have been the final authority since the apostolic age. Further, it is quite an admission for the Protestant to argue that the Church needed a *living voice* via the Holy Spirit for the first four centuries, but not thereafter. Finally, and most devastatingly, the Protestant cannot prove his position from Scripture.

It is also clear that most of the books in the New Testament were written to address specific moral, theological or disciplinary issues in the Church. The sacred authors of Scripture had no intention of writing a theological compendium on the Christian religion, and would be utterly shocked to know that many

---

[22] Theologically speaking, it is not proper to refer to these communities as "churches" because they are severed from the Body of Christ and unity of the successor of Peter, upon whom Christ built His one Church.

Protestants view their writings in such a light. While forming a complete whole, the books of the Bible are fragmentary and issue-specific, which is why we call it "the Bible" (from the Greek *biblia*, which means "the books"). Collecting the writings of the apostles and evangelists into one volume to serve as the formally sufficient rule of faith would have been the farthest thing from the evangelists' minds.

Sola Scriptura also presupposes that those who followed the apostles had the ability to read. However, we know that literacy during the Roman Empire and for some time thereafter rarely exceeded ten percent of the total population on average. Since most Christians could not read, are Protestants ready to argue that God was creating a rule of faith that most people could not follow? Even those who could read would first need access to the Scriptures and the time to read them, not to mention an education in the original biblical languages and critical thinking skills to discern their meaning. Is this what God really expects from each and every Christian in order to save their souls from damnation?

What should be even more perplexing to our Protestant friends is that the Bible as we know it didn't exist until more than 1400 years after Jesus ascended into heaven. Why? Because the printing press wasn't invented until A.D. 1450.[23] If God really intended for the Scriptures to be the exclusive means of spreading the gospel, then why didn't He lead men to invent the printing press earlier? This historical fact means that most people, *for fifteen centuries*, didn't read or have ready access to the Bible until it was reprinted in their own languages. Instead, they had the Catholic Church,

---

[23] The printing press was invented by Johann Gutenberg who was a Roman Catholic. Gutenberg printed the first Bible.

whose bishops and priests read the Scriptures from the parchment or vellum manuscripts which were translated copies of the original Hebrew and Greek texts.[24]

These were the same bishops who interpreted the Scriptures, handed on the Tradition, and celebrated the sacraments for the faithful. After all, the life of the Church was the Holy Sacrifice of the Mass, not Bible studies. Jesus never said, "Write this in remembrance of me," or "Read this in memory of me." He said, "*Do this* in remembrance of me."[25] While Scripture had an important place in the life of the Christian (and for many years, this was the Old Testament Scriptures only, because there wasn't a New Testament), the Christian truly came to know Jesus "in the breaking of the bread" (Lk 24:35).

Throughout the centuries, the Church has always followed the apostolic pattern of spreading the gospel: "And they devoted themselves to the apostles' teaching and fellowship, to the breaking of bread and the prayers" (Acts 2:42).[26] While holding in highest regard the inspiration of the Scriptures, the Church has converted sinners primarily through "the apostle's teaching" (the Tradition) and the "breaking of the bread" (the Holy Mass). In fact, if the Scriptures were never written, we would still have the Catholic religion

---

[24] For an excellent historical account of the compilation of Scripture, see Henry G. Graham's *Where We Got the Bible* (San Diego, CA: Catholic Answers, 1997; original edition by B. Herder Book Company: St. Louis, MO, 1911). See also John A. O'Brien's *The Faith of Millions* (Huntington, IN: Our Sunday Visitor, 1963,1974), pp.125-141.

[25] Lk 22:19; 1 Cor 11:24.

[26] The article "the" (Greek, *ho*) before the word "prayers" (*proseuche*) indicates that the apostles had a formal set of prayers to celebrate the Holy Mass and the other sacraments (which is also evidence of their divine and apostolic origin).

because we would have the Church, against whom "the powers of death shall not prevail (Mt 16:18).

If the Bible is indispensable for the salvation of one's soul as most Protestants contend, then what happened to the souls of the untold millions of people who were born before the Bible was printed? Did God, who desires all men to be saved and come to the knowledge of the truth, leave their salvation to chance? The Protestant understanding of the Bible leads us to the ridiculous and blasphemous conclusion that God failed to provide men in every generation the means necessary to save their souls through the knowledge of His truth. It also risks treating as ignorant the countless uneducated saints and missionaries who were martyred for their faith as they spread the gospel through their oral words and good deeds without any recourse to the Bible.

Jesus commanded the apostles to preach, not write

From the very beginning, the apostles understood that they were to imitate their Master. They were to do precisely what Jesus did: preach, heal and forgive sin. After all, Jesus never wrote any Scripture during His earthly ministry, nor did He command His apostles to write anything down. This is quite odd if Jesus really intended for His religion to be entirely committed to a book. Since only five apostles wrote Scripture, Protestants would have us believe that Jesus gave the other seven nothing to do. Scripture tells us a different story. Right before He ascended to the Father, Jesus commanded His apostles, "Go into all the world and *preach* the gospel to the whole creation" (Mk 16:15).

Jesus commanded the apostles to preach, not write, because He never intended for Scripture to be the sole rule of faith for Christians. This is why the Holy Ghost descended upon the apostles as "tongues of fire" so that they could "speak" the gospel message (Acts 2:3-4). After Pentecost Sunday, the apostles and their successors transmitted the gospel to the masses "by word of mouth" (Acts 15:27). The Christian faith developed from what was heard, not written, and what was heard came by "the preaching of Christ" (Rom 10:17).

After a couple decades of preaching, establishing churches and ordaining successors, the apostles Matthew and John were inspired to memorialize some of the events of Christ's life in their gospels. Peter, John, James and Jude also wrote letters to address specific issues in the various churches. Mark and Luke, the two other gospel writers, also decided to document important events and teachings in Jesus' life, based largely upon the oral teaching they had already received from the Virgin Mary and the apostles. John's Apocalypse, the last book of Scripture, is the only book where Jesus actually commands His revelation to be written down (and note that Jesus gives this order only to John, while in heaven, after His earthly ministry is completed).[27] Presumably, Jesus gave the order because John was exiled on the island of Patmos and could not preach.

Luke explains at the beginning of his gospel that he wrote it because "many have undertaken to compile a narrative of the things which have been accomplished among us" (Lk 1:1). Because there were many phony gospels circulating about Judea as false teachers sought to cash in on the new Christian religion, Luke says that "it seemed good to me also, having followed all things closely for some time past, to write an orderly account for you, most excellent Theophilus, that you may know the truth concerning the things of which you have been

---

[27] See Apoc 1:11,19.

informed" (Lk 1:3-4). Note also that Luke is not writing to replace the Tradition that Theophilus had received, but to provide an additional witness to "the truth" of the things he had *already* learned.

Luke's gospel, and the rest of the New Testament Scriptures, was written to address special circumstances and specific needs of the times. Surely, the seven apostles who didn't write Scripture weren't less obedient to Jesus. The Scriptures were never intended to be collected at a later date to be the final authority for Christians, and the faithful never heard of such a thing until Martin Luther introduced the idea 1500 years after that first Pentecost.

Even when writing Scripture, the apostles preferred to hand on the gospel orally. In his first letter to the Thessalonians, St. Paul says the he and his fellow bishops were "praying earnestly night and day that we may see you *face to face* and supply what is lacking in your faith" (1 Thess 3:10). As Paul was giving the Thessalonians inspired Scripture, Paul claims that they still lacked elements that would make their faith complete. If the Scriptures were to be formally sufficient for the Thessalonians, Paul would not have "prayed earnestly" to see the Thessalonians to provide them what was lacking. Scripture would have taken care of it.

Similarly, Paul tells Timothy that he was coming to teach him in person and was writing his letter only in the event he is delayed: "I hope to come to you soon, but I am writing these instructions to you so that, if I am delayed, you may know how one ought to behave in the household of God, which is the church of the living God, the pillar and bulwark of the truth" (1 Tim 3:14-15). Paul's letter is a backup to the instructions he will give Timothy in person.

In his second letter, St. John also prefers to teach the faithful orally (Tradition) rather than in writing (Scripture): "Though I have much to write to you, I would rather not use paper and ink, but I hope to come to see you and *talk with you face to face*, so that our joy may be complete" (2 Jn 12). In his third letter, John says the same thing: "I had much to write to you, but I would rather not write with pen and ink; I hope to see you soon, and we will *talk together face to face*" (3 Jn 13-14).

A personal example

This subject of being taught "face to face" reminds me of my late grandmother Rose Salza. Rose, who was the matriarch of the Salza family, handed down to us many prayers, recipes and other traditions that she received from her parents and wanted me to pass on to my children. During her life, Rose memorialized some of these traditions in a letter she wrote to me which I have safely preserved in a family album. In the letter, she also provided a brief history of how my great grandparents found their way to America from Italy in 1910. I recall many conversations I had with my grandmother about these wonderful stories. Rose was a devoted Catholic wife, mother and grandmother. God called her home in 1995.

Now that she is gone, I cannot help but think about all she has given me in the context of *sola Scriptura*. How could I possibly pass on to my children everything that my grandmother gave me by following her letter alone? Certainly, I could not. And what about the people who knew Rose the best (like my father and aunt)? These people are still with me, and I relish the opportunity to ask them questions about my grandmother's traditions whenever I have a question.

Of course, I cherish my grandmother's letter to me.
It is a tangible reminder of who she was and what she
gave me. But the letter in no way represents everything
that my grandmother wanted me to know and hand on
to my children. I will be most faithful to my
grandmother's request by personally teaching my
children – "face to face" – what my grandmother
taught me, both from what I remembered and what I
learn from my living relatives who knew her. My
grandmother's letter will serve only as a supplement to
what we have received.

It is no different with Sacred Scripture. Scripture is
a witness to the truth that Jesus Christ gave to His
apostles, but it does not represent the totality of what
Jesus taught or did. Moreover, the Scriptures were
written by different authors, from many geographies,
in foreign languages, to address many different issues.
How can one possibly argue that we should ignore the
oral Tradition of the apostles and rely solely upon their
written Word? Such a view is neither biblical nor
prudent or practical.

In connection with His command to preach, Jesus
ordered His apostles to teach the world "to observe *all*
that I have commanded you" (Mt 28:20). This was
quite a monumental task. Jesus, the Word of God made
flesh, gave an incredible amount of information to His
apostles during the three years that He was with them.
Whether it was about doctrine, discipline, or the
sacraments, Jesus taught His apostles everything
necessary to bring God's gift of salvation to the world.
If they were going to be faithful to their Master, the
apostles were to teach and implement *all of it*. No
exceptions.

The Apostle John, who was with Jesus every step of
the way, describes the enormity of the information
Jesus had given the apostles. John ends his gospel

rather dramatically by writing, "But there are also many other things which Jesus did; were every one of them to be written, I suppose that the world itself could not contain the books that would be written" (Jn 21:25).

Jesus commanded His apostles to teach everything He taught, and yet Scripture says most of what Jesus did and taught is not recorded in Scripture. This means that Scripture cannot be our only authority (in fact, the gospels record only about 100 days of Jesus' three-year ministry). While John says the *entire world* could not hold the books needed to explain the life and teachings of Jesus, Protestants would have us believe that everything we need to know has been committed to a quarter-inch thick collection of writings called the New Testament. Again, such a view defies both Scripture and logic.

The Bible needs an authentic interpreter

While Scripture and Tradition are two distinct sources of God's self-revelation, they flow from the same divine source which is God. Thus, they are two witnesses to the one Truth. Scripture itself teaches that "two or three witnesses" are required to verify truth.[28] Jesus said, "I bear witness to myself, and the Father who sent me bears witness to me" (Jn 8:18). Just as Jesus calls on the witness of the Father, Scripture calls on the witness of Tradition, and vice versa. Further, as Scripture and Tradition serve as witnesses to the truth, the Church, guided by the Holy Ghost, serves as the third witness *as well as the judge.*

Unlike what Protestants contend, Scripture *cannot* serve as judge. Scripture cannot be the "final court of appeal" for questions on the Christian faith. Why?

---

[28] See Dt 19:15; 2 Cor 13:1; 1 Tim 5:19; 1 Jn 5:7-9.

Because, unlike the Church, Scripture is not a living being with a thinking personality. Scripture cannot interpret itself. Scripture serves as a testimonial or witness to the truth, but not the judge of truth. Because Scripture is a "dead letter"[29] and the Church is a "living voice," we can understand Jesus and Paul's teaching that the Church, *not Scripture*, is the foundation and arbiter of truth. Scripture has an author (God) but it also needs a teacher (the Church).

Our system of government provides a useful analogy. Our Founding Fathers knew that an ordered government required a central authority. The Fathers couldn't simply give every citizen a copy of the Constitution and tell them to figure it out themselves. That would result in anarchy. No, the Founding Fathers created the interpreting office of the Supreme Court to have the final say. Because the Constitution is a "dead letter," it needs a "living voice" to tell us what it actually means. If a living authority is necessary for the United States government, how much more necessary is it for the worldwide family of God, the Catholic Church!

Scripture itself teaches very plainly that it requires an outside authority to interpret its testimony. For example, in the book of Acts we see the Ethiopian eunuch reading from the prophet Isaiah, where Isaiah writes: "As a sheep led to the slaughter or a lamb before its shearer is dumb, so he opens not his mouth."[30] When Philip saw the eunuch reading this passage, he asked him, "Do you understand what you are reading?" (Acts 8:30). The eunuch responded, "How can I, unless someone guides me?" (v.31). Philip

---

[29] By describing Scripture as a "dead letter," we mean that the words of Scripture are fixed and cannot change, as God Himself cannot change.

[30] Acts 8:32; see Isaiah 53:7-8.

explained to the eunuch that the passage he was reading was about Jesus Christ, and then baptized him (vv.35-38).

What does God teach us in this story? *That Scripture must be interpreted by one who has apostolic authority.* Did Philip have apostolic authority? You bet he did. Philip was ordained by the apostles through the "laying on of hands" (Acts 6:6). Through his ordination, Philip became a bishop of the nascent Catholic Church. Philip preached with authority, had the power of exorcism and the gift of healing (Acts 8:5-7). Because Philip had received the oral apostolic Tradition, he could render a definitive interpretation of the prophet Isaiah. Without an authority outside of Scripture, Scripture is defenseless against interpretive errors which lead to heresy and confusion (and to the thousands of splintered sects and competing factions we see in Protestantism).

As St. Peter declares, "First of all you must understand this, that no prophecy of scripture is a matter of one's own interpretation, because no prophecy ever came by the impulse of man, but men moved by the Holy Spirit spoke from God" (2 Pet 1:20-21). Scripture itself teaches that it should not be the object of private interpretation. Instead, it is the object of the *public* interpretation of the Church. Because Scripture communicates divine truth, it must be interpreted with divine assistance.

In reference to Scripture, St. Peter also says, "There are some things in them hard to understand, which the ignorant and unstable twist to their own destruction, as they do the other scriptures" (2 Pet 3:16). While Protestants contend that Scripture is clear and self-attesting, God reveals through Peter that Scripture is difficult to understand. Moreover, God reveals that erroneous interpretations *lead to destruction*. Peter uses the word "destruction" (Greek, *apoleia*) four other times in the same epistle, and each time it refers to nothing less than *eternal damnation*.[31] In other words, erring in biblical interpretation leads souls to hell. Because God desires all men to be saved and to come to the knowledge of His truth, He gave us a Church to prevent such catastrophe.

Material versus formal sufficiency

In light of what we have learned thus far, Catholics may believe in the material, but not formal, sufficiency of Scripture. By material sufficiency, we mean that Scripture contains all the "materials" necessary to form doctrine. In other words, all the building blocks of the desired structure are available. However, because many of these doctrines are only implicit in Scripture, things outside of Scripture (namely, Tradition and the Magisterium) are required to extract the true meaning of the doctrine. The Tradition, you might say, is the glue that connects the blocks, and the Magisterium is the builder who puts it all together.

The Catholic's view of the *material* sufficiency of Scripture is to be distinguished from the Protestant's view of Scripture's *formal* sufficiency. Formal sufficiency means that all the materials in Scripture are in "usable form" such that the structure is complete. In other words, the doctrines in Scripture are presented in such a clear and understandable way that neither the Church nor Tradition is necessary to understand the doctrine's true meaning.

As we have seen, Scripture does not teach that it is formally sufficient to understand all doctrine. In fact, Scripture is formally *insufficient* for this purpose. This

---

[31] 2 Pet 2:1-3,7.

is why the Church took hundreds of years to define even the most basic doctrines of the Christian faith (the Trinity, the Divinity of Christ, the procession of the Holy Ghost, etc). This is why the sacred authors of Scripture warn us about the consequences of erroneous biblical interpretation. And this is why there are thousands of factions within Protestantism, all disagreeing with each other on the core doctrines of the Christian faith (e.g., the baptism of infants, divorce and remarriage, homosexual unions, woman pastors, etc.).

The need for correct biblical interpretation in the realm of sexual morality is particularly crucial, especially because Scripture is silent on many different issues. Consider, for example, the terribly important life issues involving abortion, contraception, sterilization, in-vitro fertilization, surrogate motherhood, polygamy, and genetic engineering, among others. Scripture is unable to render a definitive judgment on these all-important life issues because it doesn't expressly address them. Protestants have almost as many opinions on these topics as they have Bible studies. Yet, getting these questions right is a question of life and death, both physically and spiritually.

For example, consider a poor woman who is raped and becomes pregnant by the violent act. This unfortunate fact pattern raises the obvious and most profound question: When does life begin? While Scripture refers to pre-natal life,[32] it doesn't tell us the all-important question of when exactly a human life comes into being. How does the Protestant determine whether it is permissible for this woman to have an abortion? He cannot answer the question using Scripture even though he claims that Scripture is his

---

[32] Ps 22:10-11; 51:7; 139:13,15; Gal 1:15.

only authority. Scripture is formally insufficient to answer the question. And yet a wrong answer could result in the murder of one human being and the risk of eternal damnation for the other.

Jesus knew by His divine foreknowledge that Christians would wrestle with these questions. Did Jesus simply leave us on our own to figure these life issues out? Is life not important to God? We know the answers. Jesus did not leave the truth to a consensus of opinion because that would be against His own divine nature. God can neither deceive nor be deceived. Jesus promised not to leave us orphans (see Jn 14:18). He left us His Church. By Christ's authority and the gift the Holy Ghost, the Church is able to render a definitive judgment on these questions based on her examination of Scripture and Tradition.

In regard to our hypothetical, the Church definitively teaches that life begins at the moment of conception. Drawing upon the information from Scripture and the oral Tradition as conveyed in the writings of the Fathers, doctors, saints and popes, the Church has resolved the question for us. While Protestants have many different positions on abortion, God's Church has one because the truth is one, and the Church is the pillar and foundation of the truth (1 Tim 3:15).

Because Catholics submit to the Church's judgment on the proper interpretation of Scripture, Protestants argue that Catholics divest the Scriptures of authority. This is a fallacious argument. It is like saying a decedent's will has no authority because the probate judge must interpret it. Scripture is an authority because it reveals the Word of God, just like the will is an authority because it reveals the intentions of the decedent. The question is not one of authority, but about *protecting* the authority.

If there is no probate judge to interpret the will, the authority of the will would be undermined. The family would be fighting about its contents and nothing would get resolved. The same is true with Scripture. If there is no Church to interpret the Scriptures, the authority of the Scriptures will be undermined as well. The family of God will fight about its contents (which we see in Protestantism) and nothing will be resolved.

Further, to discern the proper meaning of the will, the judge may decide to subpoena witnesses to give oral testimony as well. He may desire "two witnesses" (the written will and the oral testimony) to assist him in rendering his decision. The Church does the same thing. She reviews both written Scripture and oral Tradition before rendering her verdict. She ensures the Word of God says what God intended it to say, just like the probate judge strives to ensure that the will says what the decedent intended it to say.

Thus, the Church is not above Scripture and Tradition. She is the *servant* of Scripture and Tradition. The act of interpreting Scripture does not place the Church above the Scripture, just like a judge is not above the law. The judge is the servant of the law, just as the Church is the servant of God's Law. If, according to the Protestant, the act of interpreting Scripture puts the Church above Scripture, then every single Bible-only Protestant places himself above Scripture as well!

The "Word of God"

Before we examine the many Scriptural injunctions to obey Tradition, we first address the biblical phrase "Word of God." Whenever most Protestants read the phrase "Word of God" and other similar phrases in Scripture, they automatically conclude that it refers to the Bible only. This is not true and is one of the most common errors in Protestant biblical interpretation. In fact, whenever the Bible uses the phrase "Word of God," *it usually means preaching, not Scripture.*[33] For example, we read:

> • in the high-priesthood of Annas and Caiaphas, *the word of God* came to John the son of Zechariah in the wilderness; and he went into all the region about the Jordan, *preaching* a baptism of repentance for the forgiveness of sins (Luke 3:2-3).

> • While the people pressed upon him to *hear the word of God*, he was standing by the lake of Gennesaret (Luke 5:1).

> • Now the parable is this: The seed is *the word of God.* And the ones on the rock are those who, when they *hear the word*, receive it with joy; but these have no root, they believe for a while and in time of temptation fall away. And as for that in the good soil, they are those who, *hearing the word*, hold it fast in an honest and good heart, and bring forth fruit with patience (Luke 8:11,13,15).

> • But he said to them, "My mother and my brothers are those who *hear the word of God* and do it" (Lk 8:21); But he said, "Blessed rather are those who *hear the word of God* and keep it!" (Lk 11:28).

Moreover, the phrase "Word of God" primarily refers to the preaching of the apostles and their successors. For example:

---

[33] The phrase "Word of God" appears 43 times in the New Testament and almost always refers to preaching.

• And when they had prayed, the place in which they were gathered together was shaken; and they were all filled with the Holy Spirit and *spoke the word of God* with boldness (Acts 4:31).

• And the twelve summoned the body of the disciples and said, "It is not right that we should give up *preaching the word of God* to serve tables" (Acts 6:2; see also Acts 8:14; 11:1).

• When they arrived at Salamis, they *proclaimed the word of God* in the synagogues of the Jews (Acts 13:5)

• He was with the proconsul, Sergius Paulus, a man of intelligence, who summoned Barnabas and Saul and sought to *hear the word of God* ; The next sabbath almost the whole city gathered together to *hear the word of God* (Acts 13:37,44).

• And Paul and Barnabas spoke out boldly, saying, "It was necessary that *the word of God should be spoken* first to you"; And when the Gentiles *heard* this, they were glad and glorified *the word of God*; and as many as were ordained to eternal life believed (Acts 13:46,48).

• But when the Jews of Thessalonica learned that *the word of God was proclaimed* by Paul at Beroea also, they came there too, stirring up and inciting the crowds (Acts 17:13).

• and most of the brethren have been made confident in the Lord because of my imprisonment, and are much more bold to *speak the word of God* without fear (Phil 1:14).

- Remember your leaders, those who *spoke to you the word of God*; consider the outcome of their life, and imitate their faith (Heb 13:7).

Thus, whenever Scripture refers to the "Word of God," it usually means God's revelation as handed on by preaching (Tradition) and not writing (Scripture). Of course, the "Word of God" includes both. But even Scripture itself emphasizes that God chose the oral Word as the predominant vehicle for communicating His revelation in both the Old and New Testaments. St. Peter quotes from the prophet Isaiah when he says, "The grass withers, and the flower falls, but the *word of the Lord abides forever.*" Peter then interprets the passage by proclaiming: "That word is the good news which was *preached* to you" (1 Pet 1:25).

Don't "add to" or "subtract from" the Word of God

Because Protestants equate the "Word of God" with Scripture only, whenever Scripture admonishes us not to "add to" or "subtract from" God's Word, they immediately think of extra-biblical Tradition. For example, Protestants will refer to God's statement at the end of the Apocalypse: "I warn every one who hears the words of the prophecy of this book: if any one adds to them, God will add to him the plagues described in this book, and if any one takes away from the words of the book of this prophecy, God will take away his share in the tree of life and in the holy city, which are described in this book" (Apoc 22:18-19). What are we to make of this?

First, Catholics agree that adding to or subtracting from God's Word is a violation of His Word. Any man who attempts to modify God's inspired Word with his own words comes under God's divine judgment. The problem with the Protestant's appeal to this warning is that it assumes the oral Tradition is not part of God's Word. As we will further see below, Scripture says just the opposite. Oral Tradition *is* the Word of God, just as Scripture is God's Word. They are two different sources of communicating the *same* Word.

Second, God warns us not to add to or take away "from the words of the prophecy *of this book*," (v.18). God's warning is in reference to the Apocalypse, the last book in the Bible. God issues a similar warning in the book of Deuteronomy: "You shall not add to the word which I command you, nor take from it" (4:12); "Everything that I command you you shall be careful to do; you shall not add to it or take from it" (12:32).[34] If such warnings really meant for us to avoid teachings outside of the Scripture that God was currently inspiring, then the commands in Deuteronomy should have prevented Christians from accepting any of the Old Testament books written after Deuteronomy or the New Testament books.

Let us now look more specifically at the biblical teaching on Tradition.

---

[34] See also Prov 30:6.

Chapter 2

Biblical Commands to Obey Tradition

Throughout Scripture, St. Paul gives very explicit commands to obey the oral apostolic Tradition. For example, right after Paul commands the Corinthians to "Be imitators of me, as I am of Christ," Paul says, "I commend you because you remember me in everything and maintain the *traditions* even as I have delivered them to you" (1 Cor 11:1-2).

St. Paul is commending the Corinthians for maintaining what he had *already* delivered to them. Since this was Paul's first epistle to the Corinthians, Paul is praising the Corinthians for holding to the *oral* teaching he had given them *prior* to writing his letter. Paul says nothing at all about obeying the written word only, or that his oral teaching would be inscripturated in the future.

Further, the fact that Paul exhorts the Corinthians to maintain his previously handed on oral teaching, *even as he is writing Scripture*, demonstrates that the Tradition contains vital information independent of Scripture. It also demonstrates that Scripture doesn't override Tradition. Both are witnesses to the same truth. After Paul commends the Corinthians for maintaining Tradition, Paul tells them that he will be coming to them to give additional oral instructions which are just as authoritative as his written ones (v.34).

Similarly, in his letter to the Thessalonians, St. Paul says, "Now we command you, brethren, in the name of our Lord Jesus Christ, that you keep away from any brother who is living in idleness and not in accord with the *tradition* that you received from us" (2 Thess 3:6). Again, Paul is referring to the oral Tradition that the Thessalonians had *already* received from the apostles and their successors ("from us"). Paul gives no indication to the Thessalonians that his final letter to them would someday nullify everything that he had already taught them orally. If the collection of New Testament Scriptures the Thessalonians would receive years later were to be their sole infallible authority, Paul says nothing about it.

The Catholic teaching on Tradition is further supported by two additional passages: 1 Thessalonians 2:13 and 2 Thessalonians 2:15. Let us now examine these passages below.

1 Thessalonians 2:13

In his first letter to the Thessalonians, St. Paul says, "And we also thank God constantly for this, that when you received the word of God which you *heard* from us, you accepted it not as the word of men but as what it really is, *the word of God*, which is at work in you believers" (1 Thess 2:13).

In this passage, St. Paul tells the Thessalonians that his *oral* words were inspired by God, just as his written words were inspired. Paul puts the oral Tradition on par with Scripture. *Both* are infallible because *both* are the Word of God. This is the same oral Word that Paul entrusted to Timothy to guard and hand on to successors. Once again, Paul never says that the orally inspired revelation he gave to the Thessalonians would be committed to Scripture in the future.

In order to be true to their theory that the Bible is our only authority, Protestants must argue that the Bible teaches *sola Scriptura*. If the Bible doesn't teach *sola Scriptura*, then *sola Scriptura* comes from a teaching authority outside the Bible, which destroys the whole theory. In light of these parameters, 1 Thessalonians 2:13 strikes *sola Scriptura* with a fatal blow. Why? Because 1 Thessalonians 2:13 teaches that oral revelation (proclaimed by Paul and others) is *also* an infallible authority. Thus, the Bible teaches that there are <u>two</u> sources of infallible authority (the oral and written Word) and *sola Scriptura* teaches that there is only <u>one</u> (the written Word). This means that the Bible doesn't teach *sola Scriptura*.

Protestants can respond only by saying that the oral Word existed during the period of revelation but not beyond it. But this rebuttal gets them into more hot water. Why? First, because they cannot prove their position from Scripture which *sola Scriptura* requires them to do. The Bible never teaches that the oral apostolic Tradition would cease with the death of the last apostle or be merged into Scripture when the New Testament was completed.

Second, if *sola Scriptura* were not a valid doctrine during the period of revelation (only afterward), then the Bible doesn't teach *sola Scriptura* because it was written during this very period! Scripture cannot contradict itself. What was true for the first century Christian must be true for us today. If the written revelation did not teach *sola Scriptura* when it was being inspired, then it doesn't teach *sola Scriptura* at all. The Protestant cannot alter the meaning of God's written Word between revelation and post-revelation periods to suit his novel theories.[35]

Third, as we have seen, the Bible repeatedly teaches how the successors to the apostles (e.g., Timothy, Titus, Philip) are to guard and hand on the oral Tradition, and how the faithful are to hold fast to Tradition. The Bible never modifies or rescinds these commands. Perhaps the best example of the Bible's teaching on the equality of Scripture and Tradition is found in the next passage, 2 Thessalonians 2:15.

2 Thessalonians 2:15

In his second letter to the Thessalonians, St. Paul says: "But we are bound to give thanks to God always for you, brethren beloved by the Lord, because God chose you from the beginning to be *saved*, through sanctification by the Spirit and belief in the *truth*. To this he called you through our *gospel*, so that you may obtain the glory of our Lord Jesus Christ" (2 Thess 2:13-14). Then Paul says, "So then, brethren, stand firm and hold to the *traditions* which you were taught by us, *either by word of mouth or by letter*" (2 Thess 2:15).[36] Then he says, "Now may our Lord Jesus Christ himself, and God our Father, who loved us and gave us eternal comfort and good hope through grace, comfort your hearts and establish them in every good work and word" (vv.16-17).

---

[35] Catholic apologist Robert Sungenis makes this point in his quintessential work *Not By Scripture Alone* (Goleta, CA: Queenship Publishing, 1997) at p.128, ft 24, in rebutting Protestant apologist James White.

[36] The word "tradition" used in 1 Corinthians 11:2 and 2 Thessalonians 2:15; 3:6 comes from the Greek word *paradosis*. The word has two components: *"para"* (which means "along side of") and *"dosis"* (which means "to give").

The plain meaning of St. Paul's words is clear. Paul says that the Thessalonians have been called through the "gospel" which is the "truth" that "saves" and "sanctifies" them (vv.13-14). Paul says that this gospel has come to them through both the oral ("by word") and written ("by letter") form (v.15). These oral and written "traditions" will establish them "in every good work and word" (v.17). Paul commands the Thessalonians to "stand firm" and "hold" to these oral and written "traditions" without distinction. Paul puts the written Scripture and the oral Tradition on the same level. They are *of equal value*.

As with his other references to Tradition, Paul sees the oral apostolic teaching as something come down *from the past*, not something to be crystallized in writing *in the future*. In 2 Thessalonians 2:15, Paul is commanding the church of Thessalonica to hold fast to what they have already heard, not what they will later read about. This oral teaching is the very Word of God that Paul reveals in 1 Thessalonians 2:13. Paul never rescinds his command to obey oral Tradition, nor does any author of Scripture teach that oral revelation would be retired with the compilation of the New Testament. Therefore, if Protestants are not obeying the oral apostolic Tradition, they are not following the Bible.

Wasn't all oral Tradition committed to Scripture?

In light of these clear, biblical mandates to obey oral Tradition, Protestants have come up with a number of arguments to rationalize their Bible-only position. One of the more popular arguments is that, because the New Testament had not been written at the time Paul penned 2 Thessalonians 2:15, it was necessary to hold to oral Tradition until the New Testament was completed. Once the last word of New Testament Scripture was written, the Protestant argues that the entire oral apostolic residue was instantaneously found in Scripture.

In other words, the churches in Ephesus, Thessalonica, Corinth, and Philippi were to obey the oral Tradition they had received from Paul as he commanded. However, once John finished the Apocalypse on the island of Patmos, these churches were to forget everything they heard from Paul! When John penned that last "Amen" of his book of Revelation,[37] Protestants would have us believe that a giant bell went off and Paul's disciples were to erase from their memories everything that he and his successors taught about Jesus Christ!

As we have seen, not only is such an argument unreasonable, it cannot be proven from Scripture. Notwithstanding the absurdity of such a proposition, the fact that the argument cannot be proven from Scripture is the most devastating argument against *sola Scriptura*. Nowhere in Scripture does St. Paul or any other author teach such a thing. Since the Protestant by his own standard is required to get all of his doctrines from Scripture, he is required to show, from Scripture, why Paul's Scriptural mandates to obey Tradition are no longer valid. If the Protestant cannot carry his burden by proving, from Scripture, that the oral apostolic Tradition ceased with the completion of Scripture, *then the debate about Tradition is over and the Catholic position prevails.*

This burden the Protestant cannot meet. Not only that, but Scripture teaches that all oral revelation was *not* committed to Scripture – another blow to the Protestant position. For example, in the Old Testament, two companions of Moses named Eldad and Medad

---

[37] See Apoc 22:21.

prophesied in the camp, but none of their prophecies were recorded in Scripture (Num 11:26-27). Similarly, during the reign of King David, the sons of Asaph, Heman, and Jeduthun prophesied, but not all their revelations were written in Scripture (1 Chron 25:1-3).

In the New Testament, in the book of Acts, we learn that Philip had four daughters who prophesied, but none of their revelations were recorded in Scripture (Acts 21:9). The Corinthians also received divinely-inspired prophecies and spoke in tongues, but nothing was committed to Scripture.[38] The Protestant may downplay this fact by pointing out that the people of Corinth were not apostles. But the Apostle Paul also spoke in tongues and prophesied, and we also see no evidence that all or any of these revelations were recorded in Scripture.[39]

Didn't oral Tradition have to come from an apostle's lips?

As we just alluded to, another popular Protestant argument is that the tradition St. Paul constantly referred to had to come directly from his or another apostle's own lips. Now that the apostles are deceased, the obligation to follow the Tradition no longer exists. This is another example of some people reading into the Bible what they want to see.

In 2 Thessalonians 2:15, Paul doesn't say they are "his" traditions only, but the traditions that were taught by "us" (v.15). Paul says the traditions come from "*us*" in 1 Thessalonians 2:13 and 2 Thessalonians 3:6 as well, and also refers to the instructions that "*we gave you*" in 1 Thessalonians 4:2. Paul is not referring

---

[38] 1 Cor 12:10, 28; 14:1-40.
[39] 1 Cor 13:1; 14:6,14,18.

to traditions that come from his lips only, but also from those who are associated with his ministry (that is, the apostles *and their successors*). No where does Scripture say that oral Tradition must come only from the lips of an apostle.

In his letter to the Colossians, Paul writes, "Of this you have *heard* before in *the word of the truth*, the *gospel* which has come to you" (Col 1:5). Then Paul explains that the Colossians learned this word "from Epaphras our beloved fellow servant. He is a faithful minister of Christ on our behalf" (v.7). Epaphras was not an apostle, but a *successor* to the apostles. As a successor, Epaphras received the oral apostolic Tradition which he "handed on" to the church at Colossae. This is the same "word of truth" that Paul himself preached to the Colossians (Col 1:23). Indeed, the Colossians had received the "word of truth" well before Paul wrote them his epistle.

We see the same thing with Timothy. We saw that Paul ordained Timothy as the bishop of the church at Ephesus through the "laying on of hands."[40] Even though Timothy was not an apostle, Paul charges him to "preach the word" (2 Tim 4:1). This is the revelation that Paul had received from Christ, the Holy Spirit or the apostles and handed on orally to Timothy. As we have seen, Paul also instructs Timothy, as a bishop of the Church, to hand on the Word (the oral apostolic Tradition) to other men who will in turn be able to teach others. Paul says, "what you have heard from me before many witnesses entrust to faithful men who will be able to teach others also" (2 Tim 2:2).

Thus, Paul views the revelation which he received as a Tradition to be handed on to successors of the

---

[40] See 1 Tim 4:14; 5:22; 2 Tim 1:6.

apostles through the protection of the Holy Spirit (2
Tim 1:14). In 2 Timothy 2:2, the oral apostolic Tradition
is handed on from Paul (first generation) to Timothy
(second generation) to other faithful men (third
generation) who will be able to teach others as well
(fourth generation). Paul does not view Tradition has
having to come from his own lips or from those of the
other apostles, nor is there anything in Scripture which
teaches that the handing on of oral Tradition ceased
with the death of the last apostle.

We might also ask those making this argument
why oral revelation has to come directly from the
apostles' lips, but written revelation does not have to
come directly from their hands. After all, none of the
original autographs of Scripture written by the apostles
and evangelists are extant. We have not received the
written revelation "directly from an apostle." We have
only copies of their writings, translated by fallible men
over many centuries. This demonstrates that the
Protestant argument is purely arbitrary.

Isn't Tradition fallible?

It is obvious that those who believe in *sola Scriptura*
have a problem. Because they cannot prove from
Scripture that the oral Tradition would be crystallized
into Scripture with the completion of the New
Testament, they can respond only by attacking St.
Paul's meaning of the word *tradition*. Because the
Protestant holds the Bible to be his only inspired and
infallible authority, the Protestant has to argue that the
"tradition" Paul commands the faithful to obey is not
inspired or infallible.

Such an argument is problematic for a number of
reasons. First, Scripture never says oral Tradition is
fallible. To the contrary, 1 Thessalonians 2:13 teaches
that the oral Tradition is the *infallible* Word of God.

When Paul commands Timothy to guard the oral teaching that has been entrusted to him, Paul calls the oral teaching "the truth" (2 Tim 1:13-14). "The truth" cannot be fallible for it comes from God.

Second, if someone really wishes to argue that Tradition is "authoritative but not infallible," this means that Scripture can be an "authoritative but not infallible tradition" as well. Why? Because Paul never makes any such distinction in 2 Thessalonians 2:15. He simply commands us to hold fast to the traditions, "either by word of mouth or by letter." According to St. Paul, what the Protestant can apply to Tradition the Catholic can apply to Scripture.

Is the Protestant really suggesting that Paul commands us to follow infallible Scripture on the one hand, and fallible oral traditions on the other? Would Paul actually command us, while being divinely inspired, to obey fallible teachings? Would Paul command his successors to guard and hand on teachings that had the possibility of error? Of course not. The Protestant position is defeated by any honest analysis of the applicable Scriptural texts.

Those who admit that Tradition is infallible have abandoned the theory of *sola Scriptura* (which teaches that the Bible is the Christian's *only* infallible authority). Nevertheless, even with this admission, some may contend that Scripture is a *higher* authority than Tradition because, infallibility aside, Scripture is inspired and Tradition is not. There are several problems with this argument as well.

First, the premise is false. The Tradition that was handed on during the apostolic age, like the Scriptures that were written during the same period, *was inspired.* We saw this in 1 Thessalonians 2:13 where Paul says that he was giving revelation *orally* through the process of divine inspiration. Second, as we have just seen, the Bible doesn't say that Scripture is a higher authority than Tradition. Scripture simply commands us to obey both without distinction. Third, as we have mentioned, while the original Scriptures were inspired, they no longer exist. All we have are copies of the originals. If the Protestant wants to argue that we no longer have "inspired Tradition," Catholics will point out that we don't have "inspired Scripture" either, insofar as we have only copies of the inspired text.

Isn't Tradition corruptible?

Along a similar line of argument, some contend that Tradition cannot be trusted because the oral Word is easily corruptible. First, if God knew that the oral Tradition would become completely corrupted, then why would He command us to follow it? Wouldn't God at least have given us a warning about how to deal with the corruption once it occurred? Scripture doesn't warn us that Tradition would become corrupted.

Instead, Scripture teaches that, through the grace of apostolic succession, Tradition is guarded and preserved *by the power of the Holy Spirit* as it is transmitted to the apostles' successors. We might even say that Tradition is *less* prone to corruption than Scripture, for God did not promise to protect translators of the Bible from error. Tradition has been preserved inviolate through the popes, bishops, saints and doctors of the Church.

Second, if corruption is the issue, then Scripture is not trustworthy either. Catholic and Protestant scholars agree that about 80 percent of the verses in the

New Testament have some form of corruption.[41] These include variations in letters, words and even whole phrases. We see these deviations in many verses such as John 1:18, John 7:39, Acts 6:8, Acts 20:28, Colossians 2:2 and 1 Thessalonians 3:2.[42] In fact, some Protestant scholars still debate whether or not entire passages belong in Scripture. These passages include Mark 16:9-20, John 8:1-12 and 1 John 5:7-8. There may be as many as 200,000 or more corruptions throughout the entire Bible.[43]

Some respond by arguing that corruptions in Scripture don't affect major doctrines. But if corruptions don't negatively impact Scripture, then the same can be said for Tradition. Also, corruptions *can* impact major doctrines. For example, some translations of John 1:18 say that the "Son" is in the bosom of the Father, and others say that "God" is at the Father's side, referring to the Son.[44] If one were trying to show a Jehovah's Witness that the "Son" is "God" and not merely a man based on John 1:18 alone, the corruption in translation has an impact indeed.[45]

Consider also Mark 16:9-20. In verse 16, Jesus says, "He who believes and is baptized will be saved; but he

---

[41] Notwithstanding these corruptions, most Catholic and Protestant scholars, including this author, maintain that such variants are minor and that Scripture's textual integrity is extremely high (perhaps as high as 98 percent).

[42] Bruce M. Metzger, *The Text of the New Testament: Its Transmission, Corruption and Restoration* (Oxford University Press, 1992), pp.221-225, 234-243.

[43] See Graham, *Where We Got the Bible*, p.41.

[44] Raymond F. Collins, *Introduction to the New Testament* (Garden City, NY: Doubleday & Company, Inc, 1983), p.102.

[45] There are, of course, many other verses that demonstrate Jesus Christ's divinity. See, for example, Jn 1:1-3,14,18; Acts 2:36; 3:15; 20:28; Rom 9:5; Col 2:9; Titus 2:13; 3:4; Heb 1:6,8-9; 2 Pet 1:1; 1 Jn 5:20; Apoc 2:8.

who does not believe will be condemned." In this verse, Jesus clearly connects the necessity of baptism with salvation. If we reject verses 9-20, we eliminate a very clear teaching of Jesus *on a question of salvation/damnation*. While Jesus alludes to the salvific nature of baptism in John 3:5, it is not as cut and dried as Mark 16:16. There are other passages in Scripture which teach that baptism saves,[46] but the point is this: Corruptions in Scripture *can* impact core doctrines of the faith. This means we need an authority outside of Scripture to tell us which are the true Scriptures and which are not.

Finally, the Catholic should ask the Protestant who decides which doctrines are major and which ones are not. Are not the Divinity of Christ and Baptism major doctrines? Does not eternal life depend upon our understanding of these revelations? Because Scripture makes no distinction between major and minor doctrines, the Protestant rebuttal only further undermines his Bible-only position. In short, the "major versus minor doctrine" argument is a tradition of the Protestant's own making.

Thus, we ask the question: Does the presence of corruption in Scripture mean that the Protestant should dismiss the entire Bible as unreliable? Certainly not. Therefore, if the Protestant does not reject Scripture in spite of its corruptions, then he should not reject Tradition in spite of corruptions either. This is because, in the end, the real issue is not whether Scripture or Tradition has corruptions, *but whether we can know the true meaning of Scripture and Tradition with infallible certainty.*

---

[46] Acts 2:38; 1 Cor 6:11; Titus 3:5-7; Heb 10:21-23; 1 Pet 3:21.

Isn't Scripture clearer than Tradition?

Protestants also argue that Scripture is "clearer" than Tradition. The argument is based on the assumption that the written Word is more easily understood than the oral Word. Protestants making this argument assert that Scripture is "self-attesting" and "perspicuous." These terms mean that Scripture is so clear and understandable that no resource outside of Scripture is necessary to understand Scripture.

As mentioned in the Preface, Protestants often reject the plain meaning of Scripture verses. Even though Jesus called Peter the "rock" of the Church, Protestants say Peter is not the rock (Mt 16:18). Even though Jesus said, "this is my body" and "this is my blood," Protestants say it is not His body and blood (Mt 26:26-28). Even though Jesus said, "eat my flesh" and "drink my blood," Protestants say there is no real flesh and blood to eat and drink (Jn 6:51-58).

Even though Jesus commanded His apostles to "forgive sins," Protestants say that man cannot forgive sins (Jn 20:23). Even though Peter says "baptism saves," Protestants say baptism does not save (1 Pet 3:20). Even though James says "we are justified by works and not by faith alone," Protestants say we are justified by faith alone (Jam 2:24). Even though the 2,000 year-old Catholic Church has always interpreted these verses literally, the less than 500 year-old Protestant religions reject the plain and literal meaning of these verses.

Further, as we have seen, Scripture makes no claims about being clear and completely understandable. To the contrary, Scripture teaches that it is *not* clear and *requires* an outside authority to understand its meaning. We saw this in the Acts of the Apostles, when Philip used his apostolic authority to interpret Isaiah for the Ethiopian eunuch (Acts 8:30-33). We also learned from Peter that Scripture has "some things in them *hard to understand*" (2 Pet 3:16). Similarly, after teaching about the eternal priesthood of Jesus Christ, Paul tells the Hebrews, "About this we have much to say which is *hard to explain*, since you have become dull of hearing" (Heb 5:11).

Scripture teaches that the Word of God may not be clear *even when God is speaking directly to us*. In the book of Samuel, God develops a special relationship with the young boy Samuel. Scripture says that "the boy Samuel continued to grow both in stature and in favor with the Lord and with men" (1 Sam 2:26). One day, God called upon Samuel to reveal His judgment against the house of Eli. God called Samuel by name three times: "Samuel, Samuel!"[47] Even though Samuel had favor before God, he did not recognize God's voice. The Word of God is not always clear, even to very holy people who receive God's revelation directly!

Jesus also teaches us that we need an authority to help us understand Scripture. For example, in the Old Covenant, Jesus points out to the Pharisees, "You search the scriptures, because you think that in them you have eternal life" (Jn 5:39). Even though the Pharisees knew the Scriptures by heart, they could not discern their real meaning (that Jesus was the Messiah). They were incapable of extracting the true doctrine about Jesus.

In John's gospel, we read how Peter and John ran to see Jesus' empty tomb after the resurrection (Jn 20:4-8). While Jesus was on earth, He revealed to the

---

[47] See 1 Sam 3:1-9.

apostles that He would rise from the dead.[48] The apostles also knew the Scriptures concerning His future resurrection (Lk 24:44). Yet, when Peter and John ran to the empty tomb and found only Jesus' garment, John admits that "for as yet they did not know the scripture, that he must rise from the dead" (Jn 20:9). The resurrected Jesus, once again, had to open "their minds to understand the scriptures" and explain "that the Christ should suffer and on the third day rise from the dead."[49] The Scriptures weren't formally sufficient to explain Jesus' resurrection to the apostles. They needed an authority, Jesus Himself, to help them understand their meaning.

In Luke's gospel, we read about how two disciples of Jesus met Him on the Emmaus Road after His resurrection. As they walked together, Jesus "interpreted to them in all the scriptures the things concerning himself" (Lk 24:27). Even though Jesus interpreted the scriptures, the two disciples did not completely understand until Jesus celebrated the Eucharist with them: "And their eyes were opened and they recognized him; and he vanished out of their sight" (Lk 24:31). In the cases of both the Pharisees and the two disciples, we learn that the Word of God is not always clear, even when the Word of God made flesh is leading the Bible study!

We also submit that it is arrogant to presume the absolute clarity of Scripture. While some teachings in Scripture are clear, many teachings are clear as mud. In addition to the historical, philosophical and theological complexity of Scripture, Scripture employs many different literary techniques. Scripture's language is composed of the literal, symbolic, allegorical,

---

[48] Mk 9:9,31; 10:34,48; Lk 18:33
[49] Lk 24:45-46. See also Mk 16:14.

metaphorical, historical, and apocalyptic. Who would arrogate to themselves the ability to know what Scripture means in every instance? Moreover, if Scripture is so clear, then why are there thousands of competing sects within Protestantism? Why can't Protestants agree on even the most basic Christian doctrines such as baptism? The answers are obvious.

Scripture "or" Tradition?

Some Protestant apologists correctly point out that St. Paul commands us to obey the traditions by word of mouth *or* by letter (v.15). Because Paul uses the word "or" (Greek, *eite*) and not "and" (Greek, *kai*), the Protestant concludes that Scripture is formally sufficient to convey the gospel. That is, one can follow "either" Tradition "or" Scripture."

Of course, the argument cuts both ways. If either Scripture *or* Tradition can be formally sufficient, then Scripture is not necessary per se. If this is true, *sola Scriptura* is false. Is it true? Yes. Someone can be saved by responding to a sermon about Jesus Christ and never reading a verse of Scripture. Someone can be saved through preaching alone. This is common in remote lands where missionaries preach Jesus Christ to illiterate people and administer the sacraments to them. Paul's use of "or" in 2 Thessalonians 2:15 underscores the formal *insufficiency* of Scripture, and that Scripture and Tradition are two separate witnesses to the same salvific truth.

Some Protestant apologists also point out that St. Paul commands us to "stand firm" in holding to the oral or written traditions. The Greek for "stand firm" is the verb *steko* which means to "stand firm, persevere, persist." Protestants argue that the word precludes any kind of handing down of tradition from the apostolic age. In other words, the Thessalonians were to only "maintain" what they had received orally, but not to "pass it on" to future generations. This is not only a tortured reading of the text, but it also contradicts the very meaning of the word "tradition" (*paradosis*) which means "to hand on."

Further, if *steko* precludes the passing on of oral tradition, then it would also preclude the passing on of the written tradition, since Paul applies *steko* to both of them. That would mean the Protestant would not be able to use his translation of the Scriptures which have been "passed on" to him. The argument also tacitly admits that there is an authoritative oral tradition, independent of Scripture, which contradicts the doctrine of *sola Scriptura*. Finally, if Paul were really instructing the Thessalonians to hold on *only* to what they had *already* received, the Thessalonians would have had to reject most of the New Testament Scriptures since Paul's letters to the Thessalonians were among the earliest written.

More examples of oral Tradition

Scripture provides many other examples where St. Paul exhorts his readers to obey the oral apostolic Tradition they had already received. For example, in his letter to the Galatians, Paul says, "For I would have you know, brethren, that the gospel which was preached by me is not a man's gospel. For I did not receive it from man, nor was I taught it, but it came through a revelation of Jesus Christ" (Gal 1:11-12). First, Paul emphasizes that what he orally preaches is a revelation from God, not an invention of man. Paul makes a distinction between the oral "revelation" that he "preached" (apostolic Tradition) and "a man's gospel" (a "tradition of men").

Second, St. Paul makes it clear that the Galatians *had already received* the oral revelation at some point in the past because he uses the word "preached" in the past tense. The oral revelation is a separate, independent source of communicating divine information from the letter he would later write to the Galatians. If Paul never wrote the epistle to the Galatians, the Galatians would have still received the "revelation of Jesus Christ" from Paul's oral preaching.

Similarly, in his letter to the Ephesians, St. Paul says, "In him you also, who have heard the word of truth, the gospel of your salvation, and have believed in him" (Eph 1:13). Again, Paul says that the Ephesians have received the "gospel" of "salvation" by having "heard" the "word of truth." If Scripture is the only saving source of infallible information for Christians, then how can Paul say that the Ephesians had already come to a saving faith without the Scripture?

In Acts 20:27, St. Paul further explains that he declared to the Ephesians "the whole counsel of God." This is how Paul brought them to their saving faith in Christ. However, in Ephesians 3:3, Paul says that he has only "written briefly" about the revelation he has communicated to them.[50] In other words, Paul gave the Ephesians the "whole counsel of God" orally, and committed only *some* of the revelation to Scripture. Both Ephesians 1:13 and 3:3 refer to the same oral revelation that Paul "handed on" to the church at Ephesus.

In his letter to the Corinthians, St. Paul writes, "Now I would remind you brethren, in what terms I preached to you the gospel, which you received, in which you stand, by which you are saved, if you hold it fast – unless you believed in vain" (1 Cor 15:1-2).[51]

---

[50] See Sungenis, *Not By Scripture Alone*, p.230.
[51] See also Col 1:23.

Again, Paul explains that the Corinthians are currently saved by the "word of faith" which he *preached* to them, not what he wrote to them. In fact, because this was Paul's first letter to the Corinthians, they were saved without Scripture. Paul says the same thing to the Romans: "So faith comes from what is heard, and what is heard comes by the preaching of Christ."[52]

St. Paul's preaching to the Corinthians included a detailed catechesis on the sacrament of the Eucharist. Paul prefaces his instruction by saying, "For I received from the Lord what I also delivered to you" (1 Cor 11:23). Even though this was Paul's first letter to the Corinthians, Paul says that he had *already delivered* the oral revelation about the Eucharist to them, which he received directly "from the Lord." Paul's letter simply serves as an additional witness to the truths he has already communicated. Moreover, Paul most likely received this instruction from the apostles, even though he says it came "from the Lord." Paul is acknowledging that the oral revelations of Christ have been preserved through the apostolic Tradition.

After explaining how the Eucharist should be celebrated (by recounting Jesus' words of consecration) and the consequences of receiving Christ's body and blood unworthily, Paul says, "About the other things I will give directions when I come" (1 Cor 11:34). Just as Paul received Christ's instructions through the oral teaching of the apostles, he will pass on the same instructions through his own oral teaching. We can only imagine what additional directions Paul gave the Corinthians when he met with them face to face. These instructions may have included further details on the canon of the Mass, the required prayers, the postures

---

[52] Rom 10:17; see also Rom 10:8; 1 Cor 15:11.

of the priest and the people, the manner of receiving the Eucharist, and many other crucial elements.

Because the celebration of the Eucharist is the renewal of the New Covenant[53] and some of the Corinthians had become sick and even died for abusing the Eucharist, St. Paul's additional instructions were of paramount importance (see 1 Cor 11:30). Do Protestants really expect us to believe the Corinthians were supposed to erase from their memories Paul's oral instructions when the New Testament was completed? Especially when Paul's instructions regarded the epicenter of Christian worship and the life (or death) of the Corinthian church?

In his letter to the Romans, St. Paul says, "you yourselves are full of goodness, filled with all knowledge, and able to instruct one another. But on some points I have written to you very boldly by way of reminder" (Rom 15:14-15). Because the Romans are *already* "filled with knowledge," Paul writes only about "some points" in his letter. This means that the Romans' in-depth "knowledge" of Christianity came primarily from oral Tradition and not Scripture.[54]

In his second letter to the Thessalonians, St. Paul warns them of the anti-Christ when he writes that "the man of lawlessness is revealed, the son of perdition, who opposes and exalts himself against every so-called god or object of worship, so that he takes is seat in the

---

[53] Mt 26:28; Mk 14:24; Lk 22:20; 1 Cor 11:25.

[54] The Romans were "filled with all knowledge" because Peter had already established the Church in Rome. In 1 Peter 5:13, Peter says he is writing from "Babylon," which was a code name for Rome (Apoc 14:8; 16:9; 17:5; 18:2,10,21). This is why Paul says that he doesn't want to "build on another man's foundation" (Rom 15:20) and will be visiting Rome only in passing (vv.23-24,28).

temple of God, proclaiming himself to be God" (2 Thess 2:3-4). In the next verse, Paul writes, "Do you not remember that when I was still with you I told you this?" (v.5). The word "This" in verse 5 refers to the warnings about the "son of perdition" in verses 3 and 4.

While St. Paul exhorts the Thessalonians to remember his teaching on the "son of perdition," there is no such reference or instruction in 2 Thessalonians, 1 Thessalonians, or *any* of Paul's 12 other letters. Instead, Paul is referring them to the oral Tradition he had already "handed on" to them. Paul does not say that, with his writing of Scripture, the Thessalonians were to purge from their memories what they had previously learned from Paul. If there was any doubt, Paul removes it ten verses later when he commands the Thessalonians to stand firm and hold fast to the oral traditions he had given them (v.15).

In his letter to the Galatians, St. Paul warns them about avoiding immoral behavior such as "envy, drunkenness, carousing, and the like" (Gal 5:21). In the next verse, Paul says, "I warn you *as I warned you before*, that those who do such things shall not inherit the kingdom of God" (v.6). But there is no written record of Paul's previous warning to the Galatians, which means that Paul was reminding them to obey his oral instructions that he had already "handed on" to them.

In the beginning of his gospel, St. Luke explains to Theophilus that he is writing an orderly account of the life of Christ "that you may know the truth concerning the things of which you have been informed" (Lk 1:4). In other words, Luke acknowledges that Theophilus and the rest of the believers had *already received* the truth of Jesus Christ even though they didn't have the New Testament Scriptures. Luke is writing his gospel to supplement, not supplant, the oral Tradition they had received. Both Scripture and Tradition serve as independent witnesses to the same truth of the gospel.

In his second epistle, St. Peter writes to the churches in Asia Minor, "And I will see to it that after my departure you may be able at any time to recall these things" (2 Pet 1:15). Peter tells the faithful that he will, *in the future,* leave with them a method of recalling the truths about which he preached and wrote. However, this was Peter's last canonical epistle. Thus, the additional information Peter would later communicate would not come from Scripture. Instead, this "means to recall" would come from the oral Tradition that Peter would "hand on" to his successors as well as his teaching office. Of course, if Scripture were formally sufficient to teach the faithful, Peter would have no need to leave them another authority outside of Scripture to teach them.

Note also that St. Peter is writing to Christians who are already "established in the truth" (2 Pet 1:12). What these Christians know, which makes them established in the truth, cannot simply refer to Peter's first or second epistle since these epistles do not contain everything a Christian needs to know for salvation. Like the Romans, who were "filled with all knowledge" from their reception of Tradition, these Christians were "established in the truth" from the same Tradition they had already received. Peter writes them simply to "remind you of these things" (v.12). This shows that Scripture, far from being an exclusive source of divine information, serves as an additional witness to complete the "handing on" of the gospel.

What are the Traditions?

In the face of all of the evidence, some Protestants often shoot back at their Catholic friends by asking them to provide a laundry list of the Traditions. If the

Catholic cannot produce a complete, numerical list, their antagonism toward Tradition remains. After all, the list of Scriptures is clear. Why isn't there a list of the Traditions as well? How should a Catholic respond?

The Catholic might reply with a similar question: "What are the Scriptures"? In addition to the pervasive corruptions throughout Scripture, we don't have the original autographs of the inspired text. Instead, we have about 5,300 copies of the originals, which are numerous and varied. How does the Protestant know what are the true Scriptures? His 20th or 21st century English translation of the Bible certainly doesn't tell him, which means he needs an authority outside of Scripture to tell him.

The Church has not issued official interpretations of all 30,000-plus verses in the Bible, just as she has not issued a list of all of the apostolic Traditions. Such an exercise, while possible, would be unnecessary. The Church officially interprets Scripture and Tradition only when it is necessary to safeguard the Deposit of Faith. This generally occurs when there is much debate about a doctrine (like the Trinity) or a heresy (like Arianism) that must be dispelled. The bottom line is this: Catholics have an authority to tell them what are the true Scriptures and Traditions, and Protestants do not. If it would ever be necessary for the Church to definitively enumerate every single authentic Scripture and Tradition, she could do so.

That having been said, the Church has proclaimed the apostolic Tradition from the very beginning. As we alluded to, we find apostolic Tradition in the writings of the early Church Fathers and the medieval theologians.[55]   We   find   Tradition   in   the pronouncements of ecumenical councils and papal encyclicals. We find Tradition in the Church's liturgies and prayers. We find Tradition in the Church's creeds and catechisms. Far from being nebulous and esoteric, the apostolic Tradition is an objective body of knowledge that permeates Catholic teaching and praxis. Paul did not command us to "stand firm and hold fast" to the unknowable or impossible. All one needs is a little time and effort to become familiar with Tradition, just like one needs time and effort to become familiar with Scripture.

For those who want to know where to find the Tradition, here is my response: Get the *Catechism of the Catholic Church* (Second Edition, Washington, D.C.: United States Catholic Conference, Inc. 1997). This is the single-most comprehensive modern resource for learning about the Church's Tradition. The Church explains the meaning of Tradition in paragraphs 75-84, 95, 97, 113, 120, 126, 174, 1124 and 2651 and presents the Tradition over 688 pages (excluding indices and glossaries) in the following format:

Part One: The Profession of Faith (transmission of divine revelation, the creeds)
Part Two: The Celebration of the Christian Mystery (the liturgy, the seven sacraments)
Part Three: Life in Christ (dignity of man, grace, the Ten Commandments)
Part Four: Christian Prayer (meaning and manner of prayer, the Our Father)

---

[55] As noted, the Church (at the Ecumenical Councils of Trent and Vatican I) assures us that when the Fathers are unanimous in their teaching based on an interpretation of Scripture, such teaching comes from Christ and the apostles.

I encourage both Catholics and Protestants to become familiar with the *Catechism*. It presents the apostolic faith in an easy and understandable format and addresses an incredibly wide range of subject matter. Most Christians searching for truth will not only find nothing objectionable in this material, but will discover the richness, depth and beauty of Christianity like never before.

More "Protestations"

The Protestant's antagonism toward Tradition is often demonstrated by his attempt to slice and dice the meaning of Tradition into many different components. For example, some Protestant apologists create distinctions between the Tradition revealed directly by God to the apostles versus "uninspired tradition" that originated with the apostles or with the post-apostolic Church. They may also distinguish between Tradition that is dogmatic and tradition that is merely disciplinary. Some even distinguish between Tradition that can be found explicitly in Scripture versus that which can be found either only implicitly or not at all. By creating all these distinctions, the Protestant apologist thinks he can water down the authority of Tradition while confusing his Catholic opponents.

This type of approach does nothing for their case. First, by acknowledging the existence of divinely revealed Tradition, they admit that the Scriptures are not the only source of divine and infallible revelation. Second, which is a related point, by acknowledging that some core doctrines of the Christian faith are found only implicitly in Scripture (or perhaps not at all), the Protestant necessarily admits that these doctrines must be found elsewhere (that is, explicitly in the apostolic Tradition). Third, we have already pointed out the distinction between capital-T Tradition (which refers to revelation) and small-t tradition (which refers to the Church's non-dogmatic practices). Fourth, Scripture never divides Tradition into such hair-splitting categories, which means the Protestant's approach is another "tradition" of his own making.

At the other extreme end is the Protestant's effort to limit the definition of Tradition to merely the "interpreter of Scripture." By arguing that Tradition is an interpreter only and serves no other purpose, the Protestant wants us to believe that oral revelation has not survived outside of Scripture. First, with this argument, the Protestant admits that Scripture cannot interpret itself, which means that it cannot be formally sufficient to teach all the truths of Christianity. Second, arguing that Tradition is an "interpreter" begs many questions. For example, where is this Tradition housed? How are final decisions on doctrine reached? And why hasn't Tradition as an "interpreter" created unity within Protestantism? This argument only underscores that Tradition is *not* an interpreter of, but a *witness* to the Deposit of Faith.

Third, if Tradition is really the "interpreter" of Scripture, then why don't Protestants follow the "interpretations" that Tradition has produced? All of the early Church Fathers believed in baptismal regeneration, confession of sin, the propitiatory sacrifice of the Mass, the Real Presence of Christ in the Eucharist, the papacy, apostolic succession, intercessory prayer, purgatory and many other Catholic doctrines that Protestants reject. These were the "interpretations" that the "Tradition" led the Church Fathers to espouse. This presents an embarrassing dilemma for Protestant apologists. Fourth, Scripture never says that Tradition is the "interpreter of Scripture." Instead, Scripture reveals that Tradition is no less than the Word of God which the apostles handed on to their successors.

Even though they insist that the Bible is their only authority, Protestants believe in a fair share of apostolic Tradition. Their Bible is perhaps the best example. The canon of Scripture (the books that belong in the Bible) is an apostolic Tradition. The Bible does not tell us what books should be in the Bible. The core doctrines of Jesus Christ are also part of Tradition. These include the doctrines of the Incarnation, the divinity of Christ, His co-equal status with the Father, His two natures, His two wills and the hypostatic union. While these doctrines are not expressly defined in Scripture, they are believed by both Catholics and Protestants alike. Thus, the only real difference is that Catholics know they are following Tradition and Protestants do not (or are not willing to admit it).

"Traditions of men"

To rebut the Catholic view of Tradition, Protestants often refer to the Scripture passage where Jesus condemns the "traditions of men." When the Pharisees and scribes noticed that Jesus' disciples did not wash their hands before they ate, they said to Jesus, "Why do your disciples transgress the tradition of the elders?" (Mt 15:2).[56] Jesus responds by saying:

> 'And why do you transgress the commandment of God for the sake of your tradition? For God commanded, `Honor your father and your mother,' and, `He who speaks evil of father or mother, let him surely die.' But you say, `If any one tells his father or his mother, What you would have gained from me

---

[56] See also Mk 7:1-13. That Christians do not have to wash their hands to be ritually pure is an oral Tradition that the apostles received from Christ and handed on to their successors. The teaching is not explicit in Scripture.

is given to God, he need not honor his
father.' So, for the sake of your tradition,
you have made void the word of God.
You hypocrites!' (Mt 15:3-7).

Because Jesus condemns the traditions of the
Pharisees, some wrongly conclude that Jesus
condemns all "tradition."[57] Thus, when Catholics refer
to apostolic Tradition to explain a particular Catholic
belief or practice, some immediately label it a
Pharisaical "tradition of men." Most obviously, in
condemning the Pharisees' tradition, Jesus was not
speaking about the oral Tradition of the apostles. They
are two completely separate types of tradition. Bible-
only Protestants are also quick to condemn all
traditions even though Jesus does no such thing, and
even though Protestants have their own non-biblical
traditions (e.g., altar calls, women pastors). Let's look
at Jesus' rebuke of the Pharisees some detail.

First, Jesus does not condemn the Pharisees'
tradition of hand-washing before meals. Washing one's
hands before eating is a highly recommended practice.
Rather, Jesus condemns the Pharisees' prideful
motivations for washing their hands. The Pharisees
engaged in hand-washing and other similar traditions
to publicly display their purported holiness, but on the
inside they were corrupt and evil men (Lk 11:39).
While they pretended to love God and neighbor, they
had contempt in their hearts. Jesus was condemning
the Pharisee's hypocrisy, *not their tradition per se*. This is
why Jesus quotes from Isaiah who says, "This people
honors me with their lips, but their heart is far from

---

[57] See also Keating, *Catholicism and Fundamentalism* (San Francisco,
CA: Ignatius Press, 1988), p.139.

me; in vain do they worship me, teaching as doctrines the precepts of men" (vv.8-9).[58]

Second, in His rebuke of the Pharisees, Jesus condemns any tradition that transgresses God's commands (see vv. 3-4,6). To drive His point home, Jesus reminds the Pharisees of God's Fourth Commandment to "honor your father and your mother" (v.4). The Pharisees were setting aside God's commandment by their tradition called the law of Corban. This tradition allowed the Pharisees to avoid taking care of their parents by dedicating their wealth to the Temple.

Jesus condemns this tradition by declaring that the Pharisees "have made void the word of God" (v.6). Unlike the hand-washing tradition, which the Pharisees corrupted because of their prideful motivations, the tradition of Corban *was evil in itself*, for it nullified God's holy commandment to honor father and mother. The bottom line is this: *Any* tradition that sets aside God's Word is a condemnable "tradition of men." This could be a good tradition that is practiced for the wrong reasons or a bad tradition that replaces God's laws with human laws. In either case, such traditions violate God's supreme law which is to love God with one's whole heart, mind, strength and soul, and to love one's neighbor as oneself (Mk 12:33).

Third, we note that the Pharisees had the Scriptures which set forth God's law, and yet they practiced traditions that transgressed the law. It took Jesus, an authority *outside* of Scripture and Tradition, to render a judgment on their Old Covenant practices. This is precisely what Jesus does in the New Covenant through His Church. The Church, under the guidance

---

[58] See Isaiah 29:13.

of the Holy Ghost, makes judgments based on Scripture and Tradition to ensure that God's law is upheld. Scripture and Tradition are two witnesses to God's one revealed truth as interpreted by the authority of the Church.

The need to avoid "traditions of men" is as true in the New Covenant as it was in the Old. For example, St. Paul provides the following warnings:

> •   See to it that no one makes a prey of you by philosophy and empty deceit, according to human tradition, according to the elemental spirits of the universe, and not according to Christ (Col 2:8).

> •   Now the Spirit expressly says that in later times some will depart from the faith by giving heed to deceitful spirits and doctrines of demons (1 Tim 4:1).

> •   I know that after my departure fierce wolves will come in among you, not sparing the flock; and from among your own selves will arise men speaking perverse things, to draw away the disciples after them (Acts 20:29-30).

> •   John also says: Any one who goes ahead and does not abide in the doctrine of Christ does not have God; he who abides in the doctrine has both the Father and the Son (2 Jn 1:9).

How do we determine whether we are following authentic, apostolic Tradition or mere "human tradition"? How do we know we are abiding in the "doctrine of Christ" and not the "doctrine of demons"? Jesus answers by telling us to "listen to the church" (Mt 18:17). This is the Catholic Church, the authentic interpreter of Scripture and Tradition, which is built upon the rock of Peter and guided by the Holy Spirit. This is why the Apostle John teaches, "Whoever knows God listens to us, and he who is not of God does not listen to us. By this we know the spirit of truth and the spirit of error" (1 Jn 4:6).

What does John mean when he says "listen to us"? After all, when John wrote this epistle, the rest of the apostles were most likely dead. Yet "us" includes men who have the same authority as the Apostle John. So who is "us"? "Us" refers to the successors of the apostles. "Us" refers to those men who were entrusted with the oral Tradition. "Us" refers to the unbroken lineage of bishops united to Peter and his successors from the apostolic age to our present day. By listening to those who have received the apostolic Tradition, we will know "the spirit of truth and the spirit of error."

In summary, there is a difference between apostolic Tradition and "traditions of men." The former is God's revealed truth in Christ which the apostles passed on orally to their successors. The latter is the corrupt, human inventions that transgress this revealed truth. The former we must accept and the latter we must reject.

Chapter 3

Examples of
Extra-Biblical Tradition

Throughout Scripture, we see the sacred authors not only commanding the faithful to obey Tradition, but also drawing upon oral Tradition themselves to teach the gospel message. In both the Old and New Testaments, oral Tradition was the principal way in which God chose to communicate His divine Word. Let us now look at some of these examples.

Oral Tradition in the Old Testament

There is no doubt that much of the material in the Old Testament was taken from oral Tradition.[59] While all of the authors were inspired by God to write the words they did, they nevertheless drew from many sources of extra (and pre-) biblical information in composing their books. These included stories from antiquity, the teachings of the patriarchs, and the oral revelations of the prophets.

---

[59] We will use Tradition with a capital letter T to describe God's revelations in the Old Covenant as well, even though the word "traditionally" refers to the apostles' oral teaching which they handed on through apostolic succession.

For example, Moses wrote the first five books of the Bible called the *Pentateuch*.[60] Yet many of the events in the Pentateuch occurred over 2,000 years before Moses was born! How did Moses know about the six-day creation account, the Fall, and the Flood? How did he know about God's covenant promises to Adam, Noah and Abraham? How did he write such meticulous and detailed genealogies of the human race in Genesis 5 and 11? These questions could go on and on, but you get the point. Since there is no written record of any of these events before Moses recorded them, Moses received much of this information from the Tradition that was handed down to him.

Moses also relied on Tradition in his own dealings with God. For example, when God first appears to Moses on Mount Horeb and reveals that He will deliver the Israelites from Egypt, He tells Moses, "I am the God of your father, the God of Abraham, the God of Isaac, and the God of Jacob" (Ex 3:6). Abraham, Isaac and Jacob lived several hundred years before Moses was born. However, Moses knew of these great patriarchs even though nothing had yet been written about them. How? Through oral Tradition.

When Moses responds to God's directive to lead the people out of Egypt, Moses wishes to "offer sacrifice to our God."[61] How does Moses know that animal sacrifice is the worship that God desires? In fact, Scripture records very little about *how* the Jews regularly gathered to worship God (their customs, practices and procedures). Their understanding of liturgical worship came almost exclusively from the oral Tradition they had received from their forefathers.

---

[60] The Catholic Church has affirmed the Mosaic authorship of the Pentateuch (*Replies of the Pontifical Biblical Commission*, June 27, 1906).

[61] Ex 5:8; see also Ex 3:18; 5:3.

We can point out the same things about the information in the books of Joshua, Judges, 1 and 2 Kings and 1 and 2 Chronicles. The authors of these books recounted events in history that occurred long before their time. They received most of their information from oral Tradition and not Scripture, for almost nothing was written down before God moved them to do so. They and the people they taught followed the instructions of the prophet Joel: "Tell your children of it, and let your children tell their children, and their children another generation" (Joel 1:3).

While some admit that the Old Testament authors relied upon oral information that was *historical*, they deny that such information was *divinely-inspired*. Scripture tells a different story. For example, in the second book of Chronicles, King Hezekiah orders a burnt offering and a sin offering to be made for Israel. We read:

> And he stationed the Levites in the house of the Lord with cymbals, harps, and lyres, according to the commandment of David and of Gad the king's seer and of Nathan the prophet; *for the commandment was from the Lord through his prophets* (2 Chron 29:25).[62]

At the time of Hezekiah's mandate, David, Gad and Nathan were dead for centuries, and yet Hezekiah follows their detailed instructions. Because these commands are not found elsewhere in Scripture, they were passed on as authoritative oral Tradition. Moreover, they are treated as nothing less than "the commandment from the Lord through his prophets."

---

[62] See a similar appeal to extra-biblical authority by Josiah in 2 Chronicles 35:4.

Far from rebuking Hezekiah for not following Scripture alone, the Jews accepted Hezekiah's oral instruction as *the very word of God*.

The same book of Chronicles records that Solomon reigned in Jerusalem over all Israel for forty years (2 Chron 9:30). While Solomon received many revelations from God during his reign, they are not all recorded in inspired Scripture. Yet, we read: "Now the rest of the acts of Solomon, from first to last, are they not written in the history of Nathan the prophet, and in the prophecy of Ahijah the Shilonite, and in the visions of Iddo the seer concerning Jeroboam the son of Nebat?" (v.29).

Thus, many of the teachings of King Solomon were preserved through the prophetical oral Tradition. In fact, the phrase "the *rest* of the acts of Solomon, from the first to last," indicates that *all* of Solomon's oral unscripturated instructions were divinely preserved through prophecies and visions. These instructions, while existing apart from inspired Scripture, were nevertheless equally authoritative for the Jews.[63]

In the first book of Samuel, we learn about Israel's practice of consulting with God through seers: "Come, let us go to the seer" (1 Sam 9:9). The seers would enjoy divine visions and issue oral revelations from God (Isaiah 30:10). At some point in history, Israel changed the title of the divine consultant from "seer" to "prophet" without any Scriptural mandate (1 Sam 9:9). This brief account records both Israel's Tradition of petitioning a seer/prophet to consult with God, and the effect of a binding oral instruction to change the

---

[63] We learn the same thing about Rehoboam in 2 Chron 12:15 and Manasseh in 2 Chron 33:19-20.

consultant's title which was also preserved through Tradition.

These examples only scratch the surface. There are many other examples in the Old Testament where prophets communicate divine revelation that is not recorded in Scripture.[64] There are also many examples in the Old Testament where God and His chosen ones command the faithful to obey oral Tradition.[65] There is never any indication in the Old Testament that Scripture overrode Tradition, or that all oral revelations were committed to Scripture, or that obedience to oral Tradition should cease. To the contrary, God reveals that His Word will be orally preserved through His chosen ones forever.

Through the prophet Zechariah, God asks the rhetorical question: "And the prophets, do they live forever?" (Zech 1:5). Then, in the next verse, God says, "But my words and my statutes, *which I commanded my servants the prophets*, did they not overtake your fathers?" (v.6). God teaches us that His Word is preserved *forever* through the oral Tradition. This is the case in both the Old and New Covenants. As the great prophet Isaiah said, from whom Peter quotes in his first epistle: "the word of our God will stand forever" (Isaiah 40:8). This is the Word that is "preached to you" (1 Pet 1:25).

The Old Testament "church"

We have described how God's Word in the New

---

[64] Num 11:27; 1 Sam 10:5,11,13; 19:20; 1 Kgs 22:10,13; 1 Chron 25:1-3; 2 Chron 18:9,12; Ezra 6:14; Neh 6:14; Jer 20:1; 28:8; Ezek 11:13.
[65] 1 Sam 28:6,15; 1 Kgs 20:41; 22:6; 2 Kgs 9:1; 17:13,23; 21:10; 23:2; 24:2; 2 Chron 18:5,9,11-12,21-22; 20:20; 24:19; 36:16; Ezra 5:1-2; 9:11; Jer 7:25; 25:4; 26:5,7-8; 27:18; 35:15; 44:4; Ezek 38:17; Dan 9:6,10; Hos 12:10; Amos 2:11; Zech 1:4; 7:7,12; 8:9.

Covenant comes to us in a triune pattern of (1) Scripture and (2) Tradition as interpreted by the (3) Magisterium of the Catholic Church. The need for an authentic interpreter of God's Word is not unique to the New Covenant. The need existed in the Old Covenant as well. God didn't love the Jews any less or leave the questions of truth and error to the consensus of opinion. Thus, it is no surprise that we see a similar arrangement of authority in the Old Covenant. Just as God has given the successors to the apostles access to His infallible judgments through the Church, He gave the same divine provisions to the leaders of ancient Israel.

For example, God appointed Moses and the Levitical priests over the people of Israel to infallibly interpret Scripture and Tradition and exercise judgments in His name. God killed anyone who disobeyed His chosen leaders' infallible decrees. In the book of Deuteronomy, we read:

> And coming to the Levitical priests, and to the judge who is in office in those days, you shall consult them, and they shall declare to you the decision. Then you shall do according to what they declare to you from that place which the LORD will choose; and you shall be careful to do according to all that they direct you; according to the instructions which they give you, and according to the decision which they pronounce to you, you shall do; you shall not turn aside from the verdict which they declare to you, either to the right hand or to the left. The man who acts presumptuously, by not obeying the priest who stands to minister there before the LORD your God, or the

judge, that man shall die; so you shall purge the evil from Israel. And all the people shall hear, and fear, and not act presumptuously again (17:9-13).

Moses, a living voice, had plenary authority over the people of Israel. He would (1) teach Tradition; (2) interpret Scripture; and, (3) act as a Magisterium by rendering infallible decrees. In fact, during his tenure, Moses had the written law read only every seven years, during the feast of booths (Dt 31:9-11). For the rest of the time, Moses taught God's people using oral Tradition and his own teaching authority. The people never complained that they lacked Scripture, for Moses taught them the Word of God orally. Moreover, Moses commanded the people to pass on the Tradition to their children so that they "may hear and learn to fear the Lord your God" (Dt 31:13).

Even when the people of Israel read the law, they could not interpret it on their own. For example, the people read that they were to "keep holy the Sabbath day."[66] One day, when the people were in the wilderness, they found man gathering sticks on the Sabbath (Num 15:32). Although they knew the Scriptures, the Israelites brought the man to Moses and Aaron "because it had not been made plain what should be done to him" (v.34). The Scriptures were not formally sufficient to resolve what they were to do to the man. Instead, God had to provide divine assistance to Moses to help His people understand the Scriptures: "The man shall be put to death; all the congregation shall stone him with stones outside the camp" (v.35).[67]

---

[66] Ex 34:1,4,28-29; Dt 4:13; 5:22; 9:9-11,15,17; 10:1-5. See also Ex 16:23,25-26,29; 20:8,10-11; 31:13-16; 35:2-3; Lev 16:31; 19:3,30; 23:3,11,15-16,32,38; 24:8; 25:2,4,6; 26:2,34-35,43; Dt 5:12,14-15.
[67] God provided similar divine intrusions through the Urim and Thummim, ephod, seer, visions and prophets.

One day, a man named Korah rose up against Moses and attempted to usurp his divine authority (Num 16:2). Korah and his followers sought the priesthood without being formally commissioned (Num 16:10). They thought they could interpret God's Word on their own, outside of the living teaching authority God appointed over them. As a punishment for their rebellion against the authority of Moses, God killed Korah and his fellow rebels by causing the earth to swallow them alive (Num 16:32-33).[68]

It is very important to note that the Apostle Jude warns the Church not to "perish in Korah's rebellion" (Jude 11). This raises a most critical question for Protestants: If the Bible is the only authority for Christians, how can we rebel against an authority other than the Bible? Korah didn't rebel against Scripture; he rebelled against God's chosen leaders. St. Jude's warning makes absolutely no sense unless there is a hierarchy in the Church with divine authority that we must obey. Indeed, there is: The successors to the apostles who are "keeping watch over your souls" (Heb 13:17).

To preserve his divine authority for future generations, Moses commissioned Joshua whom all the people of Israel obeyed (Num 27:18-20). Not surprisingly, Moses implemented the plan of succession by laying "his hands upon him" (Dt 34:9). Through the laying on of hands, Moses' divine authority passed from Joshua, to the Kings and Judges, all the way down to the Sanhedrin of Jesus' time. Jesus acknowledges the Sanhedrin's authority when He says,

---

[68] There are many examples in Scripture where false prophets rise up against God's authorized leaders and are judged as working for Satan. See, for example, Jer 14:14; 27:10,14-16; 29:9,21,27.

"The scribes and the Pharisees sit on Moses' seat; so practice and observe whatever they tell you (Mt 23:2-3). Further, Jesus' knowledge of "Moses' seat" came from oral Tradition, not Scripture. There is nothing in the Old Testament Scriptures about "Moses' seat.""

The "seat of Moses" represented the scribes and Pharisees' authority to interpret the Mosaic law. Through the "seat of Moses," God would provide Israel with access to His infallible judgments. We see this with Caiaphas who was high priest at the time of Jesus' Passion. From the "seat of Moses," Caiaphas infallibly prophesied Jesus' death by declaring, "it is expedient for you that one man should die for the people, and that the whole nation should not perish" (Jn 14:50). Caiaphas' prophecy was binding on the Sanhedrin because "from that day on they took counsel how to put him to death" (v.53).

By giving St. Peter "the keys to the kingdom of heaven" and the authority to "bind and loose," Jesus was annulling the old teaching authority of the Sanhedrin and creating a new teaching authority, the Church (Mt 16:18-19). The "seat of Moses" would be replaced by the "chair of Peter," and the scribes and Pharisees in the Old Covenant system of law would be superseded by the apostles and their successors in the New Covenant of grace.

While the Jews had both Scripture and Tradition as two witnesses to God's truth, they always had a living voice to be their final spiritual authority. They always had a divine interpreter of the Divine Word. As they transitioned into the New Covenant, it would have been unthinkable for them to be governed by Scripture (especially when the New Testament Scriptures didn't exist, and would not be settled for centuries). After nearly 2,000 years and 264 successors to the chair of Peter, history proves that God has continued to provide His people one divine authority in the Roman Catholic Church.

The living voice of the Catholic Church, which would be established by the Redeemer Jesus Christ for all generations, fulfills the prophecy of Isaiah:

> And he will come to Zion as Redeemer, to those in Jacob who turn from transgression, says the Lord. 'And as for me, this is my covenant with them, says the LORD: my spirit which is upon you, and my words which I have put in your mouth, shall not depart out of your mouth, or out of the mouth of your children, or out of the mouth of your children's children, says the LORD, from this time forth and for evermore' (59:21).

Oral Tradition in the New Testament

As in the Old Testament, the sacred authors of the New Testament drew from oral Tradition to teach the Word of God. This Tradition included both the prophetical Tradition passed on through the Old Covenant and the apostolic Tradition of the New Covenant. Further, the sacred authors relied upon Tradition not only in their preaching, *but also in writing Scripture.*

For example, after the Apostle Matthew recounts how Joseph was warned in a dream to protect the baby Jesus and the Virgin Mary by withdrawing to the district of Galilee, he writes: "And he went and dwelt in a city called Nazareth, that what was spoken by the prophets might be fulfilled, 'He shall be called a Nazarene'" (2:23).

While some of the prophets revealed in writing that Jesus would be a righteous "branch" (in Hebrew, *nazar*),"[69] the prophecy "He shall be called a Nazarene" is not found in Scripture. It was an oral revelation that God gave through His Old Testament prophets that was preserved through the prophetical Tradition. St. Matthew was not giving a *new* inspired prophecy; he was simply providing another witness (Scripture) to what had already been handed on orally (Tradition).

The Apostle James draws from oral Tradition when he recalls that Elijah "prayed fervently that it might not rain, and for three years and six months it did not rain on the earth" (Jam 5:17). While the First Book of Kings records how Elijah revealed the impending drought to Ahab, it says nothing about Elijah petitioning God through "fervent prayer" (see 1 Kg 17:1). Elijah's prayerful petition was part of the Jewish oral Tradition that James incorporates into his New Testament epistle.

The Apostle Jude also relies upon oral Tradition in his epistle. After revealing the Sodomites are undergoing a punishment of eternal fire for their sin of homosexuality, Jude writes, "But when the archangel Michael, contending with the devil, disputed about the body of Moses, he did not presume to pronounce a reviling judgment upon him, but said, 'The Lord rebuke you'" (Jd 9).

Where does Scripture reveal this dispute between the archangel Michael and Satan over Moses' body? Nowhere. It is an Old Testament Tradition that was passed down by word of mouth. God inspired Jude to provide an additional written witness to what He had already given in Tradition. The non-inspired

---

[69] Is 4:2; 11:1; Jer 23:5; 33:15; Dan 11:7; Zech 3:8; 6:12.

apocryphal work called *The Assumption of Moses* also records this Tradition, further demonstrating that the story in Jude 9 was preserved outside of inspired Scripture.

Five verses later, after Jude warns us about Korah's rebellion, he appeals to another oral Tradition, this time concerning a prophecy of Enoch: "It was of these also that Enoch in the seventh generation from Adam prophesied, saying, 'Behold, the Lord came with his holy myriads, to execute judgment on all, and to convict all the ungodly of all their deeds of ungodliness which they have committed in such an ungodly way, and of all the harsh things which ungodly sinners have spoken against him'" (Jd 14-15).

Once again, this prophecy is not found in inspired Scripture, but in a non-inspired work called the *Book of Enoch*. According to a literal reading of the genealogies in Genesis chapters 5 and 11, Enoch lived about 3,500 years before the birth of Christ. However, most scholars say the *Book of Enoch* was written within a century and a half of Christ's birth. Thus, Enoch's inspired prophecy of God's harsh judgment upon evil doers was preserved through the oral prophetical Tradition for many centuries, independently of Scripture.[70]

In his first epistle, St. Peter writes that Jesus "went and preached to the spirits in prison, who formerly did not obey" (1 Pet 3:19-20). These "spirits" included the rebellious "angels" over whom Jesus has dominion and authority (v.22). Elsewhere, Peter writes that God cast these angels "into hell and committed them to pits

---

[70] Enoch lived a life that was so pleasing to God that God translated him into heaven. See Gen 5:24; Sir 44:16; 49:14; Heb 11:5.

of nether gloom to be kept until the judgment."[71] Jesus' judgment of these evil angels mirrors Enoch's judgment of the evil angels in the *Book of Enoch*. The source for Peter's analogy between Jesus and Enoch is an extra-biblical oral Tradition.

Jesus also refers to an extra-biblical Tradition. In St. John's gospel, Jesus refers to "scripture" which says, "Out of his heart shall flow rivers of living water" (7:38). While the prophet Isaiah alluded to how God would pour spiritual water upon His people, this verbatim quotation is not found in canonical Scripture.[72] It was preserved in the prophetical Tradition and recorded outside of the Bible.

Because St. Paul never knew Jesus during Jesus' earthly ministry, Paul's knowledge of Jesus Christ came primarily from oral apostolic Tradition. While Paul did receive revelations directly from Jesus (which is what makes him an apostle),[73] he didn't learn everything about Christianity on the Damascus Road. Paul was able to declare the "whole counsel of God" from what he learned from the apostles.[74]

Paul reveals that he "went up to Jerusalem *to visit* Cephas (Peter), and remained with him fifteen days" (Gal 1:18). The phrase "to visit" (Greek, *historesai*) means a lot more than spending time with someone. The Greek verb *historesai* comes from its related noun *histor* and means "to examine." When Paul uses this verb to describe how he went "to visit" Peter, Paul means that he went to examine Peter *to obtain knowledge*

---

[71] 2 Pet 2:4; see also Jud 6.
[72] See Isa 44:3; 55:1; 58:11.
[73] Acts 9:3-6; 18:9-10; 22:6-10; 26:13-18; 2 Cor 12:4; Gal 1:12; 2:2; Eph 3:3.
[74] See Acts 15:2; Gal 1:18.

from him. That is, Paul went to receive the Tradition from Peter.

Based on what he received from Peter and the other apostles, Paul writes about many of the doctrines that were eventually formulated into the Apostles' Creed (which is also a Tradition of the Catholic Church). For example, Paul writes about:

- God the Father Almighty, creator of heaven and earth (1 Cor 8:6)
- Jesus Christ, His only Son our Lord (Col 1:3)
- who was born of the Virgin Mary (Gal 4:4)
- suffered under Pontius Pilate (Acts 13:8)
- was crucified, died and was buried (1 Cor 2:8; Acts 13:29)
- descended to the dead (Eph 4:9)
- rose from the dead (Rom 8:34; 1 Thess 4:14)
- intercedes for us at the right hand of the Father (Rom 8:34)
- will come to judge the living and the dead (2 Tim 4:1)
- the Holy Spirit (2 Cor 13:14; Eph 4:30; 1 Thess 4:8)
- the Catholic and apostolic Church (1 Cor 12:28; Eph 3:10,21)
- the communion of saints (Heb 12:1)
- the forgiveness of sins (Col 1:14)
- the resurrection of the body (1 Cor 15:12-13,21,42; Phil 3:11)
- and life everlasting (Rom 2:7; 6:23; Titus 3:7).

St. Paul was also conversant in a variety of complex, theological doctrines which the Church would later define in her councils. These include the doctrines of Original Sin;[75] the Divinity of Christ;[76] the salvific nature of baptism;[77] the Real Presence;[78] the Eucharist as a sacrifice;[79] the indissolubility of marriage;[80] justification by grace;[81] the supersession of the Old Covenant,[82] and, purgatory.[83] Further, Paul enforced various liturgical traditions that he surely received from the apostles. These included the requirements for women to cover their heads while praying[84] and keep silent in church,[85] as well as setting strict parameters around tongue-speaking.[86]

St. Paul demonstrates his reliance upon oral Tradition when he recalls these famous words of Jesus: "In all things I have shown you that by so toiling one must help the weak, remembering the words of the Lord Jesus, how he said, 'It is more blessed to give than to receive'" (Acts 20:35). Even though Paul most likely never heard Jesus speak these words, he nevertheless provides a *verbatim quote from Jesus*. This is only possible if Jesus' words were preserved and handed down to Paul in tact by the apostles (which they were).

In his letter to the Ephesians, Paul refers to a Christian hymn that is not recorded in Scripture: "Therefore it is said, 'Awake, O sleeper, and arise from the dead, and Christ shall give you light'" (Eph 5:14).

---

[75] Rom 5:12,19-20; 1 Cor 15:22,45.
[76] Col 1:15-19.
[77] Titus 3:5-7; Heb 10:22.
[78] 1 Cor 10:16; 11:27-30.
[79] 1 Cor 10:18-22; Gal 3:1; Heb 9:24.
[80] Rom 7:3; 1 Cor 7:12-15.
[81] Rom 3:24; 5:1-2; 6:14; 11:5-6; 2 Cor 6:1; 12:9; Gal 2:16; 5:4; Eph 2:8-9.
[82] Heb 7:18; 8:13; 10:9; 2 Cor 3:14.
[83] 1 Cor 3:12-15.
[84] 1 Cor 11:3-16.
[85] 1 Cor 14:33-38.
[86] 1 Cor 14:26-36.

Paul even appeals to pagan poets as he records his teaching experience in Athens: "Yet he is not far from each one of us, for 'In him we live and move and have our being'; *as even some of your poets have said*, 'For we are indeed his offspring.'" (Acts 17:27-28). James also appeals to a document outside the New Testament when he says, "Or do you suppose it is in vain that the scripture says, 'He yearns jealously over the spirit which he has made to dwell in us'"? (Jas 4:5). That Paul and James draw on sources of authority outside of Scripture tells us that they didn't believe in *sola Scriptura*.

Before St. Paul writes about the manner of celebrating the Eucharist, he says, "For I received *from the Lord* what I also delivered to you" (1 Cor 11:23). Paul then recounts the words Jesus used at the Last Supper to change the bread and wine into His body and blood (vv.24-26).[87] While Paul was not at the Last Supper, he declares that he received this information "from the Lord." This means that the Word of the Lord was preserved and handed down to him by the apostles. Although Paul commits this Word to Scripture, would it have been any less a part of the Deposit of Faith if he didn't? And were Paul's further, face-to-face instructions on the Eucharist (v.34) less authoritative than the eleven verses he penned in 1 Corinthians 11:23-34? The answers are obvious.

Here is another important point. While the twelve original apostles were present at the Last Supper, Matthew is the only apostle to record Jesus' words of

---

[87] Paul's statement in verse 23 ("I received from the Lord...") is about the celebration of the Holy Mass. This demonstrates that the liturgy is not a discipline that can be tampered with at will, but is part of the Divine Law.

consecration in Scripture (26:26-28).[88] Yet all of the apostles gave oral instructions to the many churches on the Eucharist, for the Eucharist was at the heart of the Christian faith. These instructions would have addressed doctrinal, disciplinary and liturgical matters of great significance, including the form and matter for the consecration.

Are we to believe that once the New Testament was completed, these churches were to completely dismiss the apostles' oral instructions in favor of their written ones? Do Protestants really believe that no residue of apostolic Tradition was preserved and passed on to future generations? How could these churches have possibly survived without relying upon the oral apostolic instruction they received? Again, such a position is not only ludicrous, but it cannot be proven from Scripture.

St. Paul goes on to write about the Real Presence of Christ in the Eucharist using some of the most powerful words in Scripture. Paul warns the Corinthians, "Whoever, therefore, eats the bread or drinks the cup of the Lord in an unworthy manner will be guilty of profaning the body and blood of the Lord. Let a man examine himself, and so eat of the bread and drink of the cup. For any one who eats and drinks without discerning the body eats and drinks judgment upon himself. That is why many of you are weak and ill, and some have died" (1 Cor 11:27-30). The word for "judgment" (Greek, *krima*) is nothing less than eternal damnation.[89]

---

[88] The other gospel narratives are found in Mark 14:22-24 and Luke 22:19-20.
[89] See, for example, Rom 5:16; 1 Tim 3:6.

While Matthew records Jesus' words at the Last Supper and John records Jesus' teaching about His Real Presence in the Eucharist (chapter 6), neither of them, nor any other apostle, writes about the eternal consequences of receiving the Eucharist unworthily. Where did Paul get such an incredible teaching? From the oral apostolic Tradition. This Tradition which Paul received and transmitted was just as authoritative as his letters.

Of course, the risk of receiving the Eucharist unworthily wasn't limited to the Corinthian churches. The possibility of abusing the Eucharist existed in *all* the churches as the faithful grasped the full meaning of the sacrament. People were even dying because of sacrilegious communions (see 1 Cor 11:30). The possibility of abuse also existed beyond the apostolic age. Did the teaching of Paul's successor bishops on the Real Presence have any less authority because it came from oral Tradition and not Scripture? Again, the answer is obvious. Scripture and Tradition are two witnesses to the same truth.

In the same first letter to the Corinthians, St. Paul addresses a number of abuses that were occurring in their churches. After Paul explains that it is "shameful for a woman to speak in church," he says that "what I am writing to you is *a command of the Lord*" (1 Cor 14:37). Although Paul would have received this teaching from the apostles, he considers it "a command of the Lord." This means that God's word was preserved through the apostolic Tradition. Just as the Chronicler declared "for the commandment was from the Lord through his prophets,"[90] Paul could have said, "for the commandment was from the Lord through His apostles."

---

[90] 2 Chron 29:25.

St. Paul also appeals to his non-canonical writings to teach the Word of God. For example, in his first letter to the Corinthians, Paul says, "*I wrote to you in my letter* not to associate with immoral men; not at all meaning the immoral of this world, or the greedy and robbers, or idolaters, since then you would need to go out of the world. But rather *I wrote to you* not to associate with any one who bears the name of brother if he is guilty of immorality or greed, or is an idolater, reviler, drunkard, or robber -- not even to eat with such a one" (1 Cor 5:9-11).

Even though this was Paul's *first* canonical epistle to the Corinthians, Paul refers to a *previous* letter he wrote them regarding associating with immoral people.[91] For Paul to hold as authoritative a letter outside of the New Testament shows that Paul didn't believe in *sola Scriptura*. Although this previous letter was not divinely inspired, it contained infallible truths that made up the Deposit of Faith. In other words, it taught the apostolic Tradition.

St. Paul appeals to another of his non-canonical writings in his letter to the Colossians. He says, "Give my greetings to the brethren at Laodicea, and to Nympha and the church in her house. And when this letter has been read among you, have it read also in the church of the Laodiceans; and see that you *read also the letter from Laodicea*" (Col 4:15-16). Although Paul's letter from Laodicea was not included in the New Testament, Paul commands it to be read to the churches, just as his inspired letter to the Colossians. While one is inspired and the other is not, they both teach the infallible,

---

[91] Paul's use of "letters" (plural) in 2 Corinthians 10:9-10 may also suggest that Paul wrote other epistles to the churches at Corinth which are not part of the New Testament.

apostolic Tradition that Paul is now passing on to them.

It also seems possible that St. Paul wrote more than one letter to the churches at Philippi, even though there is only one letter to the Philippians in the New Testament. In the first verse of chapter three, Paul says, "Finally, my brethren, rejoice in the Lord. *To write the same things* to you is not irksome to me, and is safe for you." Paul says he is writing "the same things" to the Philippians and yet what immediately precedes and follows this verse is not repeated elsewhere in the letter. At the end of chapter two (vv.25-30), Paul writes about how Epaphroditus almost died for the faith. At the beginning of chapter three (vv.2-7), Paul writes about the defunct Jewish ritual of circumcision. If "the same things" refer to these bookends to Philippians 3:1, Paul must have written about them in another authoritative (but not inspired) letter.

Just as Jesus appeals to Old Testament Tradition when He describes the "seat of Moses," Paul also appeals to Old Testament Tradition in his letters. For example, Paul writes, "As Jannes and Jambres opposed Moses, so these men also oppose the truth, men of corrupt mind and counterfeit faith; but they will not get very far, for their folly will be plain to all, as was that of those two men" (2 Tim 3:8-9). We already learned about Korah's rebellion against Moses, but what about "Jannes and Jambres"? Who are they? Some scholars say Paul is referring to Pharoah's magicians in the book of Exodus, but Scripture doesn't identify these men.[92] Yet both Paul and Timothy know about them because they were a part of the constant, oral Tradition.

---

[92] See Ex 7:11. Jannes and Jambres are named in the apocryphal book *The Gospel of Nicodemus*.

St. Paul relies upon another Old Testament Tradition when he recalls the Exodus: "and all ate the same supernatural food and all drank the same supernatural drink. For they drank from the supernatural Rock which followed them, *and the Rock was Christ*" (1 Cor 10:3-4). While the book of Exodus describes the rock from which the Israelites drank,[93] it says nothing about the rock following them on their journey, or being or symbolizing the coming Messiah. Instead, Paul is relying upon an oral Tradition which allegorized the Exodus as a spiritual deliverance of God's people by His Christ.

St. Paul also relies upon an Old Testament Tradition as he recounts the brutality inflicted upon the Jews by Antiochus Epiphanes during the Maccabean period.[94] Paul writes, "Women received their dead by resurrection. Some were tortured, refusing to accept release, that they might rise again to a better life. Others suffered mocking and scourging, and even chains and imprisonment. They were stoned, *they were sawn in two*, they were killed with the sword; they went about in skins of sheep and goats, destitute, afflicted, ill-treated…" (Heb 11:35-37). While the book of Maccabees describes in great detail the manner in which the Jews suffered for their faith, it says nothing about women being sawn in two. This disturbing detail was preserved for 200 years through oral Tradition.

In his letter to the Galatians, St. Paul says that God gave the Jews the Mosaic Law through "angels." He writes," Why then the law? It was added because of transgressions, till the offspring should come to whom the promise had been made; and it was *ordained by angels* through an intermediary" (Gal 3:19). In his letter

---

93 Ex 17:6; Num 20:11.
94 See 2 Macc 7:1-42.

to the Hebrews, Paul also says, "Therefore we must pay the closer attention to what we have heard, lest we drift away from it. For if the message *declared by angels* was valid and every transgression or disobedience received a just retribution, how shall we escape if we neglect such a great salvation?" (Heb 2:2-3)

No where in the Old Testament does it say that the Mosaic Law was given by or through "angels." At most, the book of Exodus explains how God used angels to lead the Israelites to the Promised Land.[95] Paul is not relying upon Scripture, but on Tradition, as he explains the institution of the Old Covenant.

While Paul could have received his information from Jewish Tradition, he may have received it from Stephen whom Paul heard preach the gospel before the Jews stoned him to death. Filled with the Holy Ghost, Stephen declared, "Which of the prophets did not your fathers persecute? And they killed those who announced beforehand the coming of the Righteous One, whom you have now betrayed and murdered, you who received the law as *delivered by angels* and did not keep it." (Acts 7:52-53). Scripture then says, "Then they cast him out of the city and stoned him; and the witnesses laid down their garments at the feet of a young man *named Saul [Paul]*" (v.58). Whether from Old Testament Tradition or Stephen, Paul did not receive his infallible information from Scripture.

---

[95] Ex 14:19; 23:20,23; 32:34; 33:2.

Chapter 4

Tradition and the Development of Doctrine

We have briefly mentioned the concept of the "development of doctrine." This is a theological concept which describes how the human side of the Church grows in her understanding of the Deposit of Faith as she is guided by the Holy Ghost into all truth. This growth occurs as the Church prayerfully reflects upon both the Scriptures and the Tradition that she has received from the apostles. In this process, there is never a recession from the doctrine's original meaning or an "evolution" of dogma. Rather, the development always proceeds from its own genus with the same sense and understanding. Through the ongoing guidance of the Spirit, the Church is able to articulate the meaning of Christian doctrine with greater clarity and profundity as she moves toward the end of time.

While the study of Scripture has been called the soul of the Church's theology, any authentic development of doctrine always occurs in light of the Tradition. In fact, oral Tradition, as preserved and transmitted by the councils and Church Fathers, often takes the lead in doctrinal development and the resolution of controversy. Let us now take a brief look at some key developments of doctrine that were drawn primarily from the apostolic Tradition.

The Council of Jerusalem

Perhaps the best biblical example of a development of doctrine is found in chapter 15 of the Acts of the Apostles.[96] This chapter describes the proceedings of the council of Jerusalem which was convened about A.D. 49. At this council, the Church had to resolve her first doctrinal question regarding whether or not Christians had to be circumcised to be saved by Christ.

As we recall, the early Church was exclusively Jewish until Peter loosed the kingdom to the Gentiles. The Gentiles began to convert to Christianity about ten years after Christ's ascension into heaven. As the Gentiles entered the Church, many of the Jewish converts believed that they had to be circumcised like themselves. Although they had no apostolic authority,[97] these Jewish teachers proclaimed, "Unless you are circumcised according to the custom of Moses, you cannot be saved" (Acts 15:1). The Gentiles resisted the circumcision party and a controversy ensued.

Although they were converted Christians, the belief of these particular Jews was understandable. After all, God had given Abraham circumcision as a sign of His everlasting covenant with him (Gen 17:10). The covenant of circumcision was affirmed throughout the book of Genesis.[98] Paul favorably describes the circumcision requirement given to Abraham as "a sign

---

[96] Although the Acts of the Apostles covers about a 30 year period from Christ's Ascension to St. Paul's deportation to Rome, there is not a single mention of either Luke's Gospel or Paul's major epistles which were written before the Acts of the Apostles. If the Bible was to be the "sole rule of faith," why weren't these books, or any reference to a future compilation of books, ever mentioned by the only historical record of the doings of the first century Church?

[97] See Acts 15:24; Rom 10:15.

[98] See also Gen 17:12,14,23-24,26-27; 21:4; 34:15,17,24.

or seal of the righteousness which he had by his faith" (Rom 4:11). God also renewed the covenant of circumcision with Moses (Lev 12:3).

Hence, all the Patriarchs, judges, kings and prophets were circumcised, the apostles were circumcised, and even the Lord Jesus Christ was circumcised (Lk 2:21). Moreover, Jesus told His disciples to "practice and observe whatever" the Pharisees taught, which would have included circumcision (Mt 23:2). Jesus also said that He didn't come to "abolish the law" but to "fulfill" it, and that "not an iota, not a dot, will pass from the law until all is accomplished" (Mt 5:17-18). Circumcision was part of "the law." Thus, based on these precedents, circumcision appeared to be a prerequisite to entrance into the New Covenant. Moreover, there is no place in Scripture where Jesus exempts the Gentiles from circumcision and other ritual laws of Moses.

Having heard the Judaizers' teaching, Paul, Barnabas and a number of other bishops went to Jerusalem to see "the apostles and the elders about this question" (Acts 15:2). Note that even though Paul is an apostle who received revelation directly from Jesus, he does not take matters into his own hands. Neither does Barnabas, a bishop himself, nor the other bishops accompanying them. They do not decide to study Scripture and form a consensus of opinion. Instead, they recognize the authority of the Church and her Tradition and travel to Jerusalem to meet with Peter and the rest of the bishops.

After much debate, St. Peter rose up and declared, "Brethren, you know that in the early days God made choice among you, that by my mouth the Gentiles should hear the word of the gospel and believe. Now therefore why do you make trial of God by putting a yoke upon the neck of the disciples which neither our fathers nor we have been able to bear? But we believe that *we shall be saved through the grace of the Lord Jesus, just as they will.*"[99] After Peter spoke, "all the assembly kept silence" (v.12). Thus, in resolving the question, Peter definitively teaches that we are saved by grace, not law, in the New Covenant of Jesus Christ.

Did the Church resolve the circumcision question using *sola Scriptura*? Quite the contrary. Even though the circumcision requirement was backed by 2,000 years of Scripture (as well as Jewish Tradition), the Church eliminated the practice in one fell swoop. Obviously, neither Peter nor anyone else believed the Scriptures were formally sufficient to resolve the question. In fact, Peter never refers to Scripture in making his decision at all. He never conducts an Old Testament Bible study of the books of Genesis and Leviticus.

Instead, Peter renders his definitive judgment based on Tradition and his Christ-delegated authority as the rock of the Church. Through the power of the keys which Peter alone holds, Peter "looses" the circumcision requirement and "binds" the Church to his teaching. No one in the assembly questions Peter's authority. No one says, "Hey, Peter, what about Scripture?" Moreover, no one says, "Hey Peter, why did it take you 20 years to teach this most basic doctrine?"

After Peter resolves the issue, Paul and Barnabas speak in support of Peter's teaching (v.12). But they don't appeal to Scripture either. Rather, Paul and Barnabas refer to the "signs and wonders God had done through them among the Gentiles" (v.12). In other words, they appeal to their apostolic authority

---

[99] Acts 15:7,10-11.

and the divine intrusions of the Holy Spirit – two authorities that exist *outside* of Scripture.

It is only after they speak that James, the bishop of Jerusalem, refers to Scripture.[100] However, James does not appeal to Scripture as a *judge* of Peter's teaching but as a *witness* to it (vv.16-18). It is only through Peter's teaching authority and the apostolic Tradition that James can understand what these Old Testament verses really mean. After submitting to Peter's dogmatic teaching, James offers a pastoral suggestion, namely, that the Gentiles more easily transition into the New Covenant by following the Noachide laws. These laws included refraining from meat sacrificed to idols, from things strangled and from blood (vv.19-20).

The Council of Jerusalem teaches us two things. First, the council did not believe in *sola Scriptura*. Instead, the council drew upon the oral teachings of Jesus Christ (Tradition) and the authority of the bishops in union with Peter (Magisterium) in rendering her decision. The council recalled Christ's commandment to preach the gospel to the Gentiles (Mt 28:19). The council remembered the Lord's revelation to Ananais that Paul would bring the gospel to the Gentiles (Acts 9:15). It also learned from Peter's visions and his baptism of Gentile converts,[101] and from Paul and Barnabas' preaching to the Gentiles.[102] The council drew from all of these facets in proclaiming that the Gentiles were saved by grace and exempt from circumcision.

Second, the Church's definitive teaching is guided by the Holy Ghost. After Peter set forth his definitive

---

[100] James cites Amos 9:11-12; Jer 12:15 and Is 45:21 to support Peter's teaching.
[101] Acts 10:9-16;44-48. See also Acts 11:1,18.
[102] Acts 13:46-48.

teaching, the Church issued a letter declaring: "For it has seemed good *to the Holy Spirit and to us* to lay upon you no greater burden than these necessary things..." (Acts 15:28). With Peter at the helm, the apostles and those they ordained collaborated with the Holy Spirit in reaching the decision. Under Peter's leadership and the Holy Spirit's guidance, the council viewed the Scriptures (which commanded circumcision) in the context of Tradition and apostolic authority (which rescinded circumcision) and came to its definitive conclusion. The Church had the final say.

The Council of Jerusalem provides us the biblical pattern of doctrinal development: Christ gives His apostles a teaching; the apostles hand it on to their successors; a controversy eventually arises; the apostles and/or their successors assemble to address the controversy; Scripture and Tradition are consulted; and, the Church, under the authority of the pope, resolves the controversy through a dogmatic pronouncement. We see the same pattern of development for *all* of the Church's doctrines throughout her 2,000 year history.

As we alluded to previously, the term "development of doctrine" refers not to the Church creating *new* doctrines, but to the process by which the Church makes more explicit her understanding of what she has *already* received from the apostles in Scripture and Tradition. Because the Church is the living Body of Christ, she grows in her explication of the Deposit of Faith that she has received, both in depth and clarity.

This growth is necessary as the subjective and human side of the Church strives to understand and articulate the objective and divine truth of God. This process happens through prayerful contemplation and study, the preaching of the successors to the apostles, and the guidance of the Holy Ghost. As each century passes, the Church responds to exigencies that require doctrinal clarification as she moves toward the consummation of the New Covenant at the end of time.

Jesus describes the Church as a mustard seed that grows into a large tree, like bread that is leavened, and like a net which catches fish of every kind.[103] These metaphors for the Church tell us that she is a living organism, that is, the Body of Christ. This means her appearance changes over time, but her essence remains the same. The Church of the 21st century does not externally resemble the Church of the 1st century, but it is organically the same Church. Similarly, the manner in which the Church explicates doctrine may change subtly over time, but the essence of the doctrine never changes.

The Church clarifies a doctrine in one century, and builds upon it in another century when the circumstances so require. What the Church definitively proposes in the past is never changed in the future – only more complete explanations are added. The Church enjoys a natural progression of understanding as she provides greater clarity and deeper insights into Scripture and Tradition. There are not multiple routes and changes in course, but a single journey along a single road.

This pattern of development follows the very pattern God used to transmit His revelation. God would give an initial message and then build upon it over time. For example, after the Fall, God revealed that He would send the world a Savior when He told Satan, "I will put enmity between you and the woman,

---

[103] Mt 13:31-33,47.

and between your seed and her seed" (Gen 3:15).[104] God built upon His message by later revealing that the Messiah would be the Son of God.[105] God's revelation was fulfilled with the actual coming of His Son, Jesus Christ, "who is God over all, blessed forever" (Rom 9:5). There are many more examples of "progressive revelation" in Scripture (the Trinity, the Person of the Holy Spirit, the resurrection of the body, etc.)

The Council of Jerusalem's doctrine that we are saved by the grace of Jesus Christ and not the Mosaic law of circumcision continued to develop over time. Paul used the Council's letter as precedent for his future teaching[106] and continued to explain and refine the doctrine over many years.[107] The seed doctrine planted in Jerusalem grew into an oak tree of dogmas for the universal Church. These include her teaching on Original Sin,[108] the supersession of the Old Covenant,[109] and justification by grace.[110]

While Scripture is materially sufficient to discern these truths, it would take future councils to present them in a formally sufficient and understandable fashion. Scripture alone would not suffice. Thus, we see the Council of Orange (A.D. 529) issue dogmatic canons on Original Sin, (which were further refined by

---

[104] This is called the First Gospel, or *Protoevangelium*.

[105] 2 Sam 7:12-14; 1 Chron 17:11-15.

[106] Acts 21:25.

[107] Rm 2:25-29; 3:1,30; 4:9-12; 1 Cor 7:19; Gal 5:6; 6:15; Phil 3:3; Col 2:11; 3:11; Tit 1:10.

[108] Rom 5:12; 19; 1 Cor 15:22,45.

[109] 2 Cor 3:14; Heb 7:18; 8:13; 10:9.

[110] Rom 1:5; 3:24; 4:16; 5:2,17,20-21; 6:1,14-15; 11:5-6; 12:3,6; 15:15; 16:20; 1 Cor 1:3-4; 3:10; 15:10; 16:23; 2 Cor 1:2,12; 4:15; 6:1; 8:1,9; 12:9; 13:14; Gal 1:3,6,15; 2:9,21; 5:4; 6:18; Eph 1:2,6-7; 2:5,7-8; 3:2,7-8; 4:7,29; 6:24; 2 Thess 1:2,12; 2:16; 3:18; 1 Tim 1:2,14; 6:21; 2 Tim 1:2,9; 2:1; 4:22; Tit 1:4; 2:11; 3:7,15; Phlm 3,25; Heb 2:9; 4:16; 10:29; 12:15; 13:9,25.

the Council of Trent (1545-1563)); the Council of Florence (1442) on the abolition of the Old Covenant; and, the Council of Orange on grace (also further refined by the Council of Trent).

Like the Council of Jerusalem, each of theses pronouncements was prompted by theological controversy and debate (i.e., Pelagius at the Council of Orange; Judaizers at Florence; Luther at Trent). And like the Council of Jerusalem, the Church rendered her decrees and ended the debate. Just because many centuries pass until councils render decrees does not mean the Church's teachings are new. Some doctrines are defined early and some later, but they *all* follow this same process of development. They always flow naturally from the Deposit of Faith as the Holy Ghost guides the Church into all truth.

Other developments of doctrine

One of the most important developments of Catholic doctrine after the apostolic age occurred at the Council of Nicea (A.D. 325). At this moment in history, a priest named Arius was preaching that Jesus Christ was not co-equal to the Father. Like today's Protestants, Arius and his followers based their doctrine on their own interpretation of Scripture. When the Arians read Jesus' words, "the Father is greater than I"[111] and the Proverb "The Lord created me at the beginning of his work" (8:22), they concluded that Jesus could not be of the same substance as God the Father. Instead, the Arians claimed that Jesus was of "like substance" (Latin, *homoiousios*) as the Father.

Arius and his followers were educated men. Many were seasoned theologians and great debaters. They

---

[111] Jn 14:28.

also had Scripture to back up their claims. Because their argumentation was so persuasive, many in the Church fell into their error. The error became one of the most damaging heresies in Church history. As a result of this major controversy, the Church called her first ecumenical council (Nicea, A.D. 325) to put an end to the dispute. After examining Scripture and Tradition, the Church condemned the views of Arius and his followers as heretical. In addition, the Church issued a number of dogmatic decrees concerning the Divinity of Christ, including the decree that Jesus was of the "same substance" (Latin, *homoousios*) as the Father.[112]

Once again, we see the Catholic Church acting as the *final* authority in resolving a major doctrinal dispute. Scripture was formally insufficient to discern the true doctrine. In fact, an erroneous interpretation of Scripture created the controversy in the first place. While the apostles had been dead for more than two centuries, the bishops of the Church had been entrusted with their Tradition. Under the leadership of Pope Sylvester I and the guidance of the Holy Ghost, the Church put Scripture and Tradition on the witness stand, and, after reviewing the testimony, issued her infallible judgment.[113]

---

[112] Notice that the single letter i was the difference between the true and false description of Christ's nature (*homoousios* versus *homoiousios*) and caused a *de facto* schism in the early Church. Yet Protestants think they can correctly interpret the 30,000 verses in the Bible?

[113] Using Tradition and her Magisterial authority (and *not* Scripture alone), the Church had to condemn many other heresies dealing with the nature of God, Christ, grace and salvation. These included Modalism (1st century); Docetism (1st century); Gnosticism (1st / 2nd century); Montanism (2nd century); Marcionism (2nd century); Manichaeism (3rd century); Donatism (4th century); Apollinarianism (4th century); Nestorianism (5th century); Monophysitism (5th century); Pelagianism (5th century); Semi-Pelagianism (5th century);

If Arius could make such an error, why do some think they are immune from error? What guarantee do those people have that their interpretation of Scripture is correct? At a minimum, they must admit that Scripture is not formally sufficient to resolve the Arian controversy. Scripture does not explicitly say that Jesus is of the "same substance" as the Father. Scripture says nothing about *homoousios*. If Scripture is insufficient to resolve a basic doctrine about Christ, Scripture is insufficient for articulating many other dogmas as well. If that is the case, *sola Scriptura* must be abandoned and the Church must be embraced.

Another key development of doctrine after the apostolic age is the canon of Scripture (more on this in the next chapter). The canon of Scripture is the list of the inspired books that make up the Bible. While many don't give this much thought, the Bible does not tell us the canon. There is no inspired table of contents page. Thus, Scripture alone is insufficient to tell us what Scripture is.

During the first three centuries of the Church, there were certain books that were generally held to be apostolic. These were the four gospels (by Matthew, Mark, Luke and John), the Acts of the Apostles, and thirteen of Paul's fourteen epistles. These books were unanimously recognized by the East and the West as inspired Scripture and read at the celebration of Holy Mass.

There were other inspired books that did not garner unanimous recognition in certain parts of the Christian world. These included the letter to the Hebrews, James, 2 Peter, 2 and 3 John, Jude and the

---

Monothelitism (7th century); Iconoclasm (7th and 8th centuries); and, Catharism (11th century).

Apocalypse. Some thought these books did not contain apostolic doctrine. Others doubted the authenticity of their authorship. In fact, there were many books, like Pope Clement's letter to the Corinthians, the Didache, and the Shepherd of Hermas, that were regarded by many as inspired even though they were not. Similar reverence was given to the Epistle of Barnabas and the seven letters of Ignatius. For a Bible-only Christian, it is hard to imagine that some of the inspired books of the Bible were actually disputed or rejected by many Christian communities, while non-inspired books were regularly read in churches along side Sacred Scripture.

Influential Fathers such as Eusebius, Jerome, Epiphanius and Augustine had slightly different lists of what were the canonical Scriptures. There were also many "spurious" books floating around toward the close of the fourth century. These were false and non-canonical writings that contained heretical doctrines and included about 50 different "gospels" (like that of James, Judas and Thomas), about twenty different "Acts," (like that of Paul and Pilate) as well as other letters, epistles and apocalypses.

On top of top of that, the Emperor Diocletian in A.D. 303 issued his "Edict against the Christians." This edict forced Christian soldiers to leave the army, razed churches and burned Scriptures. But the question was obvious: What *was* divinely-inspired Scripture? Faithful Christians knew they *had* to give up their lives for Christ or risk losing their souls for eternity. But how would they really know whether they were dying for the Word of God or the word of man?

With Scripture silent on the issue of the canon, the Church had to look to the apostolic Tradition. After reviewing the many writings that claimed to be authentic and listening to the testimony of the bishops, the Church, *through the lens of Tradition*, authoritatively determined which manuscripts were apostolic and which ones were not. Under Pope Damasus, the Council of Rome in A.D. 382 finalized the canon which included 46 books in the Old Testament and 27 books in the New Testament. After Pope Damasus spoke, *the canon was settled*.[114] The pope's decree was affirmed at the regional Councils of Hippo (393) and Carthage (397 – 419), and again at the Council of Carthage (419), the Second Council of Nicea (787) and the Council of Florence. Once again, the Catholic Church, and not Scripture, had the final say.

The Church's determination of the canon of Scripture definitively proves that *sola Scriptura* is a false doctrine. Why? Because while Protestants believe that all the saving truths of the Christian faith are found in the Bible alone, the canon of Scripture is a saving truth of the Christian faith *that comes to us from outside the Bible*. Knowing the canon is necessary for our salvation because, if we didn't know it, all those heretical books could have been mixed up with inspired texts. If the erroneous books would have been accepted as canonical, Christians would have been led into error. God's revelation would have been compromised, and our salvation jeopardized.

---

[114] Fifteen years before Pope Damasus' decree, Athanasius drew up his own list of the New Testament canon (A.D. 367). Because Athanasius was an Eastern bishop, some advance the argument that the Eastern Orthodox, and not the Catholic Church, determined the canon. However, the Orthodox didn't exist until A.D. 1054 when certain Catholic bishops broke away from the Church! Before the schism, there was only one Church around – the Catholic Church – which existed in the East and the West as she does today. This is the same Catholic Church to which Athanasius claimed membership. Moreover, Pope Damasus didn't categorize the Scriptures the same way Athanasius did (more on this later).

During the so-called Protestant "Reformation," as he invented the novel doctrine of *sola Scriptura*, Martin Luther attacked many of the Church's teachings including purgatory and intercessory prayer. However, Luther had a big problem. He saw explicit support for the Church's teaching in some of the Old Testament books. For example, in the second book of Maccabees it says that Judas "made atonement for the dead, that they might be delivered from their sin" (2 Mac 12:45). Since there is no deliverance from sin for those in hell, and no need for deliverance from sin in heaven, Maccabees proves that there is another state after death (which the Church calls purgatory).

In the same book, we see intercession of the saints as Judas prays with the high priest Onias and the prophet Jeremiah, even though they were dead for centuries (2 Mac 15:12-16). In the book of Tobit, we also see angels interceding for Tobit and Sarah by presenting their prayers before God (Tob 12:12,15). Because these and other verses in the deuterocanonical books did not fit Luther's theology, he eventually decided to remove them from the established canon.

Luther's brash arrogance didn't end there. When he translated the Bible into German in A.D. 1536, Luther also removed the book of Hebrews, James, Jude and the Apocalypse from the New Testament canon and placed them in an appendix, declaring that they were less than canonical! The Founder of *sola Scriptura* thought he knew better than the decisions of sainted popes of the previous millennium as well as the entire Christian world who obeyed these decisions.

For example, Luther called James' letter "an epistle of straw, compared to these others, for it has nothing evangelical about it."[115] Luther wanted the letter of James removed because it directly contradicted his new-fangled theory that man is justified by faith alone (*sola fide*). James, on the other hand, clearly teaches that "a man is justified by works and not by faith alone" (Jam 2:24). Jesus even teaches that "by your words you will be justified, and by your words you will be condemned" (Mt 12:37).

Luther also removed Hebrews because Paul referred to the New Covenant sacrifice of Christ as "sacrifices" (in the plural) as he described the sacramental re-presentation of Jesus' sacrifice in the Mass (Heb 9:23). In his faulty exegesis of Hebrews, Luther said, "it is certain that Christ cannot be sacrificed over and above the one single time when He sacrificed Himself." Luther thus concluded, "No other sin, manslaughter, theft, murder or adultery is so harmful as this abomination of the popish Mass."[116]

In light of the controversy caused by Luther, the Council of Trent in A.D. 1546 infallibly affirmed the canon of Scripture first decided at the regional council of Rome in A.D. 382. As we can see, Trent was not issuing a *new* teaching. Based on the apostolic Tradition, Trent was affirming the decisions that had been handed down from the early councils in Rome, Hippo and Carthage, to Nicea II to Florence. The doctrine of the canon of Scripture developed from the debates in the second and third centuries, to the decisions in the fourth century, to an infallible definition in the sixteenth century. This also means that

---

[115] Hartmann Grisar, *Martin Luther: His Life and Work* (Westminster, MD: The Newman Press, 1961), p.426.
[116] Martin Luther, *Werke*, Weimar ed., vol. 15, 774, quoted in Francis Clark, *Eucharistic Sacrifice and the Reformation* (The Newman Press: Westminster, MD, 1960), p.101.

the canon of Scripture *is a Tradition of the Catholic Church.*

The Esdras issue

Because the Church's infallible determination of the canon of Scripture is so damaging to *sola Scriptura*, Protestant apologists are forced to attack the infallibility of the Church's decision, while at the same time holding to the infallibility of the canon. One of their more clever arguments is that Trent's declaration on the canon of Scripture is inconsistent with the Church's earlier decisions at the regional councils in Rome and Carthage. They point out that both councils at Rome and Carthage accepted "Esdras, two books,"[117] while the council of Trent accepted "the first book of Esdras, and the second which is called Nehemias."[118] Based on the difference in nomenclature, the Protestant apologist argues that Trent's canon is not the same as the canon determined by Rome and Carthage. The Protestant argument is not only built upon un-provable assumptions, but is refuted by the weight of historical facts.

First, some background. There is a distinction between the nomenclature used in the Septuagint and that used in the Latin Vulgate. In the Septuagint nomenclature, "Esdras, two books" could include not only the canonical books Ezra and Nehemiah, but also the non-canonical book of Esdras.[119] Because Esdras was not included in the canon determined by Trent, the Protestant's argument requires him to assume that Rome and Carthage were using a Septuagint

---

[117] See Denz., 84, 92.
[118] See Denz., 784.
[119] For additional information on this issue, see Gary Michuta's *Why Catholic Bibles Are Bigger* (Port Huron, MI: Grotto Press, 2007), pp.238-242.

translation which included Esdras. In other words, he argues that Rome and Carthage's use of "two books" really means the "three books" of Edras, Ezra and Nehemiah. This premise, which is odd on its face, cannot be proven. The early councils could have used the Vulgate (which Trent later affirmed to be the official translation of the Church) which identifies the first and second book of Esdras as Ezra and Nehemiah, excluding the non-canonical Esdras. Thus, "Esdras, two books" does not necessarily include the non-canonical Esdras, and the preponderance of evidence suggests that it *excludes* Esdras (although it ultimately depends upon what manuscript of the Septuagint one uses).

That both the councils of Rome and Carthage refer to "Esdras, two books" (Latin, "*Esdrae ii libri*") actually indicates that the councils affirmed only Ezra and Nehemiah and not Esdras. This is because the Septuagint translation doesn't use numbers 1 and 2, but rather "a Esdras" and "b Esdras."[120] By using the phrase "two books" (*ii libri*) strongly suggests that the councils were referring to the two books within 2 Esdras which are Ezra and Nehemiah, also known as "2 Esdras." Protestants assume that "two books" automatically refer to "a Esdras" and "b Esdras," but this is an assumption that cannot be proven.

Moreover, the Septuagint also includes another book called "3 Esdras" which is the non-canonical Apocalypse of Ezra. If, in using the phrase "two

---

[120] "a Esdras" is a manuscript that includes material from Ezra, Nehemiah, and 2 Chronicles, in addition to its own material. Some of the early Church Fathers quoted from Esdras until the councils of Rome and Carthage, which indicates that the Fathers understood the councils to have rejected its canonicity. Also, the Fathers' references to Esdras was generally limited to the canonical material within Esdras, which does not affirm the book as a whole.

books," the councils were not referring exclusively to Ezra and Nehemiah, then their declarations would be uncharacteristically ambiguous (another bad assumption for the Protestant to make). It would not be clear if the councils meant 1 and 2 Esdras, 1 and 3 Esdras, or 2 and 3 Esdras, since any of these combinations could refer to "two books" (and that assumes that Ezra and Nehemiah would be viewed as one book). If the councils intended to include the non-canonical Esdras, they would have been more specific than simply referring to "Esdras, two books." Finally, Protestants admit that St. Augustine exercised much influence over the council of Carthage. Since Augustine rejected the canonicity of Esdras (and affirmed the canonicity of Ezra and Nehemiah), it is extremely unlikely that he would have approved the council's inclusion of the "two books" if they included Esdras, and without any comment.

While it is unclear what nomenclature these early councils used (Septuagint or Vulgate), the council of Trent used the Vulgate nomenclature (while declaring the Vuglate free from doctrinal error). Based on the Vulgate, Trent dogmatically declared that the canon of Scripture included "the first book of Esdras, and the second which is called Nehemias" (Latin, "*Esdrae primus et secundus, qui dicitur Nehemias*"). It seems clear that Trent was giving clarity to the Church's earlier decisions by identifying the "two books" of Esdras as Ezra and Nehemiah, *excluding* Esdras (the Protestant argument also assumes that the Tridentine Fathers didn't understand the differences in the nomenclature which is absurd). In fact, Trent does specifically exclude Esdras from the canon by referring to "3 and 4 Esdras" as apocryphal books ("*Libri apocryphi*") in a footnote in its proceedings. We recall that "3 Esdras" in the Vulgate is the Book of Esdras, which Trent specifically excluded.

Thus, the Protestant's argument that Trent's canon contradicts the canon determined by Rome and Carthage is completely unfounded. It improperly assumes that the early councils included Esdras in the canon. The assumption is not only un-provable, but is also contradicted by the weight of the evidence.[121] Moreover, the Protestant fails to recognize that the Council of Trent was the first to issue an infallible, dogmatic decree on the canon of Scripture. Technically, the decisions of Rome, Hippo and Carthage did not invoke the Church's charism of infallibility (which is why there were still some minor debates after these decisions). Even if Rome and Carthage did include Esdras in its canon (the evidence indicates they did not), Trent could overrule their decisions without compromising either the infallibility of the canon or the Church's infallibility.

Closing comments about Scripture and Tradition

The foregoing historical facts raise an obvious question: Why do some Christians accept some teachings of the Catholic Church *but not all of her teachings?* Hopefully by now, any honest Christian will realize that rejecting a teaching of the Church on the ground that it is "unbiblical" is silly. There is nothing particularly "biblical" about the doctrine of the Trinity, and yet Protestants believe in the Triune God with all

---

[121] If we were to play devil's advocate and argue that Rome and Carthage included Esdras in the canon, we could also argue that Trent did not expressly reject Esdras. This is because the Tridentine Fathers voted to pass on making an explicit judgment on Esdras *"sub silentio"* (this fact is part of the historical record of Trent's proceedings). That being the case, there would be no inconsistency between Trent and the earlier councils. The Fathers passed on making a specific judgment on a number of the apocryphal books as a diplomatic gesture to facilitate reunion with the Eastern schismatics who held Esdras (and other books like 3 Maccabees) as canonical.

their heart. There is nothing in the New Testament that tells us what books are inspired, and yet Protestants accept the 27-book canon without question.

Such doctrines as the Blessed Trinity (Nicea, A.D. 325), the two natures of Christ (Chalcedon, A.D. 451), and the divine and human wills of Christ (Third Council of Constantinople, A.D. 680-681) are not clearly taught in Scripture and were defined well beyond the apostolic age. In fact, Mary as the Mother of God and her Perpetual Virginity (doctrines some Protestants oppose) were defined at the Council of Ephesus (A.D. 431) and Second Council of Constantinople (A.D. 553) respectively, well *before* the Church defined the divine and human wills of Christ (a doctrine Protestants accept). These are all "developments of doctrine" springing forth from the seed of Tradition under the authority of the pope and the guidance of the Holy Ghost.

We have already mentioned the doctrines of baptismal regeneration, papal infallibility, the Real Presence of Christ in the Eucharist, the sacrifice of the Mass, intercessory prayer and purgatory. On what basis do Protestants reject these teachings? While addressing all of these doctrines is beyond the scope of this book, these doctrines are found throughout Scripture and Tradition, have an abundance of support from the Church Fathers (as we will see in Chapter 11), and were proclaimed by the same councils that determined the canon of Scripture and the dogmas of Christ.

Moreover, doctrines such as papal infallibility and the Real Presence of Christ in the Eucharist have much stronger patristic support than, say, the dogmas of the

Trinity and the Divinity of Christ.[122] The Church had always interpreted the Scripture passages about the Eucharist in their literal and obvious sense, and thousands of Christians were martyred for this belief. The early Church Fathers were also unanimous in their belief about the Eucharist. The very fact that the Church waited until the Fourth Lateran Council (1215) to define transubstantiation of the Eucharist was because the doctrine of the Real Presence was *already well-settled.*

In fact, there was no opposition to the Church's understanding of the Eucharist until the eleventh century in the writings of Berengar of Tours. This complete absence of opposition to the Eucharist for a millennium should be alarming to Protestants. The purpose of Lateran IV's teaching was to exclude false explanations about the transformation of bread and wine into Christ's body and blood. Hence, the Church adopted the term *transubstantiatio* (to describe that the "substance" of the bread and wine becomes Christ's body and blood while the "accidents" remain the same). The Church affirmed the doctrine at the Council of Lyons (1274), and added further clarity and dogmatic decrees at the Council of Trent.

We see the same thing with the doctrine of papal infallibility. For nineteen centuries, the Church operated under the assumption that the pope was protected from error whenever he officially taught on matters of salvation. The Church's understanding was based on the plain meaning of Jesus' words that "whatever Peter bound or loosed on earth would be bound or loosed in heaven" (see Mt 16:19). The

---

[122] For extensive quotes from the early Church Fathers on the dogmas of papal infallibility and the Real Presence, please see my books *The Biblical Basis for the Papacy* and *The Biblical Basis for the Eucharist* (Our Sunday Visitor), respectively.

Church's understanding was also supported by a unanimous consensus of the early Fathers and medieval theologians.

Because popes over the centuries made a number of doctrinal errors in their private letters and non-dogmatic teachings, the Church decided to define the parameters of papal infallibility at the First Vatican Council (1870). The Church declared that the pope is infallible only when he speaks on faith and morals either from his chair (*ex cathedra*) or through an ecumenical council and manifestly invokes his intention to speak infallibly.[123] Again, the doctrine was always believed, but needed to be "developed" with further clarity and elucidation.

The Catholic dogmas regarding Mary are perhaps the most troubling to Protestants. These include Mary's Immaculate Conception and her Assumption into heaven. Admittedly, there is less Scriptural support for these dogmas, and they were defined later in Church history. But as we have seen, *when* a dogma is officially promulgated and how much *biblical support* there is for the dogma is not relevant to whether the dogma is part of the Deposit of Faith.

If people would read the early Church Fathers, they would discover the basis for all Marian dogmas in Tradition. The Immaculate Conception is a great example. Even though the dogma wasn't pronounced until the 19th century, we find many allusions to it in the writings of the Church Fathers.

---

[123] As we have mentioned, the Church also teaches infallibly without an *ex cathedra* or conciliar decree when she consistently pronounces upon a matter of faith and morals throughout the centuries (e.g., condemnation of abortion, contraception, homosexuality, women priests). Such teachings are said to come from the "ordinary and universal Magisterium."

For example, Hippolytus said Mary was "exempt from putridity and corruption" (c.A.D. 235); Origen said she was "immaculate of the immaculate" (A.D. 244); Ephraim called her "the pure Mary" (A.D. 370); Ambrose said she was "free of every stain of sin" (A.D. 388); Proclus of Constantinople said she was formed "without any stain of her own" (A.D. 446); Theodotus said she was spotless, "free of all defect, untouched, unsullied" (A.D. 446); and James of Sarugh said that no "stain had disfigured her soul" (A.D. 521). Quotes similar to these could be multiplied many times over.

It is the same with the Assumption of Mary into heaven. For example, Gregory of Tours said Mary's body was "taken in a cloud into paradise" (c.A.D. 575); Modestus of Jerusalem said God "has raised her from the tomb and has taken her up to himself" (A.D. 634); Theoteknos of Livias similarly said Mary was "raised up to heaven in glory" (c.A.D. 650); Germanus of Constantinople said Mary's body was "changed into the heavenly life of incorruptibility" (c.A.D. 773); John Damascene also said that Apostles believed Mary was assumed into heaven after discovering her tomb was empty (c.A.D. 747).

While these quotations only scratch the surface, they reveal that the dogma of the Immaculate Conception and the Assumption were part of the Deposit of Faith. That the Church didn't formally dogmatize the Immaculate Conception and the Assumption until the 19th and 20th centuries respectively is irrelevant to whether these teachings come from Tradition. The Church decides when to officially promulgate teachings based on the needs of the faithful and the surrounding facts and circumstances. When theologians began to debate what was always held as a pious belief, the Church decided that the time was right to settle the matters once for all. Thus, Blessed Pius IX dogmatized the Immaculate

Conception in his Constitution *Ineffabilis Deus* (1854), and Pius XII did the same with the dogma of the Assumption in his Bull *Munificentissimus Deus* (1950).

How did the Church decide that the Immaculate Conception and the Assumption were dogmas of the faith? The same way she determined the circumcision exemption, the Divinity of Christ, the canon of Scripture and all the rest of her dogmas. The same way she knows who wrote the gospels (all four are anonymous). The same way she knows the Eucharist is a sacrament and the washing of feet is not (even though the Jesus told the apostles to do both at the Last Supper).[124] The same way she knows that there are seven sacraments and not one or two as is believed by most Protestants. Guided by the Holy Spirit, the Church prayerfully considers the witnesses of both Scripture and Tradition. She scrutinizes the Deposit of Faith and plumbs the depths of the Word of God. After examining the witnesses and reviewing the testimony, she renders her judgment.[125]

---

[124] See Jn 13:14-15.

[125] Just as there is no way to the Father but through His Son, there is no way to the Son but through His Mother. Thus, I believe that some day the Church will dogmatize the traditional Catholic belief that Mary is the Mediatrix of All Graces by virtue of being Mother of the Church and uniquely participating in the Mediatorial role of Her Son Jesus Christ. The belief is deeply rooted in Scripture (1 Kg 2:17-20; Jn 2:3-5) and Tradition (Irenaeus, Gregory of Nazienzen, Epiphanius, Peter Chrysologus, Basil of Seleucia, Romanos the Singer, Theoteknos of Livias, Germanus of Constantinople, Andrew of Crete, Ambrose Autpert, Paul the Deacon, John the Geometer, Peter Damian, Anselm, Bernard) and has been taught by the Magisterium (Pope Leo XIII, *Octobri mense* (1891); *Iucunda semper expectatione* (1894); and, *Adiutricem populi* (1895); Pope Pius X, *Ad diem illum* (1904); *Pii X Pontifici Maximi Acta* (1908); Pope Pius XI, *Miserentissimus* (1928); Pope Pius XII, radio message (May 13, 1946); Second Vatican Council, *Lumen Gentium*, No. 62 (1962-1965).

To date, the Catholic Church has convened 21 ecumenical councils in her 2,000 year history (from Nicea in A.D. 325 to the Second Vatican Council in A.D. 1962-1965). An ecumenical council is a special gathering of the pope and all of the world's bishops for the purpose of teaching faith and morals. The regional Council of Jerusalem served as the blueprint for how the Church would conduct its future ecumenical councils by exhibiting the following traits:

- It is an assembly of the pope and bishops.
- It addressed a question of faith or morals.
- It promulgated a doctrine that was binding on the entire Church.
- It recorded its teaching in a written document for the entire Church.
- It declared that its teaching was confirmed by the Holy Spirit.
- The pope presided over the council and approved its teachings in order for the council to be valid.

II.
The Bible and *Sola Scriptura*

Chapter 5

The Inspiration of Scripture

In the first section, we demonstrated the biblical basis for Tradition. We showed that Tradition is the oral transmission of the gospel that the apostles handed on to their successors through the process of apostolic succession and the protection of the Holy Ghost. We also showed that Scripture commands us to obey Tradition and not Scripture alone. In this second section, we address in more detail the errors of *sola Scriptura* and provide further proofs that the Bible is not the sole rule of faith for Christians.

But first, let's step back and ask a more fundamental question: Why should we believe the Bible is a rule of faith at all? After all, the Bible can only be a rule of faith if it teaches the Word of God. Does it? Christians will respond by claiming that the Bible is divinely inspired. But the question is not what the Bible *is*, but how we *know* what it is. How do we know the Bible is divinely inspired? How do we know it is the Word of God? Surprisingly, many non-Catholic Christians, who stake their entire spiritual lives on the teachings of the Bible, have not given these questions much, if any, thought.[126]

---

[126] Catholic apologist Karl Keating provides an excellent analysis of this question in *Catholicism and Fundamentalism*, pp.121-126.

Many Christians simply accept the authority of the Bible because their parents taught them to believe in it. Of course, accepting the inspiration of Scripture on the basis of family custom is not sufficient to prove that Scripture is in fact inspired. Muslims, for example, usually come to their faith in Islam the same way, but that does not mean that the Koran is inspired. Indeed, it is not. Further, the Christian who comes to believe in the Bible on the authority of his parents is relying upon an authority *outside* of Scripture (a family "tradition"). This undermines any claim of Scripture's ability to make itself known without outside assistance.

Other Christians explain how the Bible "inspires" or "moves" them when they read it. But Islamic jihadists are also "inspired" when they read the Koran. While many Christians undeniably feel "inspired" after soaking in some Scripture, this subjective sentiment does not prove that the Scripture is God-breathed. A good novel, or even a good motion picture, can have the same effect. Moreover, many people would rather read the newspaper than Holy Writ, even those with a sincere desire to learn about God. Some people simply find the Word tedious and dull no matter how hard they seek to be inspired. We should also admit that a fair chunk of Scripture *can be* tedious to read. For example, the ritual prescriptions in Leviticus and the genealogies in Chronicles contain little to stimulate the emotions.

Still other Christians explain how the Sacred Word has changed their lives. The Scriptures have helped many people who led habitually sinful lives to renounce evil and grow in holiness. They have also helped many people conquer fears, addictions and other harmful maladies. Because of these miraculous changes, these Christians are convinced that the Bible is the Word of God. This, of course, is the beautiful and powerful reality of God's Word. The Bible has changed my own life as well. God has given us His Word for this very purpose.

But again, a subjective, personal experience does not answer the question of how we know objectively that the Bible is the Word of God. It explains only the effects that reading the Bible has had on a particular person. Many people who read the Bible do *not* have profound conversions to Christ. This does not mean that the Bible is not inspired. In addition, there are many non-Christians who falsely believe their religious writings are inspired due to their own life-changing experiences. Mormons and Jehovah's Witnesses commonly claim inspiration for their religious writings based on their own personal "feelings" and "experiences."

Many Christians simply assert that "The Bible teaches that it is the Word of God." This knowledge, which they extract from the Bible, serves as a sufficient basis for them to accept its divine inspiration. But this response is equally inadequate to prove inspiration for a number of reasons. First, almost *none* of the books in the Bible claim to be divinely inspired. Just read it and see. The only book in the New Testament which makes any such claim is the Apocalypse of John. What about books like Paul's letter to Philemon or John's third epistle? Nothing in these letters jumps off the page to convince the reader of its divine inspiration.

Second, the response presumes that any claim of inspiration found in the Bible is true. This begs the same question. How do we know such a claim is true? If every book in the Bible contained a preface claiming divine inspiration (e.g., "Following is an inspired book"), it would prove absolutely nothing. Many books written about Christ during the first three centuries of Christianity also claimed to be divinely inspired, but did not make it into the Bible.

Mohammed also claimed to be divinely inspired (Islam), as did Joseph Smith (Mormonism), Mary Baker Eddy (Christian Science) and Ellen G. White (Seventh Day Adventistism).

After trying to "prove" the inspiration of the Bible, non-Catholic Christians ultimately resort to arguing that their belief is a matter of faith. But faith in God does not prove that the Bible is inspired either. Muslims also profess faith in God but do not believe in His written revelation. This argument also does not convince people who have not been given the gift of faith (which also means that using the "faith" argument to prove the Bible is inspired is a bad way to evangelize).

In fact, if faith were the sole criterion for the non-Catholic Christian, this should actually raise *doubts* about the Bible's inspiration. This is because, while the Bible teaches the truth and the truth is one, non-Catholic Christians are *not* one in the Christian faith. They are divided. There are thousands of different Protestant denominations which disagree with each other on basic doctrines of the Christian faith and yet all claim to be faithful to the Bible.

If the truth cannot be divided, the divisions among non-Catholic Christians undermine the "faith" argument. That is, non-Catholics cannot successfully argue that the Bible teaches the truth when the Bible is the very thing that divides them. This division actually causes unbelievers to conclude that the Bible does *not* teach the truth (which is why the lack of Christian unity is so scandalous). This is also why Jesus stated that *unity* in the Christian family would *prove* to the world that He was really the Son of God (Jn 17:21).

Since the Bible, when analyzed in isolation, is not sufficient to demonstrate it is a divinely inspired book, the Christian is forced to admit that he is (consciously or unconsciously) relying upon an authority *outside* of the Bible that attests to its inspiration. But what is it? What demonstrates to the Christian that the Bible is the Word of God? Surely it is something other than custom, experience, feeling, or even the Bible's own claims about itself. The Catholic offers the following analysis.

The Catholic approach

The Bible is approached like any other ancient writing (such as the classical writings of Plato, Herodotus and Euripides). The goal with this initial approach is to authenticate the *accuracy*, not the inspiration, of the biblical texts. Inspiration is not presumed. Based upon an analysis of all the works of antiquity, we can demonstrate without serious question that we have accurate copies of Sacred Scripture.

In fact, the evidence we have that demonstrates the accuracy of Sacred Scripture far surpasses the evidence we have for *any* other ancient writing for two principal reasons. First, the manuscripts we have were written in closer proximity to the time of their original composition. Most of the New Testament manuscripts date from the third and fourth century A.D., just several hundred years after the autographs were first composed. For works by the classical authors, the time span between the originals and the copies is much greater. For example, for Plato it is about 1,300 years, for Herodotus about 1,400 years, and for Euripides 1,600 years. Yet, the authenticity of these manuscripts is beyond dispute.

Second, we have many more manuscripts – about 5,300 – from which to conduct our study. These manuscripts, which consist of entire books, partial books or fragments, can be cross referenced with remarkable accuracy. The accuracy between the manuscripts is especially extraordinary given that they were copied in many different places, under different conditions, and in a variety of different languages such as Aramaic, Hebrew, Greek and Latin. While there are textual variants throughout the manuscripts, the vast majority of these variants involve a single word, letter or gloss that crept into the text – an amazing fact given the sheer number of manuscripts and their geographical and linguistic diversity. Based on these facts, we can be confident that we are working with an accurate text.

The next step is to determine what the Bible, as an historical document only, tells us about the person named Jesus Christ. We pay particular attention to the gospels of the New Testament which record the events in the life of Jesus. In the gospels, we read about Jesus' core teaching concerning love and forgiveness, and how we must do to others what we would have them do to us. We read about Jesus' many miracles such as His raising the dead, driving out demons, giving sight to the blind, and multiplying the fish and loaves. We also learn about Jesus' own claims about Himself, namely, that He was God: "Truly, truly, I say to you, before Abraham was, I am" (Jn 8:58); "I and the Father are one" (Jn 10:30). We discover that no one in history ever taught like Jesus, spoke like Jesus, or performed miracles like Jesus did.

Because of Jesus' claims to divinity, the Jewish religious authorities handed Jesus over to the Romans to be crucified (Jn 19:7). The gospels tell us about Jesus' brutal scourging, crucifixion and death under Pontius Pilate. The gospels also reveal that Jesus rose from the dead on the third day, appearing not only to His apostles and friends, but to more than five hundred people *at once* (1 Cor 15:6). St. Paul's written account of

Jesus' appearance to these hundreds of people, particularly because these eye witnesses were *still alive* when Paul wrote his letter, is some of the strongest evidence for the historical fact of Jesus' resurrection. In a court of law, the corroborated eye witness testimony of two or three witnesses is almost always sufficient for carrying the burden of proof. In the case of Jesus' resurrection, we have *more than five hundred eye witnesses!*

We should also remember that Paul was not a believer until he encountered the risen Christ on the Damascus road. Before this encounter, Paul persecuted the Church of God and presided over the torture and murder of Christians.[127] When Jesus appeared to Paul in his resurrected state, Paul did a "180 degree turn." Paul immediately converted to Christianity and became one of the greatest missionaries the Church has ever had. St. Paul's change of heart was based entirely on the reality of Jesus' resurrection. Paul says, "if Christ has not been raised, then our preaching is in vain and your faith is in vain" (1 Cor 15:14). Jesus' conversion of *hostile witnesses* is more powerful evidence of His resurrection.

As an aside, in my opinion, the image on the Shroud of Turin is the most compelling, tangible evidence for the resurrection. The Shroud, which is believed to be Jesus' burial cloth, depicts a photographic negative of a man who bears the wounds of scourging and crucifixion. The image also shows wounds on the head (from the crowning of thorns) and a large wound in the chest cavity (from the soldier's spear). The man also appears to be suspended vertically in mid-air.

---

[127] See Acts 7:58-60; 1 Cor 15:9; Gal 1:13

Through carbon-14 dating, the age of the cloth is traced back precisely to the time of Jesus Christ. Modern science cannot explain how the image was transferred to the cloth. They compare the amount of energy necessary to burn such an image into cloth to the energy that was released during the explosions of atomic bombs (like at Hiroshima and Nagasaki). In John's gospel, when Peter went into Jesus' empty tomb, he saw the linen cloth that wrapped Jesus' dead body. Then John "also went in and *he saw and believed*" (Jn 20:8).

Through the gospels (as historical documents only), the death and resurrection of Jesus Christ is one of the most documented events in history. These accounts are also corroborated not only by hundreds of Christian writers of the first several centuries, but by at least a dozen *non-Christian* writers including the noted Flavius Josephus, the first century Jewish historian. While the Jews claimed that Jesus' disciples stole Jesus' body from the tomb, the evidence contradicts such a claim.[128]

First, the Jews knew that Jesus claimed He would rise from the dead on the third day (Mt 27:63). As a result, the Jews asked the Romans to secure the tomb to prevent Jesus' disciples from stealing the body and perpetrating an even greater "fraud" (v.64).[129]   The Romans capitulated, placing a seal on the tomb which represented the power and authority of the Roman Empire (v.66). If the Roman soldiers failed to guard the tomb and the seal was broken, the soldiers would have

---

[128] See Mt 28:11-15.

[129] Note that, as pagans, Romans generally believed that "gods" could resurrect from the dead. Hence, it is ironic to think that some of the pagan Roman soldiers who guarded Jesus' body may have actually believed Jesus could rise from the dead, while the Jews who had heard God's Word and saw Jesus' miracles did not so believe.

been immediately executed. This motivated the soldiers to pay flawless attention to their duties. The Roman soldiers' failure to guard the tomb is inexplicable given that their lives were at stake.

Further, the Romans secured the tomb with a large stone that weighed nearly two tons. All of the gospels record that this stone had been moved.[130] In fact, the massive stone "had been taken away from the tomb" (Jn 20:1). It was completely separated from the sepulcher. The improbability for Jesus' disciples to remove such a large stone and steal Jesus' body, especially in the presence of the Roman guards, is an understatement to say the least.

Second, if the apostles did steal Jesus' body from the sleeping Roman guards (an unlikely proposition for eleven terrified fishermen), the Romans would have hunted them down and murdered them. There is no record of this happening (the record actually demonstrates the apostles died much later in history, such as Peter's death in Rome in A.D. 67). Instead, the Roman guards fled the scene and the once-scared apostles went back into hostile Jerusalem to boldly proclaim Jesus' resurrection from the dead. Jesus' resurrection could have never been maintained even for an hour - and especially in Jerusalem – had the empty tomb not been established as an absolute fact.

Third, if the apostles stole Jesus' body, how would that lead to their conversions and the conversions of thousands of Christians? How would having Christ's dead and mangled body convince them that they could conquer death through faith in Him? During the first three centuries of the Church, Jesus' disciples chose

---

130 See Mt 28:2; Mk 16:4; Lk 24:2; Jn 20:1.

violent deaths at the hands of non-believers rather than betray their Master. While Jesus' own apostles abandoned Him during His Passion, they accepted martyrdom in His name after the resurrection. And they did so without any prospect of economic, social or other earthly advantage whatsoever. Why? *Because they saw something that dramatically changed their lives: the risen Christ.*

Human nature tells us that people don't willfully die for a hoax. People aren't willing to suffer for a fraud. This is especially the case when they have nothing to gain but torture and death. The seed of Christianity came forth from the blood of these martyrs, beginning with the apostles. If Jesus didn't rise from the dead, the conversion of the world to Christ, brought about by eleven uneducated men from Galilee, seems to be an even greater miracle than the resurrection!

The most desperate antagonists of Christianity say Jesus was seriously wounded during the crucifixion, but never died (often called the "swoon theory"). This is an impossible scenario for a number of reasons. First, secular sources record Jesus' death. Even the disbelieving Jews who denied the resurrection admitted Jesus died. Second, all those crucified under Roman authority were *guaranteed to die*. This is why they broke the legs of the crucified. Breaking the legs prevented the victims from supporting themselves as they gasped for oxygen which ensured their death through asphyxiation. Jesus' suffering was so intense that He died before the soldiers needed to break His legs (Jn 19:33).

It would have been impossible for Jesus to survive the torture He endured (scourging, crowning with thorns, crucifixion, and receiving a lance through His heart). Even if He had theoretically survived the cross,

He would have suffocated to death in His burial cloth
(Jewish custom required the face of the decedent to be
tightly wrapped along with the rest of the body). If
Jesus really didn't die, then the apostles were either
liars or delusional. These are not reasonable
alternatives, for there would have been absolutely no
motive for all of them to lie, and equally improbable
that they would have all suffered delusions from
seeing the wounded and near-dead Jesus. Again, how
would seeing Jesus in such a condition convince all of
them to preach the resurrection from the dead and
accept violent martyrdoms?

Based on the evidence, we are compelled to
conclude that Jesus Christ rose from the dead. Of all
the theories advanced to describe the origins of
Christianity, the historical reality of Christ's
resurrection is the most tenable and most supportable.
This also means that Jesus was not merely a "great
moral teacher" or a "good man," for great teachers and
good men don't claim to be God and rise from the
dead. Rather, our reasoning leads us to conclude that
Jesus Christ was indeed who He said He was – the
Incarnate Son of God. If Jesus was God, then His
claims and promises are trustworthy. So what did He
promise?

One of the things Jesus promised to do was *build a
Church*. According to the Bible (again, viewing the
Bible only as an historical document), Jesus established
His Church upon the apostle Simon whom Jesus
renamed Peter ("rock"). Jesus also gave Peter "the keys
to the kingdom of heaven." By giving Peter "the keys,"
Jesus established a supreme teaching office over the
Church that would be occupied by Peter and his
successors until the end of time. We see the unbroken
lineage of 264 successors to Peter since the time of
Jesus Christ in both Christian and secular sources. The
game plan that Jesus drew up 2,000 years ago has been

implemented by the Catholic Church and her alone. The evidence is indisputable.

Further, the Bible tells us that Jesus also told Peter, "whatever you bind or loose on earth will be bound or loosed in heaven" (see Mt 16:19). In other words, Jesus gave Peter the authority to speak for heaven itself as he exercised his teaching office. This means Peter's teachings must be error-free, for Jesus cannot lie and heaven cannot confirm error. Thus, still looking at the Bible as merely an historical (but not yet an inspired) book, we conclude that Jesus Christ *established an infallible Church*.

This last part of the equation, of course, is the key. Once we establish an infallible Church, we can believe that her teachings are also infallible. Because the Church teaches that the Bible is inspired, we accept the Bible as an inspired book. We do so based on the authority of the Church, not the authority of the Bible. We base it on the Church's authority to infallibly "bind and loose" as promised by the God-man Jesus Christ. It is only after we establish the Church's infallibility that we can accept the Bible's inspiration. This is the only logical method of ascertaining the Bible's divine inspiration. It is the only analysis that can satisfy the intellect. As Augustine said, "I would not believe in the Gospel if the authority of the Catholic Church did not move me to do so."[131]

Is the Catholic position "circular reasoning"?

Some accuse the Catholic position of circular reasoning. "Circular reasoning" means that the premise of the argument is restated in the conclusion. The Protestant argument goes like this: The Catholic

---

[131] *Against the letter of Mani*, 5:6, A.D. 397.

claims that the Church is infallible and thus she gave us the Bible. However, because the Catholic gets this information from the inspired Bible, it is really the Bible, not the Church, that is infallible. If this were the Catholic argument, it would be circular reasoning indeed. But it is not the Catholic argument.

The trajectory of the Catholic argument is not circular. Rather, it is ascending or escalating, like a staircase, because it reaches its destination only after traversing firmly established steps.[132] That is, Catholics do *not* approach the Bible as an inspired book as a first step, but as a conclusion that results from three preliminary steps. It is only after these three steps are satisfied that we can take the final step and conclude that the Scriptures are inspired.

First, we establish that the Bible is an historical and reliable book, which is a point of agreement for all Christians. As we have seen, the Bible's reliability has been established by virtue of the massive number of translated manuscripts, their proximity in time to the original authors, their internal consistency, and their support in secular sources. Second, the historically reliable Scriptures reveal that Jesus Christ established an infallible Church. Third, the infallible Church teaches that the Bible is inspired. Absent a revelation from God, we would never know what Scriptures are inspired without a divinely-appointed authority to tell us.

Not willing to see the logic of the Catholic rejoinder, some argue that if we need an infallible Church to tell us the Scriptures are infallible, then we need an infallible authority (the Scriptures) to tell us

---

[132] Catholic apologist Karl Keating calls it a "spiral argument" (*Catholicism and Fundamentalism*, p.126).

the Church is infallible, and so on to infinity. This argument, while clever, is flawed for the reasons we just cited. We cannot use history and reason to prove that the Scriptures are infallible like we can with the Church. Thus, the premise of their argument, that we need an infallible source to demonstrate the infallible Church, is false. Further, the Scriptures *do* point to an infallible Church, but *not* to an infallible canon of Scripture.

We must also point out that the "circular reasoning" argument does not apply to the Church because her authority comes from God Almighty. When God reveals a truth or commands us to do something, we should not ask "why." And we certainly don't dare accuse God of faulty reasoning. The problem of circular reasoning is eliminated when one is dealing with legitimate authority.

Ultimately, the Protestant says, "Who cares how we know the Bible is inspired. The most important thing is that we know it is." But here is where we get to the crux of the issue. If the Church has the authority to determine what the inspired Scriptures are, then she also has the authority to *interpret* those Scriptures. If the Protestant doesn't know what the Scriptures *are* without the Church, then he cannot know what the Scriptures *mean* without the Church. Both prerogatives flow from her charism of infallibility. Thus, the issue of how we identify Scripture goes to the very heart of how we approach Scripture and, ultimately, how we understand Scripture.

Chapter 6

The Canon of Scripture

The word "canon" comes from the Greek *kanon* which means "a measure, a rule for judgment, or an authoritative standard." We have already looked at how the Catholic Church relied upon the apostolic Tradition to determine the canon of Scripture at the end of the fourth century. Tradition was the Church's basis for determining what Scripture was apostolic and what "Scripture" was not.

We have also demonstrated the Catholic Church's determination of the canon proves *sola Scriptura* is a false doctrine. This is because the canon is a saving truth of the Christian faith which comes to us from outside Scripture. Without the canon, we would not know what books are from God, and this lack of knowledge would jeopardize our salvation. Because the Bible does not tell us the canon, the Bible does *not* contain all truths necessary for salvation. Even Luther, the Founder of *sola Scriptura*, said this about the Church's determination of the canon: "We are obliged to yield many things to the Papists – that with them is the word of God, which we received from them; otherwise we should have known nothing at all about it."[133] We now look at another important fact of the canon: *It is infallible.*

The canon of Scripture is infallible because it contains those books – and *only* those books – that are inspired by God. The Bible does not contain uninspired books, nor are there inspired books out there that didn't make it into the canon. The canon is the complete set of the books that God moved men to write under the inspiration of the Holy Ghost – no more and no less.

If the canon of Scripture is infallible, then the Catholic Church must be infallible as well. Why? Because an effect can never be greater than its cause. An effect is always less than or equal to its cause. For example, the creation (effect) is less than the Creator (cause). A child (effect) is equal to his parents (cause).[134] The canon of Scripture is infallible (effect) because the Church who determined it is infallible (cause). This is a principle of logic called the "principle of causality."

This fact puts Protestants into a real bind. If the Catholic Church made an infallible decision regarding the canon, that means she is capable of making other infallible decisions as well. On what basis does the Protestant reject these other infallible teachings, like the dogmas on the papacy or the Eucharist? It can be only on the basis of the Protestant's fallible private

---

[133] Luther's Works, Vol. 24, *Commentary on the Gospel of John*, discussion on 16th chapter (Concordia: St. Louis, MO, 1961), p.304.
[134] Here we mean to say that the parents participate in bringing about the child's existence as cause, but the child's being/essence (the effect of the marital union) is the same (equal to) the parents' being/essence. The child is not ontologically greater (or less) than the parents because an effect cannot be greater than its cause (who is ultimately God, the First Being and Cause of all things).

judgment, which is the same fallible judgment he uses to interpret Scripture. Admitting that the Church is infallible when it comes to determining the canon of Scripture but fallible in her other teachings is arbitrary, illogical and nonsensical. If the Protestant admits that the Church is infallible but remains Protestant, he effectively signs his own spiritual death warrant. It is that serious.

The canon is fallible?

If the Protestant wants to remain logically consistent in arguing the Church is fallible, he must conclude that the canon of Scripture is fallible as well. But if the canon were fallible, then why should we believe the books in the canon are themselves infallible? A fallible canon would mean that some books in the Bible may not actually be Scripture, and other books could be added to the Bible.

How can Protestants gather every Sunday to hear and study the Word of God if they don't really know they *have* the Word of God? How can the Protestant preacher tell his congregation to put all its hope in a book that could be wrong? Most would not dare make this argument, for it completely undermines the authority of the book upon which they stake their eternal life. Hopefully, they recognize the error in such reasoning. But this leaves them only one choice – to become Catholic. Indeed, the canon of Scripture's fatal blow to *sola Scriptura* is a common first step in leading Protestants home to the Catholic Church.

The Church could have erred but didn't?

Some non-Catholic apologists assert that the Church could have erred on the canon question, but didn't. They accuse Catholics of the "fallacy of composition." This is a term in logic that describes an argument whose conclusion is based on the erroneous transference of some attribute from a part onto the whole. As applied here, the Protestant says the Catholic erroneously transfers the infallible decision of the Church onto the Church itself and thus concludes that the Church is infallible. There are a number of problems with this argument.

First, the Protestant misapplies the fallacy of composition. The fallacy of composition involves the *erroneous* transference of an attribute onto the whole. Whether or not a transference is erroneous depends upon the facts and circumstances. For example, just because all the parts of a widget maker are light in weight does not mean the widget maker is light in weight. The widget maker could be heavy. On the other hand, if all the parts of a widget maker are heavy, the widget maker must also be heavy. The transference of the attribute (light or heavy weight) to the whole (the widget maker) depends on the facts and circumstances. It is not an "all or nothing" rule.

The Protestant argument also violates the principle of causality. Because no effect can be greater than its cause, an infallible canon necessarily requires an infallible Church. *No other conclusion is possible.* In this case, the transference of infallibility from the canon to the Church is mandated by the rules of logic.

Finally, with this argument the Protestant conveniently arrogates to himself the authority to determine when the Church errs and when she doesn't err. This position allows the Protestant to maintain the infallibility of the canon while rejecting other Catholic doctrines. Such an approach to theological questions is, of course, Protestantism *par excellence.* Using his own private judgment, the Protestant decides which teachings he will obey and which teachings he will disobey. The Protestant approach always brings us back to square one – who has the final authority? The Protestant can only say, "I do."

The Church couldn't make infallible decisions after the apostolic age?

Because revelation ceased with the death of the last apostle, some Protestants argue that no infallible decisions could have been rendered after the apostolic age. This argument confuses revelation with infallibility. Revelation is the object of faith that God has given us, while infallibility is the ability to interpret that revelation error-free. The Church's determination of the canon was not a revelation, but an infallible interpretation of revelation (here, the nature of inspired Scripture).

If the Protestant wishes to question the Church's infallible decisions after the apostolic age, he would call into question not only the canon of Scripture, but essentially *all* of the core dogmas of Christianity! The doctrines regarding the Fall, Original Sin, grace, the Trinity, and Christology were all determined after the age of the apostles. Many of these teachings were not dogmatized until after the canon of Scripture was determined. If the Church was not able to render infallible judgments after the death of the Apostle John, then Jesus' gift of "binding and loosing" authority would be meaningless, and the gates of hell would have prevailed a long time ago.

Finally, how does the Protestant know that revelation ended with the Apostle John? The Bible doesn't make this theological declaration. So how does the Protestant know this? Because the Catholic Church has told him so. The cessation of revelation with the death of the last apostle is another Catholic Tradition that is not found in Scripture but is nevertheless accepted by Protestants on the authority of the Catholic Church.

The canon is a function of Scripture, not the Church?

One of the more clever Protestant arguments is that the canon exists because God inspired the books in it. In other words, the canon is a "function" of Scripture and cannot be separated from the books themselves. This argument erroneously confuses the (epistemological) question of knowledge with the (ontological) question of being. It acknowledges that there *is* a canon, but doesn't tell us how we *know* what books should be in the canon.

Knowledge and existence are two separate things, because something can exist without us knowing about it. For example, the Blessed Trinity existed but we didn't know about it until the Catholic Church defined it for us. It is the same with the canon. When the Apostle John completed the Apocalypse toward the end of the first century, the canon came into existence. But we didn't *know* the canon until the end of the fourth century. Thus, the issue is not whether the canon exists (it clearly does), but how we *know* what books should be in it. If the canon cannot be found in the inspired books, this necessarily means that the canon is *separate and distinct* from those books.

True Christians are able to recognize true Scripture?

Along a similar line of argument, some contend that the Scriptures are of such a nature that "true Christians" are able to recognize their authenticity. This, of course, leads to more question-begging. First, they don't explain who is a "true Christian" and who is not. Who decides? The Protestant would have to argue that *no one* in the first fifteen centuries of the Church was a "true Christian" because they all believed in baptismal regeneration, purgatory and the sacrifice of the Mass, to name just a few doctrines.

This forces some to argue that the Church went into apostasy immediately after the apostolic age. Such an argument is preposterous for a number of reasons. Most obviously, this would make Jesus a liar, who promised that the gates of hell would never prevail against the Church (Mt 16:18). Also, if the Church became apostate, then we cannot trust *any* of her doctrines about God and Christ, much less the canon of Scripture, because *all* these doctrines were defined by the Church after age of the apostles. We might as well consign the Christian religion to the trash heap and start from scratch.

Further, if the Catholic Church went into apostasy, then where was the true Church? The Catholic Church has been converting nations, erecting churches, building hospitals and establishing universities for the past 2,000 years. Only the bodies of Catholic saints are incorrupt, and only Catholic churches have had Eucharistic miracles. The Catholic Church has brought forth the greatest saints and martyrs and miracles the world has ever known. So when did the "true" Church finally emerge? Under whose leadership? By what authority? And how come we see no proof of this "church" in any corner of the historical record?

The argument also doesn't explain why the canon was debated by "true Christians" for nearly 400 years before it was finally settled. Many "true Christians" rejected Hebrews, 2 Peter, 2 and 3 John and the Apocalypse. Other "true Christians" accepted the Shepherd of Hermas, the Didache, and the Apostolic Constitutions. The great saints Jerome and Augustine are perfect examples. Protestants acknowledge that they were "true Christians," and yet they vehemently disagreed with each other on the nature of the canon until Pope Damasus' decision.

Further, the argument fails to provide us with the definitive markers of canonicity. Why is Paul's letter to Philemon inspired but Clement's letter to the Corinthians is not? Paul's concern in his letter to Philemon is about Onesimus, a runaway slave, and not about the core gospel message of repentance and salvation. Clement's letter, on the other hand, speaks of the Church, authority, an ecclesiastical dispute, obedience, Christian unity and other issues that Paul commonly wrote about. How does one see the intrinsic value of Paul's letter over that of Clement?

The Protestant cannot explain the difference by reasoning that Paul was an apostle but Clement was not. Non-apostles also wrote Scripture (Luke, Mark). In addition, some of Paul's letters did not make it into the Bible canon.[135] Further, Clement was the third successor to Peter. When the church at Corinth had their dispute (about unlawful ordinations), they appealed to Clement in Rome, even though the Apostle John was most likely still living and geographically closer to Corinth! Clement's authority was supreme and absolute, and his letter to the Corinthians was read throughout the churches.

Arguing that canonicity is determined by authorship (either by an apostle or one with apostolic characteristics) gets the Protestant nowhere. The criterion is purely arbitrary, and Scripture makes no such claim that canonicity is determined by apostolicity. But even assuming this is the case (which, by the way, is true), who decides what is apostolic? Why are some of Paul's letters apostolic but others are

---

[135] See 1 Cor 5:9; 2 Cor 10:10; Phil 3:1; Col 4:16.

not? The criterion of authorship is actually self-defeating, for *none* of the gospels identify their authors. They are all anonymous. Same with the book of Hebrews. Knowledge of who wrote these books is a Tradition of the Catholic Church (another Tradition that is accepted by Protestants).

Scripture quotes canonical Scripture?

Some also argue that Scripture determined the canon because Scripture quotes canonical Scripture. This is often called the "quotation equals canonicity" fallacy. First, this argument doesn't explain how we know that the one book which cites another book is itself inspired. Second, the New Testament does *not* quote all the books from the Old Testament. Jesus did quote from Exodus, Leviticus, Deuteronomy, Psalms, Isaiah and Hosea. But neither Jesus nor any apostle quoted from Judges, Ruth, 1 Chronicles, Ezra, the Song of Songs, Ecclesiastes, Lamentations, Esther, Nahum, Obadiah, Nehemiah and Zephaniah. Does this make these Old Testament books any less canonical? The answer, of course, is no. Both Catholics and Protestants hold these books to be inspired Scripture.

The problem with the arbitrary criterion does not end here. Other than Peter referring generically to Paul's writings (2 Pet 3:16) and Paul referring to Luke's gospel (1 Tim 5:18), the New Testament books *do not* refer to each other. Yet, this is no basis to reject the non-referenced books (which would be almost the entire New Testament). Further, as we have just seen, some of Paul's letters reference his other non-canonical letters, and yet that is no basis to accept these referenced books as Scripture.

We have also seen how the sacred authors quote from non-inspired, apocryphal writings. For example, Paul refers to the *Gospel of Nicodemus*[136] and the *Ascension of Isaiah*.[137] Jude alludes to the *Assumption of Moses*[138] and the *Book of Enoch*.[139] Paul even quotes from the pagan poets Epimenides,[140] Aratus,[141] and Menander.[142] Finally, as we will further examine below, the New Testament makes many references to the deuterocanonical books, but most Protestants reject the deuterocanon.[143] Far from proving the case, the "Scripture quotes canonical Scripture" argument shows that Scripture *cannot* be used to know the canon.

Surprisingly, some even refer to 2 Peter 3:16 to support the "quotation equals canonicity" argument. In this verse, Peter describes Paul's letters as "hard to understand, which the ignorant and unstable twist to their own destruction, as they do the other scriptures." Because Peter uses the phrase "the other scriptures," Protestants argue that there was already an established canon which was determined by the Scripture itself (here, Peter's declaration in Scripture). This is another example of precisely what Peter is warning about – twisting the meaning of Scripture to one's destruction. In this passage, Peter is not defining the canon of Scripture. He is warning Christians not to privately interpret Scripture lest they risk condemning themselves.

---

[136] 2 Tim 3:8-9.
[137] Heb 11:37.
[138] Jud 8-9.
[139] Jud 14.
[140] See Acts 17:28; Ti 1:12.
[141] See Acts 17:28.
[142] See 1 Cor 15:33.
[143] As we will see, the New Testament alludes to Tobit, Judith, Wisdom, Sirach, Baruch, 1 and 2 Maccabees and Daniel 13.

The argument also ignores the obvious historical fact that the canon was debated for nearly 400 years after Peter wrote this letter. If Peter was referring to a defined canon in 2 Peter 3:16, no Christian knew about it, and no early Church Father wrote about it. Finally, not all New Testament Scripture was written at this time. So if Peter was defining the canon in his second epistle, then he would be excluding, at a minimum, Paul's letter to the Hebrews and John's Apocalypse, which were written after 2 Peter but which Protestants nevertheless consider part of the canon.

The canon was determined by individuals, not the Church?

Those who acknowledge that the determination of the canon was an infallible decision often resort to attributing the divine guidance to the individuals who made the decision but not the Church at large. In other words, they try to separate the infallible decision of the individual members of the Church from the Church itself. This is a futile proposition for them.

History reveals that the one individual responsible for rendering the final decision was Pope Damasus, the 36th successor to Peter, in his "Decree of Damasus" in A.D. 382. Pope Damasus did not consider himself separate from the Church; he considered himself the *head* of it! This was the Roman Catholic Church, which has been affirmed by secular historians and the early Church Fathers. As we have seen, later popes followed suit. Nothing in the writings of the Fathers or councils ever makes a distinction between the decisions of the members of the Church and the Church proper. The Catholic Church and the Mystical Body of Christ are one and the same.

Similarly, some acknowledge that the Holy Ghost can give His special guidance to certain individuals at certain moments in history, like the pope and bishops who determined the canon of Scripture. But these same people reserve for themselves the right to deny that the Holy Ghost guided the Church in other doctrines or continues to guide the Church today (at the same time they argue that the Holy Ghost guides each individual person who reads the Bible). Again, this is just another way for them to exonerate themselves from submitting to the authority of the Catholic Church.

While it is true that the Holy Spirit specially guides "certain individuals," these individuals are no less than the successors of the apostles - the bishops of the Holy Catholic Church. Jesus told His apostles that the Spirit would guide them into all truth and that He would be with them *"forever"* (Jesus' use of the term "forever" mandates successors because Jesus knew the apostles would die).[144] Through this divine guidance of the Holy Spirit, Jesus could promise that the gates of hell would never prevail against the Church and that the Church could infallibly bind and loose in heaven what she bound and loosed on earth (Mt 16:18-19). This is the same Holy Spirit Jesus gave to the apostles when He breathed on them and gave them the power to forgive and retain sins (Jn 20:21-23).

If Protestants rightfully acknowledge that the Holy Spirit guided the Catholic bishops to determine the Bible canon at the end of the fourth century, on what basis do they deny the Spirit's guidance of the Catholic Church on other doctrines in the second, or fifth or eighth centuries? They cannot arbitrarily decide when the Holy Spirit guides and does not guide the Church without engaging in gross private subjectivism. Further, they cannot divorce the Catholic Church from the bishops of the Church. The Holy Spirit guides the

---

[144] Jn 14:16; see also Mt 28:20.

bishops *because* they are the leaders of the Church, not *in spite* of their leadership!

The canon was determined by "historical consensus"?

Some try to downplay Pope Damasus' decision by claiming that the canon was already determined by an historical consensus. In other words, the pope simply rubber-stamped what the majority of Christians already believed. Since the canon was already established, the pope's actions were gratuitous and self-serving. The argument defeats *sola Scriptura* because it elevates the judgment of historical investigation above the judgment of Scripture. It also demonstrates a profound ignorance of the historical facts.

We have already seen that there was *not* an historical consensus on the Bible canon at the time of Pope Damasus' decision. Some of the greatest minds of the Church, like Jerome and Athanasius, had different views on the canon. Books like Hebrews, 2 Peter and the Apocalypse were debated right up until the pope's decree. That almost all of the debate about the canon stopped *after* the pope's decree underscores its significance in the Christian world.

History also shows that "historical consensuses" could be wrong. This is because they are based on the inductive reasoning of fallible men. As we have seen, during the third and fourth centuries, a majority of Catholics including the bishops embraced the Arian heresy. For a time, a consensus of Catholics believed that Jesus Christ was not co-equal with the Father. It took the infallible council of Nicea, under the leadership of Pope Sylvester I, to defeat the heresy with a definitive pronouncement. The Catholic Church, and not Scripture or the will of the majority, eliminated one of the most dangerous threats to the faith.

We can empathize with their argument, however. Many Protestant communities determine what doctrines they will teach by the will of the majority. If there are disagreements in the community, they either come to a consensus, settle on a compromise, or start a new denomination. But revealed truth is not determined by a democratic majority. Jesus didn't say, "an historical consensus will guide you into all truth." He said the Spirit "will guide you into all truth" (Jn 16:13). This is the same Spirit who led Pope Damasus and his successor popes to determine the canon of Scripture and define the core doctrines of the Christian faith.

There is no unity in Catholicism?

With their backs against the wall, many will try to downplay the Church's infallible determination of the canon by asserting that the Church has produced no unity within Catholicism. With this argument, the Protestant admits that unity is a sign of truth, and this admission indicts the very religion he cleaves to. With more than 30,000 different Protestant denominations, this is the proverbial "pot calling the kettle black."

More importantly, the assertion is false. The Catholic Church *is* united because she has one shepherd (the pope), not multiple shepherds like there are in Protestantism. Where there is one shepherd, there is also one flock. Over the past 2,000 years, 265 popes have kept the family of God one. Jesus created the office of the papacy to not only preserve and transmit the Deposit of Faith, but to keep unity within the family of God. In John 17:21, Jesus said that this unity would reveal to the world that He was indeed sent by God the Father.

The Church's miraculously consistent teaching on faith and morals over the past twenty centuries also testifies to her unity. While the Church's doctrines have developed over time, these developments have never contradicted, only clarified and enhanced, what she has always taught. This is truly incredible given the fallibility of her individual members and the persistent attacks of her enemies, both seen and unseen. In the Catholic Church alone, there is truly one mind and judgment.[145] While the Church has always had dissenters, Catholics at least know what they are dissenting from, that is, the teachings of the Vicar of Christ. Protestants have no such objective standard of faith, only their subjective interpretation of Scripture.

Finally, the Protestant's allegation that the Church has produced no unity can also be applied to Jesus Christ. Even though He was the infallible Word of God made flesh, Jesus did not create a unanimous doctrinal unity among His followers either. Quite the contrary, Jesus' teachings often alienated people by creating divisions among them. Jesus even said, "Do you think that I have come to give peace on earth? No, I tell you, but rather division" (Lk 12:51). The same can be said for the apostles. Infallibility is not a guarantee of unity, only of truth. The Church's infallible decision regarding the canon of Scripture could be rejected by everyone, but this would not affect the truthfulness of the canon. The canon is infallible because the infallible Church determined it. Truth is truth no matter who believes it.

Protestants often explain their lack of unity by attributing it to sin. They claim that *sola Scriptura* works but for the sinfulness and fallibility of its adherents. The Catholic responds by asking a very simple question: *Where*, historically, has *sola Scriptura* ever worked? The answer is: Nowhere. In fact, *sola*

---

[145] See 1 Cor 1:10; Acts 4:32; Eph 4:4.

Scriptura started with one "denomination" (Luther's) and, 475 years later, there are 30,000 more! These historical facts alone prove that *sola Scriptura* breeds disunity, not unity.

Human sinfulness and fallibility are not relevant to whether *sola Scriptura* is true. All of the authors of Scripture were fallible sinners and yet wrote and taught infallibly. Moreover, the Protestant may want to blame sin for the obvious failures of *sola Scriptura*, but the Scriptures *condemn private interpretation as a sin*.[146] This is the tragic irony of the Protestant's position. This also means that the sin of believing in *sola Scriptura* is the root cause of the divisions in Protestantism.

The canon was determined by divine providence?

Eventually, Protestants are content with simply chalking the canon of Scripture up to "divine providence." This is the Protestant's "catch-all" argument, but it does nothing for his case. It's just a convenient way to attribute the determination of the canon to God and not to His Church.

Certainly, the Church's determination of the canon was part of God's divine providence. But everything in this life happens within God's divine providence, whether good or evil. This simply means that God is in control and nothing escapes His knowledge and plan. But there is a big difference between God's permissive will and His active will in the realm of "divine providence."[147] Jesus didn't tell us the Church would

---

146 2 Pet 1:20-21.

147 Here we mean that God wills good but only permits evil. Specifically, God does not will evil to exist, nor does He will evil not to exist. Rather, God wills to permit evil to exist, for a greater good. This means that salutary acts must be attributed to God (God willing), and sin must be attributed to man (God permitting).

be passively ruled by God's divine providence. No, Jesus appointed Peter to actively rule and govern the Church by giving him the keys to the kingdom of heaven and the power to bind and loose. While part of God's providential design, the Church's determination of the canon was a specific act of authority granted by Christ to the successors of Peter.

Moreover, if Protestants want to attribute the Church's determination of the canon of Scripture to divine providence, will they also attribute the doctrines of justification by grace through baptism, redemptive suffering, the propitiatory sacrifice of the Mass, and other doctrines defined by the same Church to divine providence? What does this do for their case? It just leads us to the same old questions. Who decides what God's will is and what isn't? Who has the final authority? As always, we end up in the same place we began.

The Jews didn't need the Church to know their canon

After exhausting their "New Testament" arguments, Protestants often switch to "Old Testament" ones. For example, Protestants may ask Catholics how the Old Testament Jews could have known their Scripture canon if they didn't have the Catholic Church to tell them what it was. This line of argumentation fails for a number of reasons.

Most obviously, the Jews did *not have* an established canon of Scripture. As we have seen, the Sadducees accepted only the first five books of the Old Testament, while the Pharisees accepted the more expanded canon. There were even divisions among the Pharisees as well as among the scribes, elders and priests. There may have been as many as two dozen factions within Judaism with different canons of

Scripture. With this argument, the Protestant assumes something that isn't true.

Jesus' pedagogical methodology proves the point. When Jesus taught the Jews, He never held them to a particular canon. Jesus would quote only from the Scriptures that his particular audience held to be inspired. When Jesus dealt with the Sadducees, He would quote only from the Pentateuch. He would not quote from the larger Old Testament canon.

For example, when the Sadducees denied the resurrection from the dead, Jesus doesn't quote from Hosea 6:2 or Zephaniah 3:8 to prove them wrong, for the Sadducees rejected the inspiration of those books. Instead, Jesus quotes from Exodus 3:6 (which doesn't say anything specific about the resurrection).[148] A few verses later, when the Sadducees question Jesus about the Greatest Commandment, Jesus again quotes from the Pentateuch, here Deuteronomy 6:5 and Leviticus 19:18.[149] A few more verses later, when Jesus questions the Pharisees about who is the Christ, He quotes from Psalm 110:1 which they also held to be inspired.[150]

But even with regard to the Scriptures that all the Jews recognized as canonical, the Protestant's inquiry only highlights the truth of the Catholic position. Why? Because Scripture didn't tell the Jews what Scriptures were inspired; the *Tradition* did. The book of Genesis, for example, doesn't say it is God-breathed Scripture. Instead, the Jews were able to look back into history and see what books were used in the synagogues to teach the rule of faith. In short, the Jews looked to Tradition (the Catholic position), and not Scripture (the

---

[148] See Mt 22:29-32.
[149] See Mt 22:34-39.
[150] See Mt 22:41-45.

Protestant position) to have a general idea about what Scriptures were canonical.

The fact that the Jews had disagreements about what was Scripture demonstrates the need for a definitive authority *outside* of Scripture to settle the question. That the ecclesiastical authorities of the Old Covenant were divided on the canon does not undermine the authority of the Catholic Church in the New Covenant. The Old Covenant was nothing more than a "shadow" of what was to come in the New Covenant.[151] Just because Moses and his successors didn't render an infallible decision on the canon of Scripture doesn't mean that the Church is precluded from doing so. Such an argument engages in the "fallacy of composition," as we have seen.

But didn't we say that the Jewish leaders taught with divine authority through the seat of Moses? Yes we did, and Scripture affirms it. But there is a distinction between authority and infallibility. Jesus recognized the Pharisees' authority to teach and govern, and even commanded the faithful to obey them (Mt 23:1-3). Jesus also recognized the authority of Scripture, for He often appealed to it. While the Jewish rabbis taught with authority, God never gave the Jews infallible guidance to determine the canon of Scripture. Protestants want a free pass to reject religious authority as they cling to the authority of Scripture alone, but neither Jesus nor the apostles ever advanced such a model. Just as the Pharisees were to be obeyed on the Old Testament side of the cross, it is the same for the apostles and their successors on the New Testament side.

---

[151] See Col 2:17; Heb 10:1.

Practically speaking, while Moses did have access to God's infallible judgments, Moses and his successors didn't render an infallible decree about the canon because they had no way of knowing whether revelation had ended. The Jews didn't know whether God was going to inspire additional Scripture or raise up new prophets to communicate God's Word. The only time anyone knew that God had stopped inspiring Scripture is when the Catholic Church declared that revelation ended with the death of the last apostle. With this divine knowledge, the Church was able to render her divine decision on the canon. The Catholic Church's declaration of the cessation of revelation and determination of the canon are *both* accepted by Protestants, even though *neither* is taught by Scripture. Again, this proves that *sola Scriptura* is a false doctrine.

In light of these Scriptural and historical difficulties, Protestants inevitably resort to claiming the Catholic Church erred in its determination of the Old Testament canon. The argument, of course, doesn't explain how the Church infallibly determined the New Testament canon. Nevertheless, if the Protestant can demonstrate that the Church's Old Testament canon is wrong, he concludes that the Church could be wrong about other doctrines, and reserves the right to reject what he dislikes. As we will see, this argument actually backfires on the Protestants. We have already addressed the Protestant claim that the Church was inconsistent in her treatment of the Book of Esdras (which is false). Let us now look at other aspects of the issue in more detail by examining the deuterocanonical books.

Chapter 7

The Deuterocanonical Books

There are 27 books in both the Catholic and Protestant New Testament canons. However, while there are 46 books in the Catholic Old Testament canon, there are only 39 books in the Protestant's version. The seven books missing from the Protestant canon are called the "deuterocanonical" books.[152] They are distinguished from the "protocanonical" books primarily on the grounds that the deuterocanonical books were written later in salvation history (the oldest, Sirach, dating back only to the second century before Christ).[153] The deuterocanonical books are: Tobit, Judith, Wisdom, Sirach (Ecclesiasticus), Baruch, and 1 and 2 Maccabees; there are also parts of Daniel (3:24-90; 13:7-14,42) and Esther (10:4-16,24). Protestants erroneously call the deuterocanon the "Apocrypha."

For 2,000 years, the Catholic Church's Old Testament canon has included the deuterocanonical books. The earliest and most reliable Greek manuscripts recognized by both Catholic and

---

[152] From the Greek *deutero* which means "second."
[153] Some believe the deuterocanonical books are also distinguishable from the protocanon because they were written in Greek. However, only Wisdom and 2 Maccabees were originally composed in Greek. The remaining books were written in Hebrew. That the other deuterocanonical books were translated into Greek indicates that they were already well-accepted by Palestinian Jews.

Protestant scholars also contain the deuterocanonical books. These include the Codex Sinaiticus (4th century),[154] the Codex Vaticanus (4th century)[155] and the Codex Alexandrinus (5th century).[156] Even the Old Testament canon of the Protestant's King James Version of A.D. 1611 included the deuterocanonical books.

The Septuagint

We have already mentioned the many factions within Judaism including the separate canons of the Sadducees and the Pharisees. The Greek-speaking Jews, such as the Bereans of Acts 17, held to yet another Old Testament canon in their translation of Scriptures called the "Septuagint" which was a Greek translation of the Hebrew text.[157] In preaching the gospel, Jesus and the apostles generally used the Septuagint canon over the other canons. In fact, of the New Testament's approximately 350 quotes from the Old Testament, about 300 of them (around 85 percent) come from the Septuagint.[158]

For example, in Matthew's gospel, the apostle quotes the Septuagint translation of Isaiah 7:14, "Behold, a virgin (Greek, *parthenos*) shall conceive and bear a son" (1:23). In the Hebrew translation, it says a

---

[154] Contains all the books except Baruch.

[155] Contains all the books except 1 and 2 Maccabees.

[156] Contains all the deuterocanonical books.

[157] Many scholars believe that the Septuagint was created by about 70 Jewish scholars around B.C. 148 for the Greek-speaking Jews of the Diaspora ("Septuaginta" means "seventy" in Latin). The Septuagint is often referred to as the LXX (the Roman numerals for "70"). The need for a Greek translation of Scripture came about through the influence of Alexander the Great who conquered the region several hundred years prior.

[158] Joel Peters, *Sola Scriptura? 21 Reasons to Reject Sola Scriptura* (Rockford, IL: TAN Books and Publishers, 1999), pp.56-57.

"young woman" (Hebrew, *almah*) shall conceive.[159] In Mark's gospel, Jesus quotes the Septuagint translation of Isaiah 29:13 which says, "This people honors me with their lips, but their heart is far from me; in vain do they worship me" (7:6-7). This phrase is not found in the Hebrew translation.

Similarly, in Luke's gospel, John the Baptist quotes Isaiah 40:4-5 which says, "Prepare the way of the Lord, make his paths straight…and the crooked shall be made straight, and the rough ways shall be made smooth" (3:5-6). These phrases are also not in the Hebrew version. In John's gospel, the apostle records the Jews' reference to Psalm 78:24 in Jesus' Eucharistic discourse: "He gave them bread from heaven to eat" (6:31). The Hebrew translation uses "food" or "grain," not "bread." Also, Christians believe in the seven gifts of the Holy Spirit, but the seventh gift, "piety," is found only in the Septuagint (Isaiah 9:2). Examples like these could be multiplied 75 times over.

Why is this relevant? Because the Septuagint canon of the Old Testament *included the deuterocanonical books*. This indicates that Jesus and the apostles held the deuterocanon as Sacred Scripture. In fact, not only did their Old Testament Scriptures contain the deuterocanonical books, but Jesus and the apostles *make reference to these books many times throughout Scripture*. This is another demonstration of their

---

[159] Robert Sungenis notes that the word *almah* appears seven times in the Hebrew Old Testament and never refers to a woman who is married or has had sexual relations (Gn 24:43; Ex 2:8; Ps 68:25; Prov 30:19; Song 1:3; Isa 7:14). In fact, the Hebrew Scriptures use *almah* and *bethulah* (virgin) as synonyms (see Gen 24:16/Gen 24:43; Dt 22:23/Dt 22:28). See Sungenis, *The Catholic Apologetics Study Bible, Vol. I, The Gospel According to Matthew* (Queenship Publishing: Goleta, CA, 2003), pp. 189-190.

canonicity. Let's take a brief look at some of these examples.

Jesus, the apostles and the deuterocanon

In the gospels, Jesus alludes to five of the seven deuterocanonical books. For example, Jesus' statement "lay up for yourselves treasures in heaven" in Matthew 6:20 follows Sirach 29:11. Jesus' warning, "you will know them by their fruits" in Matthew 7:16 follows Sirach 27:6. Jesus' use of "powers of death" and "gates of Hades" in Matthew 16:18 is an allusion to Wisdom 16:13. Jesus' description of seeds falling on rocky soil and having no root in Mark 4:5 follows Sirach 40:15.

Jesus' description of hell as "where their worm does not die, and the fire is not quenched" refers to Judith 16:17. Jesus' statement "they will fall by the edge of the sword" in Luke 21:24 follows Sirach 28:18. Jesus' explanation, "No one has ascended into heaven but he who descended from heaven" in John 3:13 is an allusion to Baruch 3:29. Jesus' explanation of fruitless branches being cut down in John 15:6 follows Wisdom 4:5. Jesus' observance of the Feast of Hanukkah in John 10:22 is based on His acceptance of 1 Maccabees 4:59 where the divine establishment of this feast is recorded.

Paul's quote that Abraham is "the father of many nations" in Romans 4:17 is taken from Sirach 44:19. Paul's description of sin and death entering the world in Romans 5:12 follows Wisdom 2:24. Paul's reference to the potter and the clay making two kinds of vessels in Romans 9:21 follows Wisdom 15:7. Paul's question, "For who has known the mind of the Lord so as to instruct him" in 1 Corinthians 2:16 references Wisdom 9:13. Paul's statement "what pagans sacrifice they offer to demons and not to God" in 1 Corinthians 10:20 comes from Baruch 4:7. Paul's teaching about being baptized on behalf of the dead in the hope of resurrection follows 2 Maccabees 12:43-45.

Paul's prayer for a "spirit of wisdom" in Ephesians 1:17 follows the prayer in Wisdom 7:7. Paul's use of "armor," "helmet," "breastplate," "sword" and "shield" in Ephesians 6:13-17 is from Wisdom 5:17-20. Paul's description of God as "Sovereign" and "King of kings" in 1 Timothy 6:15 is found in 2 Maccabees 12:15; 13:4. Paul's reference to a "crown of righteousness" in 2 Timothy 4:8 is similar to Wisdom 5:16. Paul's teaching that Enoch was taken up into heaven in Hebrews 11:5 is also found in Wisdom 4:10 and Sirach 44:16. Paul's account of the martyrdoms of the mother and her sons in Hebrews 11:35 is taken from 2 Maccabees 7:1-42. Paul's use of "drooping hands" and "weak knees" in Hebrews 12:12 is taken from Sirach 25:23.

James' teaching that "every man be quick to hear, slow to speak" in James 1:19 follows Sirach 5:11. James' quote "it was reckoned to him as righteousness" in James 2:23 is taken from 1 Maccabees 2:52. James' instruction to perform "works in the meekness of wisdom" in James 3:13 follows Sirach 3:17. James' teaching about silver that rusts and laying up one's treasure in James 5:3 follows Sirach 29:10-11. James' reference to killing the "righteous man" in James 5:6 is from Wisdom 2:12.

Peter's teaching about testing faith by purgatorial fire in 1 Peter 1:6-7 is also found in Wisdom 3:5-6 and Sirach 2:5. Peter's teaching that God judges us "according to his deeds" in 1 Peter 1:17 refers to Sirach 16:12. Peter's reference to God's rescue of "righteous" Lot in 2 Peter 2:7 is taken from Wisdom 10:6.

John's description of the seven spirits before God's throne in Apocalypse 1:4 is an allusion to Tobit 12:15.

The reference to God's word as a "two-edged sword" in Apocalypse 2:12 follows Wisdom 18:16. John's description of God "seated on the throne" in Apocalypse 5:7 is the same description in Sirach 1:18. The angels' presentation of the saints' prayers to God in Apocalypse 8:3-4 tracks Tobit 12:12,15.

John's vision of the raining of "hail and fire" in Apocalypse 8:7 follows Wisdom 16:22 and Sirach 29:39. The raining of "locusts on the earth" in Apocalypse 9:3 follows Wisdom 16:9. The "Hallelujah" cry in Apocalypse 19:1 follows Tobit 13:18. The description of the Lord on a "white horse" in Apocalypse 19:11 follows 2 Maccabees 3:25; 11:8. John's description of the New Jerusalem with precious stones is prophesied in Tobit 13:17. There are many other similar examples. [160]

The Church Fathers and the deuterocanon

Based upon the apostolic Tradition and the teachings of the Catholic Church, the early Church Fathers also referred to the deuterocanon in their teachings on Sacred Scripture. In fact, *all* of the deuterocanonical books are cited in patristic commentaries. While the Fathers were not unanimous in their view of the deuterocanon before Pope Damasus rendered his decree, these books were held as canonical by a majority of the Fathers.

Quoting all of these Fathers is beyond the scope of the book. Nevertheless, to give you a "big picture" of the patristic testimony, I have prepared a list of the deuterocanonical books and the Fathers who quoted them during the first six centuries after Christ's

---

[160] For an extensive list of deuterocanonical references in the New Testament, please see Appendix A of my book *The Biblical Basis for the Catholic Faith* (Our Sunday Visitor).

ascension. This list is not exhaustive. For more information on this subject, I recommend reading the books on the early Church Fathers which are referenced at the end of Chapter 11. I also have more information on the Fathers and the deuterocanon on my website at www.ScriptureCatholic.com. The list demonstrates that the deuterocanonical books were commonly used by the Fathers in their commentaries on Sacred Scripture, as well as in the councils of the early Church.[161]

- *Tobit*: Polycarp, Clement of Alexandria, Hippolytus, Origen, Cyprian, Dionysius the Great, Athanasius, Hilary of Poitiers, John Chrysostom, Ambrose, Jerome, Innocent, Augustine, Leo the Great and Gregory the Great.
- *Judith*: Origen, Methodius, the Council of Nicea, Athanasius, Hilary of Poitiers, Basil, Ambrose, Gregory of Nazianzus, Innocent and Augustine.
- *Wisdom*: Barnabas, Clement, Melito of Sardis, Irenaeus, Tertullian, Hippolytus, Clement of Alexandria, Hippolytus, Origen, Cyprian, Dionysius the Great, Archelaus, Methodius, Eusebius, Hilary of Potiers, Athanasius, the Council of Sardica, Cyril of Jerusalem, Gregory of Nyssa, Basil, Ambrose, Gregory of Nazianzus, Epiphanius, John Chrysostom, Rufinus, Jerome, Augustine, John Cassian, Leo the Great, Theodoret, Gregory the Great, Leontius, and John Damascene.
- *Sirach*: Didache, Tertullian, Clement of Alexandria, Origen, Cyprian, Dionysius the

---

[161] For a thorough study of the Fathers' usage of the deuterocanonical books, I highly recommend Gary Michuta's *Why Catholic Bibles are Bigger* (Grotto Press).

Great, the Council of Antioch, Methodius, Lactantius, Alexander of Alexandria, Aphraates the Persian Sage, Cyril of Jerusalem, Athanasius, Hilary of Poitiers, Basil, Gregory of Nazianzus, Epiphanius, John Chrysostom, Ambrose, Rufinus, Jerome, John Cassian, Augustine, Vincent of Lerins, Anastasius II, Leo the Great and Gregory the Great.

- *Baruch*: Athenagoras, Irenaeus, Tertullian, Hippolytus, Clement of Alexandria, Cyprian, Origen, Methodius, Eusebius, Aphraates the Persian Sage, Cyril of Jerusalem, Athanasius, Hilary of Potiers, the Council of Laodicea, Hilary of Poitiers, Basil, Gregory of Nazianzus, Epiphanius, Ambrose, Rufinus, Jerome, John Chrysostom, Rufinus of Aquileia, Augustine, Innocent, John Cassian, Primasius and John Damascene.

- *1 Maccabees*: Hippolytus, Cyprian, Origen, Aphraates the Persian Sage, Ambrose, Innocent and Augustine.

- *2 Maccabees*: Hermas, Tertullian, Origen, Cyprian, Aphraates the Persian Sage, Athanasius, Basil, Hilary of Poitiers, Gregory of Nazianzus, Epiphanius, Ambrose, Jerome, Innocent and Augustine.

- *Daniel (deuterocanonical part)*: Irenaeus, Tertullian, Hippolytus, Origen, Cyprian, Julius Africanus, Cyril of Jerusalem, Methodius, Athanasius, Hilary of Potiers, Basil, Gregory Nazianzus, Epiphanius, Ambrose, Jerome, Gregory of Nyssa, John Chrysostom, Rufinus, Augustine, Theodoret and Leo the Great.

- *Esther (deuterocanonical part)*: Origen and the Council of Laodicea

Notwithstanding this substantial patristic evidence, some Protestants still contend the deuterocanon was always disputed. For example, they point to

Athanasius (A.D. 295-373) who drafted the earliest canon of New Testament books in his *Festal Letter 39* (A.D. 367). In his list, Athanasius does not cite the deuterocanon as "canonical," but this is because he had an idiosyncratic method of categorizing Scripture that nobody else used. It involved three groupings: those books that were read in both the synagogues and churches Athanasius called "canonical" (protocanon); those that were read only in the churches were called "read" or "necessary" books (deuterocanon); and, those that were heretical were called "apocryphal" (everything else).[162]

Thus, Athanasius distinguished the deuterocanon from the protocanon on the grounds that they were read only in the churches, while the protocanon was read both in the churches and synagogues (which was practiced only after the mid-second century). While Athanasius categorized the deuterocanon separately from the protocanon, he did not label the deuterocanon apocryphal as he did with other books. There is no compelling evidence that Athanasius rejected the deuterocanon. That Athanasius quoted the deuterocanonical books along side the protocanonical books demonstrates that he accepted them as canonical and inspired.[163] Finally, Athanasius never claimed he was authoritatively determining the canon. He was simply giving his opinion. Pope Damasus, who reigned during the time of Athanasius, settled the canon, not Athanasius. And the pope made no distinctions between the protocanon and the deuterocanon the way Athanasius did.

---

[162] See Michuta, *Why Catholic Bibles are Bigger*, pp.106-113.
[163] In Athanasius' writings, he quotes from Baruch, Wisdom, Sirach, Tobit, Judith, Maccabees and Daniel (the story of Susanna).

Protestants also like pointing to Jerome (A.D. 340-420) when discussing the canon. Because he was an expert in Latin, Hebrew, Aramaic and Greek, Pope Damasus commissioned Jerome to translate the Scriptures into a new Latin translation which is known as the Latin Vulgate. The hallowed Douay-Rheims English translation is based on the Vulgate. In his translation of the Old Testament Scriptures, Jerome relied upon the Hebrew translation instead of the Septuagint because he believed it was a more accurate translation of the originally-inspired Hebrew text.[164] Because the deuterocanonical books were written later in salvation history and not part of the oldest Hebrew Scriptures, Jerome originally doubted their canonicity. What do we say about this?

Jerome's negative judgment of the deuterocanon put him at odds with the rest of the Western Fathers and the entire Church. As we have just seen, the overwhelming majority of the Church Fathers accepted the deuterocanon as Sacred Scripture. An exception does not make the rule. Moreover, in his writings, Jerome quotes from many of the deuterocanonical books – even declaring some of them to be inspired Scripture – which makes his position confusing if not duplicitous.[165]

We also note that Jerome's opinion about the translation of the Old Testament Scriptures should not have affected his opinion about canon of those Scriptures. Scholars even agree that the Septuagint translation, which included the deuterocanon, is a much more faithful translation of the original Hebrew in many places. Finally and most importantly, when

---

[164] These Hebrew Scriptures are often called the "Masoretic" text (translated from a group of Jews known as the Masoretes).
[165] Jerome quotes from Baruch, Sirach, Wisdom, Tobit, Judith, Maccabees and the deutercanonical sections of Daniel.

Pope Damasus declared the deuterocanon to be Scripture at the Council of Rome, Jerome acquiesced to the decision. Jerome submitted to the Vicar of Christ. This fact hurts, not helps, the Protestant's reliance on Jerome.

Luther and the Jewish council of Jamnia

The foregoing information is damaging to the Protestant contention that the Church erred in her inclusion of the deuterocanon. Based upon the teachings of Jesus and the apostles, the entire Christian Tradition has always included the deuterocanonical books as part of the Old Testament canon. In light of this historical fact, how can Protestants accept Martin Luther's decision to reject the deuterocanon? Doesn't the fact that Luther sought to remove the New Testament books of Hebrews, James, Jude and the Apocalypse from the established canon give Protestants pause about his views of the Old Testament books? How does Luther's decision in the 16th century carry more weight than the Catholic Church's decision in the 4th century?

Protestants try to rationalize Luther's novel modifications to the Old Testament canon by arguing that his actions had an earlier precedent. They point to a Jewish gathering held around A.D. 90 in Jamnia near the Mediterranean coast in Israel. This gathering is often known as the "council of Jamnia" (also known as Javneh).[166] Under the leadership of a rabbi named Akiba ben Joseph, this council is said to have rejected the canonicity of the deuterocanonical books. In so doing, the Jews adopted the mid-sized canon used by

---

[166] Technically, there was not a "council" of Jamnia like we see with the councils of the Catholic Church. Jamnia was a place where Jews studied the Law and Jamnian rabbis exercised legal functions in the community.

the Palestinian Pharisees.[167] What should we say about this?

Something very obvious: The Jews formally gathered at Jamnia sixty years after the resurrection of Jesus Christ to oppose Christianity, not support it. To prove the point, Rabbi Akiba not only rejected the deuterocanonical books, but also the New Testament Scriptures. Moreover, Akiba declared Jesus to be a false Messiah and held one Simon Bar Cochba to be the true Messiah.[168] Akiba and his successors also codified Jewish oral tradition into the anti-Christian *Talmud* which says that Jesus Christ is in hell boiling in excrement and the Virgin Mary was a whore.

We must ask our Protestant friends why a council of disbelieving Jews should serve as a precedent for Christian belief? How could Luther or any Christian accept the council of Jamnia's decision about the Bible canon when this same council rejected every facet of the Christian religion? Protestant reliance upon the anti-Christian council of Jamnia proves only their desperation in rejecting the deuterocanon and the legitimate authority of the Catholic Church.

Of course, the Jews were theologically motivated to reject the deuterocanonicals in the Septuagint because Jesus and the apostles were converting Jews to Christianity *using the Septuagint*. We saw this with

---

[167] Scholars point out that many Jews rejected Jamnia on the grounds that it did not have any national authority over Jewish belief and practice. Some scholars even question whether Jamnia issued any decrees on the Scriptures. Further, the Jews continued to debate their canon well into the third century, which demonstrates that Jamnia didn't settle the issue (for example, the Jews continued to debate the canonicity of Ruth, Proverbs, Ecclesiastes, Ezekiel and Canticles).
[168] Michuta, *Why Catholic Bibles are Bigger*, p.63.

Isaiah 7:14. Because the Jews denied the Virgin Birth of Jesus Christ, the Jews rejected the Septuagint translation of Isaiah 7:14 which says a "virgin" shall conceive (the Hebrew says "young woman"). Because they denied that only a remnant of their people would be saved, the Jews rejected the Septuagint translation of Isaiah 10:22 which says a remnant of Jews "will be saved" (the Hebrew says a remnant "will return"). Because they denied Jesus was God, the Jews rejected the Greek translation of Deuteronomy 32:43, which alludes to the Messiah and how the angels "worship him" (the Hebrew omits this phrase).[169] In short, the Jews rejected the Septuagint *because they rejected Jesus Christ.* Jamnia was about derailing conversions, not determining canons.

Some Protestants try to defend the Jews' decision at Jamnia by pointing to Romans 3:2 where Paul says that "the Jews are entrusted with the oracles of God." This is a silly argument. Paul's use of "entrusted" (Greek, *pisteuo*) is in the aorist tense which means that the Jews had already been entrusted with God's oracles *prior* to his letter to the Romans. As we have seen, the Jews did not have an established canon at this time which means that the "oracles" did not include this divine provision. Moreover, the Jews' possession of the oracles of God prior to Paul's authorship of Romans would mean that Romans 3:2 is non-canonical and should be disregarded.

While the Jews possessed the oracles of God in the Old Covenant, they no longer possess them in the New Covenant.[170] The New Covenant has replaced the Old, and the oracles of God now reside in the Catholic

---

[169] St. Paul refers to Deuteronomy 32:43 in Hebrews 1:6.
[170] We should also point out that the "oracles" included not just Scripture, but oral Tradition, Urim and Thummin, prophets, visions, seers and other media of divine revelation.

Church, the new Israel (Gal 6:16). God manifested the nullification of the Old Covenant by tearing the Temple Curtain in two at Jesus' death and allowing the Romans to destroy the Temple in A.D. 70. That the Jews at Jamnia rejected Christ and His written revelation proves they no longer have the oracles of God.

In summary, the deuterocanon was used by Jesus and the apostles 60 years before Jamnia took place. The Septuagint translation was in force 250 years before Jamnia convened. Jamnia deliberately tried to *wipe out* the well-established authority of the deuterocanon, not to mention everything else about the Christian faith. For Protestants to appeal to Jamnia to justify their Old Testament canon means that they follow an anti-Christian "council" and not the Tradition of the apostles. If the Jews called a council next week to remove the book of Jeremiah because it says that God was going to give them a "New Covenant,"[171] would the Protestants follow this decision? If Protestants would reject such a decision in the 21st century, why do they accept such a decision in the 15th century?

Didn't Jesus define the Old Testament canon?

Some say Jesus determined the Old Testament canon which excluded the deuterocanonical books. They point to Jesus' statement in the gospel of Luke: "These are my words which I spoke to you, while I was still with you, that everything written about me in the law of Moses and the prophets and the psalms must be fulfilled" (Lk 24:44).[172]

---

[171] See Jer 31:31.
[172] See also Mt 5:17; 7:12; 11:13; 22:40; Lk 16:16,29,31; 24:27.

According to the Protestant, when Jesus refers to the "law," He means the Pentateuch; when Jesus refers to the "prophets," He means all of the major and minor prophets as well as the books of Joshua, Judges, Samuel and Kings; and, when Jesus refers to the Psalms, He includes the rest of the Old Testament Scriptures except for the deuterocanon. Notwithstanding Jesus' very generic language, the Protestant confidently concludes that Jesus reveals a three-fold division of the Old Testament Scriptures which excludes the deuterocanonical books.

This is a classic example of reading into a text what one wants to see. First and most obviously, when Jesus refers to the "law, prophets and Psalms," He never says He is defining the Old Testament canon, nor does He define these categories for us. Identifying the books in these categories is pure speculation, and it assumes without any proof that the deuterocanonicals would necessarily be excluded from the "canon." Second, if Jesus really wanted to reveal the Old Testament canon to the apostles, He would have done so. But He didn't. That is why the canon was debated for nearly 400 years until the Catholic Church settled the question. That no apostle, nor any early Church Father, pope or council ever alleged that Jesus defined the Old Testament canon when referring to the Scriptures shows the novelty of the Protestant argument.

Some Protestants push the issue by emphasizing that the book of Sirach also refers to "the law and the prophets and the other books."[173] Thus, they conclude that Jesus in Luke 24:44 was simply affirming the Old Testament canon that was already established centuries before. This argument actually causes more confusion for the Protestant. Why? Because Jesus'

---

[173] See Sirach prologue verses 1,7,24-25; see also 2 Macc 15:9.

description in Luke 24:44 is *narrower* than the statement in Sirach. While both refer to "the law and prophets," Sirach refers to the "other books" while Jesus refers to the "Psalms." The Psalms refer to the revelations of King David only and not to the "other books" of the Old Testament.

If Protestants contend that Jesus is affirming the Old Testament canon in Luke 24:44, this canon would have arguably excluded inspired books like Joshua, Judges, Ruth, Samuel, Kings, Job, Proverbs, Ecclesiastes, and the Song of Solomon (since these books were not considered the "law, prophets or Psalms"). Thus, it is obvious Jesus was not defining or even alluding to the canon of Scripture. Instead, Jesus was focusing on those Scriptures that contained *the Messianic prophecies*. After Jesus alludes to these Scriptures right before His ascension, He explains, "Thus it is written, that the Christ should suffer and on the third day rise from the dead" (Lk 24:46). In fact, Jesus' reference to the "law, prophets and Psalms" follows the pattern of the New Testament as more than half of the Old Testament quotations in the New Testament come from Deuteronomy (the Law), Isaiah (the Prophets) and the Psalms.

Protestants also contend that Sirach is distinguishing itself from the canonical Scriptures when it refers to "the law, prophets and other books." This is another faulty argument. It automatically assumes that books like Sirach are not part of the "law and the prophets and other books," without any foundation for doing so. Sirach is the oldest of the deuterocanonical books and was originally written in Hebrew. The fact that Sirach was later translated into Greek strongly suggests that it was one of the "other books" already accepted by Palestinian Jews. The author's rather generic reference to "other books" also indicates that a canon was *not* firmly established at this time in history.

The Protestant's argument also assumes that when a book makes a reference to another book (like when Sirach refers to the "law, prophets and other books"), the referring book is making a statement about canonicity. We know this is not true. Canonical Old Testament books refer to other canonical books but this doesn't mean that they are separate or distinct in their canonicity, and it surely doesn't mean they are non-canonical. It can mean just the opposite. The argument also assumes the referring book is making a true statement, but this cannot be established without evaluating the referring book on its own merits.

The second book of Maccabees (15:9) also refers to "the law and the prophets," but without any reference to either the "other books" or the "Psalms." Following the Protestant line of argumentation, the Catholic could respond by saying since 2 Maccabees does not mention the "other books" or the "Psalms," it is not distinguishing itself from those books. Therefore, just as the "other books" and "Psalms" are inspired, 2 Maccabees must be inspired as well. These arguments demonstrate how fruitless it is to use Scripture to prove canonicity. These Scriptures also provide further evidence that the Jews did not have an established canon of Scripture.

We have already addressed how some canonical books refer to non-canonical books. Whether a book makes a reference to another book has nothing to do with the canonicity of *either* book. We also recall that when Jesus taught the Sadducees, He limited His recognition of Old Testament Scripture to the first five books of the Old Testament. When the Sadducees wanted Scriptural proof for the resurrection, Jesus quotes from Exodus 3:6: "I am the God of your father, the God of Abraham, the God of Isaac, and the God of Jacob." Does this mean that Jesus rejected the books outside the Pentateuch? Of course not. Scriptural references to other Scriptures do not confirm or deny divine inspiration.

As an aside, Jesus' interpretation of Exodus 3:6 demonstrates the need for human beings to have divine guidance when reading the Bible. Jesus teaches us that Exodus 3:6 is about the resurrection even though the verse says nothing about "resurrection." Jesus didn't castigate the Sadducees for failing to understand the verse from Exodus, one of the five books they held to be inspired. That is because the Scriptures are not formally sufficient to explain all the truths of the faith. Jesus recognized the Sadducees' need for guidance and gave it to them, just as He recognizes our need for guidance and gives it to us through His Church.

We must also mention that, as with the protocanonicals, the deuterocanonicals were written by prophets. A prophet is someone who received God's revelation. Solomon, the author of the book of Wisdom, was one of God's greatest prophets. Many people, including the queen of Sheba, came from afar to hear his prophecies (see 1 Kg 10:1-13). One of the most vivid and stunning prophecies of the sufferings of Jesus Christ is found in Wisdom 2:12-20. Rich, prophetical and historical traditions are found throughout the deuterocanonical books, further underscoring that the Protestants' rejection of them is arbitrary and capricious.

Some Protestants respond by pointing to 1 Maccabees 14:41 which says: "And the Jews and their priests decided that Simon should be their leader and high priest for ever, until a trustworthy prophet should arise." Based on this verse, Protestants conclude that true prophets did not exist during the Maccabean period and therefore this book cannot be inspired. This is another example of going beyond the plain meaning of the text.

Just because the Jews were waiting for a trustworthy prophet during their exile does not mean true prophets didn't exist at the time. In fact, the protocanonical books make even harsher statements about the absence of prophets during their times, but this doesn't negate their inspiration. For example, in the Psalms, Asaph says "We do not see our signs; there is no longer any prophet, and there is none among us who knows how long" (Ps 74:9). Moreover, Jeremiah acknowledges the existence of prophets during the exile but complains that "her prophets obtain no vision from the Lord" (Lam 2:9).

Protestants will also point to Jesus' statement in Luke 11:50-51: "that the blood of all the prophets, shed from the foundation of the world, may be required of this generation, from the blood of Abel to the blood of Zechariah, who perished between the altar and the sanctuary." By citing the first and last murders in the Hebrew Scriptures (Abel in Genesis 4:8 and Zechariah in 2 Chronicles 24:21), Protestants argue that Jesus was determining the Hebrew canon. Although arranged differently, Protestants contend that this canon is the same as their Old Testament canon. There are a number of problems with this argument.

First, not all Protestant scholars agree that 2 Chronicles was the last book of the Hebrew Scriptures. In fact, some of the earliest codices of the Hebrew Bible do not place 2 Chronicles as the last book.[174] We have already learned that the Jews did not have a definitive canon. Certain books like Esther, Ecclesiastes and Song of Solomon were composed between Genesis and 2 Chronicles but their canonicity was debated well after the time of Christ. Other books like Ezra, Nehemiah, Esther, Joel, Zechariah and Malachi were written after the exile but are still inspired. Any argument based on the particular *order* of books in a canon, when the canon is not even *established*, is gratuitous at best.

Second, Jesus is talking about murders that the Jews committed against their own prophets, not the canon of Scripture. Because the Maccabees were slain by Greeks and not Jews, the books of Maccabees would be excluded from Jesus' discussion. It is possible that Jesus was using the murder of Zechariah as a pedagogical tool, marking the beginning of the Babylonian exile in B.C. 586 when God punished Israel decisively for its faithlessness.[175] Jesus warns the scribes, "Yes, I tell you, it shall be required of this generation" (v.51). What shall be required of this generation? The same punishment for faithlessness. In other words, just as the Jews of the Old Testament were punished by the Babylonians for their rejection of the prophets, Jesus tells the Jews of the New Testament that they too will be punished if they reject Him, the fulfillment of all prophecy. Jesus' statement has nothing to do with the canonicity or even the authority of Scripture.

Some Protestants also appeal to the first-century Jewish historian Flavius Josephus. In his famous letter

---

[174] Gary Michuta notes that the Leningrad and Aleppo Codices actually place Chronicles as the first book! (*Why Catholic Bibles are Bigger*, p.21).
[175] Robert Sungenis posits this argument in *Not By Scripture Alone*, p.283.

Against Apion, Josephus writes that the Jews have "twenty-two books." These books included the five books of Moses, thirteen books of the Prophets, and four books which included hymns to God (the Psalms). According to Josephus, these books were written during the time between Moses and Artaxerxes, the king of Persia (c.B.C. 450). The deuterocanonical books were written after the reign of Artaxerxes. Thus, the Protestant relies upon Josephus as an historical witness to support their argument that the deuterocanon is not inspired. There are many problems with this argument as well.

First, the Protestant cannot demonstrate that Josephus' twenty-two book canon corresponds to the Protestant canon. Josephus uses very generic language and does not specifically identify those books that are included in the "prophets" and "hymns to God." Second, the Protestant interprets Josephus' twenty-two book canon to mean that God sent no prophets or gave divine revelation after the time of Artaxerxes. This contention is refuted by Scripture itself. The Jews believed there were real prophets in their time.[176] Jesus referred to John the Baptist as not only a prophet, but "more than a prophet."[177] Jesus even told the Jews, "He who receives a prophet because he is a prophet shall receive a prophet's reward."[178]

Third, we note that the Hebrew alphabet has twenty-two letters. Thus, the Jewish historian may have been advancing a symbolic apologetic against his Greek foe Apion as he referred to the "twenty-two" books of the Hebrews. Finally, the Protestant is relying, not only upon an authority outside of Scripture to

---

[176] Mt 14:5; 21:11,26,46; Mk 6:15; 11:32; Jn 1:21; 4:19; 9:17; 11:51.
[177] Mt 11:9; Lk 7:26.
[178] Mt 10:41; see also Mk 6:4.

prove a truth of Scripture, but a Jewish historian who rejected God's revelation in Jesus Christ. Protestant reliance upon Josephus not only refutes the doctrine of *sola Scriptura*, it favors the opinions of first century Judaism over that of Christianity.

Do the deuterocanonical books deny their inspiration?

Some Protestants contend that the deuterocanonical books deny their inspiration because they use weak and equivocal language. For example, in the prologue to Sirach, the author's grandson urges us "to be indulgent in cases where, despite our diligent labor in translating, we may seem to have rendered some phrases imperfectly." Similarly, the author of 2 Maccabees concludes the book by saying, "If it is well told and to the point, that is what I myself desired; if it is poorly done and mediocre, that was the best I could do" (2 Macc 15:38).

That an author displays insecurity, humility or even doubt about what he is writing is irrelevant to whether his words are divinely inspired. God can inspire an author to write about his weakness or shortcomings just as much as he can inspire him to write about his strengths. For example, Paul tells the Corinthians he was with them "in weakness and in much fear and trembling, and my speech and my message were not in plausible words of wisdom."[179] Paul even says, "For I am the least of the apostles, unfit to be called an apostle"[180] and "And I am the foremost of sinners" (1 Tim 1:15). Paul's self-deprecating statements do not negate the inspiration of his words, just as the humility of the authors of Sirach and Maccabees do not negate the inspiration of their words.

---

[179] 1 Cor 2:3-4; see also 1 Cor 4:9-10.
[180] 1 Cor 15:8-9.

God can also inspire a writer to admit he has incomplete knowledge of something. For example, in his first letter to the Corinthians, Paul seems to disclaim divine inspiration when he says, "I did baptize also the household of Stephanus. Beyond that, I do not know whether I baptized any one else" (1 Cor 1:16). Do Protestants reject the canonicity of 1 Corinthians because Paul can't remember who he baptized? Of course not. Paul's statement highlights that God used the knowledge and abilities of the sacred authors as He inspired their written words. This underscores the incredible miracle of divine inspiration.

Similarly, in addressing the virtue of chastity, Paul encourages a widower to remain unmarried by saying, "But in my judgment she is happier if she remains as she is. And I *think* that I have the Spirit of God" (1 Cor 7:40). Even though Paul is writing under divine inspiration, he equivocates about it. Why? Because God inspired Paul to reveal that his teaching was his own opinion and not directly from God. Elsewhere in the same letter, God sometimes inspired Paul to preface his teachings with "not I but the Lord,"[181] and other times to write, "I say, not the Lord."[182] Again, these revelations demonstrate the profound mystery of the interaction between the Divine Author and the human authors.

Do the deuterocanonical books contain errors?

Protestants also attempt to discredit the deuterocanonical books by claiming that they contain historical and theological errors. For example,

---

[181] See, for example, 1 Cor 7:10; 11:23; 14:37.
[182] See, for example, 1 Cor 7:12; 40.

Protestants accuse the book of Judith of an historical error because it says Nebuchadnezzar was the king of the Assyrians rather than the Babylonians. Those Protestants don't realize that this is a different Nebuchadnezzar than the famous king of Babylon who succeeded Asaraddon in the Assyrian kingdom. This different Nebuchadnezzar reigned at the same time as Manasseh in Judah (B.C. 679-643).

Baruch is also accused of an historical error because it says he returned "the vessels of the house of the Lord" to the land of Judah during the exile (Baruch 1:8), while Ezra says the vessels were returned after the exile (Ezra 1:7). However, Baruch had returned only "silver vessels" while the vessels in Ezra were "of silver, with gold" (1:6). Daniel also reveals the presence of silver and gold vessels (Dan 5:2). Thus, Baruch had taken only a portion of the vessels (the silver ones) while the remaining vessels were returned upon the completion of the exile. These are two of many examples where apparent historical errors are not errors at all and can be easily reconciled with additional historical or biblical testimony.

Protestants accuse the book of Tobit of a theological error because the angel Raphael supposedly lies to Tobit about his identity. However, it is evident that Raphael initially conceals his identity to ingratiate himself with Tobit. Knowing that Tobit would respond favorably to a relative, Raphael calls himself "Azarias, the son of the great Ananias, one of your relatives" (Tob 5:12). Raphael later reveals himself to Tobit[183] and Tobit praises him (Tob 13:1-18). In fact, it appears that Tobit knows it is Raphael all along, for he refers to Azarias as "a good angel" before Raphael formally reveals himself to him (Tob 5:21).

---

[183] Tob 12:15.

Protestants also accuse Judith of a theological error because she lied to king Holofernes about how he could capture the Israelites (Jdt 11:5-19). This is more nonsense. Judith protected her people by deceiving the evil general which was morally acceptable under the circumstances. Judith asks God to bless her tactic[184] and God works with her to bring about Holofernes' demise.[185] In fact, it was Holofernes who wanted to deceive Judith and Judith played his bluff (Jdt 12:16). Judith's actions are no different than those of other holy women in Scripture. For example, the Hebrew midwives lied to Pharoah by hiding Moses;[186] Rebekah lied to Isaac in procuring his blessing of Jacob and not Esau;[187] and, Rahab lied to the king of Jericho by hiding Joshua's spies.[188] Yet Protestants have no problem accepting the inspiration of the books of Genesis, Exodus and Joshua.

Some Protestants even accuse the deuterocanonical books of having stories that are too "fanciful" to believe. For example, in the book of Tobit the angel Raphael relieves Tobit's eyes of a blinding, white film by rubbing fish gall on them.[189] Is this much different than the angel purifying Isaiah's mouth with a burning coal? (Isa 6:6-7). In the same book, Raphael reveals that the smoke from the burning heart and liver of a fish will drive away a demon.[190] Is this much different than the prescriptions in Numbers 5, where a priest would make a woman accused of adultery drink a potion of dust and water and, if she were guilty, her body would swell and thigh fall away? (vv.11-22).

---

[184] See Jdt 9:13.
[185] See Jdt 13:15-16; 16:3,6.
[186] Ex 1:17; 2:2-3.
[187] Gen 27:5-41.
[188] Josh 2:4.
[189] Tob 3:17; see also Tob 6:8; 11:7-13.
[190] Tob 6:7,16-17; 8:2-3.

Addressing the purported "errors" in the deuterocanon is well beyond the scope of this book, for examples like this could be multiplied many times over. For the Christian, the issue should not be one of reconciling the supposed errors of the deuterocanon (and they can *all* be reconciled) any more than it is addressing the alleged errors of the protocanon or the New Testament. This is because the true Scriptures contain no errors, period. Sacred Scripture is inerrant and inerrancy is the product of inspiration. God is the primary author of Scripture who cannot tell a lie. The real issue is *what are the inspired Scriptures*. Once there is a determination of inspiration, the "errors" in the text are only apparent and not real.

For example, once we know the gospel of Matthew is inspired, we can search for ways to understand our Lord's commands to "pluck out our eye" and "cut off our hand" if they cause us to sin (Mt 5:29-30). Once we establish the inspiration of Luke, we don't need to accuse Jesus of teaching the theological error of having to hate our spouses and relatives (Lk 14:26). We can chalk these seemingly erroneous statements up to the literary use of *hyberbole*, whereby our Lord deliberately used exaggerative language to make a point. Many more examples could be provided.

Once we know a Scripture is inspired, everything falls into place. We recognize that we don't need to solve every problem or reconcile every apparent contradiction because we are dealing with God's Word. If we don't know a Scripture is inspired, we need to make that determination first, or our biases and fallible judgments will cloud the truth. If, like Protestants, we start with the assumption that certain Scriptures (i.e., deuterocanon) are not inspired, no amount of proof will matter. But since our *a priori* assumption comes from our fallible intellect, we can never be certain that we are correct.

So where do we end up? You guessed it. The Church. We need an infallible authority outside of both Scripture and our intellects to tell us what writings are divinely inspired. The Church who gave us the canon of Scripture is the same Church who is able to reconcile all the apparent inconsistencies in Scripture. The Church is the divine interpreter of the divine Word. We must first know what the Scriptures *are* before we can know what they *mean*. Once we humbly accept the Church's authority in *both* matters, the wonder, splendor and beauty of the Scriptures unfold before our very eyes.

Chapter 8

Protestant Bible Verses to "Prove" *Sola Scriptura*

By now, we hope the reader can see the errors of *sola Scriptura* and the Protestant approach to the Bible. *Sola Scriptura* is not taught in Scripture and was never even contemplated as a rule of faith before the revolt of Martin Luther. As we will see, while Scripture often affirms that it is "inspired," or the "Word of God," it *never* says that it is the *only* infallible authority for Christians. As we have also seen, Scripture says that Tradition and the Church are also authorities that must be obeyed with equal deference. Nevertheless, Protestants have standard Bible verses to which they appeal when arguing their case. We now examine these verses in some detail.

2 Timothy 3:16-17

Protestants use (and abuse) this passage perhaps more than any other when attempting to prove the case for *sola Scriptura*. In this passage, Paul is exhorting his newly-ordained bishop Timothy to use Scripture in his instruction of the faithful. St. Paul writes:

> All scripture is inspired by God and profitable for teaching, for reproof, for correction, and for training in righteousness, that the man of God may

be complete, equipped for every good work (2 Tim 3:16-17).

The first thing Protestants do is focus on verse 16 where Paul calls Scripture "inspired." The word *inspired* in the Greek is *theopneustos* which literally means "God-breathed." This means that God is the primary author of Sacred Scripture. Because Scripture does not describe Tradition as "God-breathed," the Protestant contends that Paul is making a distinction between the inspiration of infallible Scripture and the human origin of fallible tradition. Such an argument is an example of "eisegeting"[191] a biblical text without regard to the rest of the Bible.

As we have seen, Paul also says that the "Word of God" is what the people "heard from us" (1 Thess 2:13). This oral Word of God was just as *theopneustos* as the written Word. We saw the same thing when the apostles "spoke the word of God with boldness,"[192] and "proclaimed the Word of God in the synagogues,"[193] as well as how the people "heard the word of God."[194] Describing the oral Tradition as the "Word of God" is just as powerful as describing Scripture as "God-breathed." Making distinctions between these descriptions is pure anachronism.

We also note that Paul describes Scripture as both "inspired and *profitable*" (v.16). The Greek word for "profitable," *ophelimos*, means "helpful" or "useful." *Ophelimos* does not mean "exclusive" or "sufficient."[195]

---

[191] *Eisegesis* refers to imposing one's own interpretation upon the text based on one's own premises and presuppositions.

[192] Acts 4:31; see also Acts 6:2; 8:14; 11:1; Phil 1:14; Heb 13:7.

[193] Acts 13:5; see also Acts 13:46,48; 17:3

[194] Acts 13:46,48; see also Acts 13:37,44.

[195] See Joel Peters, *Sola Scriptura? 21 Reasons to Reject Sola Scriptura*, p.4. See also John Henry Newman, *On the Inspiration of Scripture*,

If God wanted us to believe that Scripture was formally sufficient to teach all truths of the Christian faith, He would not have inspired Paul to use a marginal word like *ophelimos*. Catholic apologist Robert Sungenis points out that there were at least three other Greek words (*arkeo, autarkeia* and *hikanos*) that Paul could have used to describe Scripture as "sufficient" or "perfect" or "complete," but Paul didn't use any of them.[196]

For example, Paul records that Jesus told him, "My grace is *sufficient* (*arkeo*) for you, for my power is made perfect in weakness" (2 Cor 12:9). Paul also says, "And God is able to provide you with every blessing in abundance, so that you may always have *enough* (*autarkeia*) of everything and may provide in abundance for every good work" (2 Cor 9:8). Paul further says, "to one a fragrance from death to death, to the other a fragrance from life to life. Who is *sufficient* (*hikanos*) for these things?" (2 Cor 2:16). In each of these passages, Paul is referring to the *sufficiency* of God's grace to bring us to salvation. Paul was certainly aware of several words that describe the sufficiency of something, but Paul never applied such words to Scripture.

St. Paul's use of *ophelimos* to describe Scripture actually underscores that Scripture is *not* formally sufficient or even mandatory for Christian instruction. For example, in his letter to Titus, Paul describes how

eds. J. Derek Holmes and Robert Murray (Washington: Corpus Books, 1967), 131.
[196] See Sungenis, *Not By Scripture Alone* (p.113, ft 7 and p.118, ft 12) which provides an indispensable framework for this chapter. Paul would have used the Greek *arkeo* (Mt 25:9; Lk 3:14; Jn 6:7; 14:8; 1 Tim 6:8; Heb 13:5; 3 Jn 10), *autarkeia* (2 Cor 9:8; 1 Tim 6:6) or *hikanos* (2 Cor 2:6,16; 3:5) if he wanted to teach that the Scriptures were complete or sufficient for teaching.

God saves us through the regenerative waters of baptism (3:5-6). Paul then tells Titus to exhort the faithful to good deeds which are "profitable" (*ophelimos*) to their salvation (3:8). St. Paul wasn't saying that, on one hand, we were saved in baptism, but on the other hand, good deeds are the exclusive means to be saved. That would be a contradiction. Instead, Paul is teaching that good deeds are beneficial in maintaining our salvation, but not the only thing we need to do, just like knowing Scripture is beneficial for our salvation, but not the only thing we need to know.

Similarly, in his first letter to Timothy, Paul says, "for while bodily training is of some value, godliness is of value (*ophelimos*) in every way, as it holds promise for the present life and also for the life to come" (1 Tim 4:8). In this passage, St. Paul is revealing another factor, godliness, that is "profitable" and "valuable" for "the life to come." As with Scripture and good deeds, godliness is an ingredient in the salvation program, but not the only ingredient.

Verse 16 poses another problem for the Protestant's position. St. Paul's phrase "All Scripture..." comes from the Greek *pas graphe* which can be interpreted to mean "every Scripture" (not "all Scripture").[197] This would mean that every *passage* of Scripture is useful. Moreover, if the word *ophelimos* really meant "exclusive" (which it does not), then *pas graphe* can be interpreted to mean that every single Scripture passage is a formally sufficient source of teaching and instruction. This would mean that *any* single verse in Scripture gives us the totality of the Gospel (try 1 Chronicles 1:1). This, of course, is absurd.

---

[197] See Protestant author W.E. Vine's definition of *pasa* in *Vine's Expository Dictionary of New Testament Words* (Mclean, VA: McDonald Publishing House, nd), p.387.

Some Catholic apologists point out that Paul's use of "All Scripture" refers to the Old Testament Scriptures of Timothy's childhood. In the preceding verse, Paul reminds Timothy "how from childhood you have been acquainted with the sacred writings which are able to instruct you for salvation through faith in Christ Jesus" (v.15). It certainly appears that Paul is referring to the Old Testament Scriptures alone, which even means that Paul believes one can come to faith in Jesus without the New Testament Scriptures (since the New Testament canon didn't exist at this time).

But even if Paul in 2 Timothy 3:16 is referring to *all* inspired Scripture (also a plausible interpretation), he is not teaching *sola Scriptura*, for the "useful" (*ophelimos*) but not "exclusive" nature of Scripture would apply to the New Testament as well. 2 Timothy 3:16 is the one place where Paul makes a direct statement about the very nature of Scripture, and yet he limits its significance to merely "useful" (not "exclusive").

The second thing Protestants do is focus on verse 17 where Paul says Scripture makes the man of God "fit" (Greek, *artios*) and "equipped" (Greek, *exartismenos*).[198] In the New Testament, these two Greek words appear only here, in 2 Timothy 3:17, and so their meanings cannot be definitively established using Scripture. Greek lexicons provide a wide range of meanings from "fit" or "capable" to "complete" or "perfect." These variations in meaning, coupled with the aforementioned Greek words for "complete" and "perfect," suggest that *artios* and *exartismenos* refer to

---

[198] For a detailed treatment of these Greek words in the context of 2 Tim 3:16-17 and overall, see Sungenis, *Not By Scripture Alone*, pp. 111-115. See also Peters, *Scripture Alone? 21 Reasons to Reject Sola Scriptura*, pp.6-9.

capability rather than perfection.[199] But even if these words do mean "perfect" or "complete," they are referring to the "man of God," *and not to Scripture.* This grammatical fact is often missed by Protestant exegetes. This also means that 2 Timothy 3:17 cannot be used to prove that the Scriptures are sufficient or complete.

Protestants may respond by arguing that if the man of God can reach "completeness" or "perfection" by using the Scriptures, then there is nothing else he needs and *sola Scriptura* prevails. But even if we assume that these Greek words in question mean "complete" or "perfect," the Protestant still has a problem with *ophelimos.* While the man of God may ultimately reach "perfection," the Scriptures are described as merely "profitable" to that end. Scripture may be an important factor in helping the man of God reach perfection, but Scripture doesn't say it is the *only* factor.

As our Lord tells us, "perfection" is the end-game,[200] but Paul never uses that word to describe Scripture. Instead, in the very same letter, he tells Timothy to follow oral Tradition (1:13), entrust the Tradition to others (2:2) and preach the word (4:2). He also tells Timothy to suffer for the gospel (1:8), avoid godless chatter (2:16), continue in what he has already learned (3:14) and rebuke and exhort the faithful (4:2). As a "man of God," all these things, in addition to Scripture, will help Timothy reach perfection in Christ.

After Paul explains that Scripture can equip the "man of God" for every good work, he goes on to charge Timothy "in the presence of Christ Jesus...preach the word, be urgent in season and out of

---

[199] See Sungenis, *Not By Scripture Alone,* p.113.
[200] See Mt 5:48.

season, convince, rebuke and exhort, be unfailing in patience and in teaching" (4:1-2). Thus, Paul penned 2 Timothy 3:16-17 as an instruction for the clergy (bishops and priests), and not for all Christians. Protestant communities don't have priests or bishops so, technically, the passage doesn't even apply to them.

Nevertheless, even if the passage applies to all believers, how are Protestants to determine who the "man of God" really is? Is the Lutheran pastor who believes in infant baptism a "man of God," but a Baptist preacher who denies infant baptism a "man of Satan"? Or is it vice versa? Protestants have varied interpretations of the "man of God" as they do the rest of Scripture. If the Protestant cannot tell us definitively who the "man of God" is in 2 Timothy 3:17, they certainly cannot provide us with a definitive interpretation of the passage. As with all these issues, we have no resolution without an infallible authority outside of Scripture.

Notice also that Scripture helps the man of God become complete and equipped "for every good work" (v.17). St. Paul uses the identical Greek phrase earlier in the same letter: "If anyone purifies himself from what is ignoble, then he will be a vessel for noble use, consecrated and useful to the master of the house, ready *for any good work*" (2 Tim 2:21). As we can see, Paul is teaching that *both* Scripture *and* avoiding what is ignoble makes a man "complete" and "equipped," and not Scripture alone. Timothy is to draw from both sources to achieve the same goal.

This also demonstrates that St. Paul's use of "fit" (*artios*) and "equipped" (*exartismenos*) cannot mean "perfect" or "sufficient," but simply "capable" and "competent."[201] If not, then avoiding what is ignoble could make a man perfect and complete, but this is not true. Man must do many other things to bring about his perfection (baptism, faith, hope, charity, repentance, perseverance, etc.). Thus, if Protestants are not willing to argue that avoiding ignobility perfects man (which they are not), then they cannot successfully argue that Scripture perfects man either.

St. James uses similar language in his epistle: "And let steadfastness have its full effect, that you may be *perfect* and *complete*, lacking in nothing" (Jas 1:4). In this case, "steadfastness" or perseverance, and not Scripture, makes a man "perfect" and "complete." The Protestant would presumably not argue that perseverance is the only thing one must do to become perfect and complete. As with Paul, James is describing the Christian's desired outcome and identifying one of the ways to achieve that goal.

Further, the Greek words that James uses for "perfect" (*teleios*) and "complete" (*holokleros*) refer to "completeness" and "perfection" and are thus much stronger words than *artios* and *exartismenos* in 2 Timothy 3:17. For example, James uses the same adjective later in the same chapter: "Every good endowment and every *perfect* (*teleios*) gift is from above"(v.17), and "he who looks into the *perfect* (*teleios*) law, the law of liberty, and perseveres, being no hearer that forgets but a doer that acts, he shall be blessed in his doing"(v.25).

Paul also says, "May the God of peace himself sanctify you *wholly* (*holokleros*)…at the coming of our Lord Jesus Christ" (1 Thess 5:23). In these and other cases, *teleois* and *holokleros* refer to a state of completion

---

[201] See also Sungenis, *Not By Scripture Alone*, pp.116-117.

or perfection. Yet Paul doesn't apply these words to Scripture, or even to the man of God who becomes equipped using Scripture. For all of these reasons, 2 Timothy 3:16-17 does not teach *sola Scriptura*.

1 Corinthians 4:6

In Paul's first letter to the Corinthians, Protestants believe they find another "silver bullet" for *sola Scriptura*. Paul writes:

> I have applied all this to myself and Apollos for your benefit, brethren, that you may learn by us not to go beyond what is written, that none of you may be puffed up in favor of one against another (1 Cor 4:6).

Protestants automatically conclude that St. Paul is referring to Scripture when he tells the Corinthians "not to go beyond what is written." Based on this assumption, the Protestant concludes that Scripture is the sole rule of faith and that Christians are not to go "beyond" Scripture to receive the truths of salvation. From this single verse, Protestants find the entirety of God's revelation in the Bible alone. What do Catholics say about this? Several things.

First, both Catholic and Protestants biblical scholars agree that 1 Corinthians 4:6 is one of the most ambiguous, obscure and confusing passages in all of Scripture. It is thus quite ironic that Protestants who argue for Scripture's perspicuity would rely on such a non-perspicuous verse to prove *sola Scriptura*. As Catholic apologist Robert Sungenis explains, many scholars believe that the verse is corrupted so that the original Greek words are non-translatable.[202] Other scholars believe that "what is written" was not even in the originally-inspired text, but is instead a marginal gloss or other copyist error that crept into the translation. No one in the history of the Church ever used 1 Corinthians 4:6 to support even the material sufficiency of Scripture. In fact, not even the Protestant Reformers used 1 Corinthians 4:6 as a defense of *sola Scriptura* because of the verse's ambiguity. Protestant reliance on the verse to support their Bible-only theology is a relatively modern initiative.

Second, a lexical and exegetical analysis of the verse further highlights its complete inability to sustain the *sola Scriptura* position. The Greek for "what is written" (*grapho*) is a perfect passive verb. This means that the progress of the action (writing) has been completed (although the results continue on in the future). Thus, the verb *grapho* is literally translated as "what *has been* written." If "what has been written" does mean "Scripture," then Paul could have been referring *only* to the Scriptures that were written *up to that point in history* (that is, the Scriptures written up to the time of his first letter to the Corinthians). He would not have been referring to any Scripture that would be written in the future.

Paul's first letter to the Corinthians was one of the first New Testament Scriptures written. Only Paul's letters to the Thessalonians and Galatians were likely written earlier. This would mean that Paul's supposed directive in 1 Corinthians 4:6 would have excluded the rest of the New Testament corpus from the rule of faith. Paul would have been instructing the

---

[202] For an exhaustive list of the possible interpretations of "what has been written" and an in-depth exegesis of the verse, see Sungenis, *Not By Scripture Alone*, pp.139-149.

Corinthians to ignore not only his and other evangelists' future letters, but also the four gospels which were held in particular esteem in the early Church just as they are today. This conclusion, of course, is absurd.

Even if the Greek verb for "what is written" was in the present or future tense, the verse would still prove nothing for the Protestant. This is because the verb has no referent (which is also clear in the English translation). It is therefore completely gratuitous for Protestants to automatically conclude that Paul is referring to Scripture. While it is possible that Paul is referring to Scripture, this cannot be proven definitively. Some Protestant scholars even suggest that Paul was referring *not* to Scripture, but to a proverb that may have been used by Rabbis or philosophers. If this is the case, then 1 Corinthians 4:6 cannot be used to prove *sola Scriptura* because Paul would be appealing to an authority outside of Scripture.

If Paul was referring to Scripture, what about Paul's non-canonical letters?[203] Paul would presumably have those in mind as he commanded the Corinthians "not to go beyond what is written." In fact, Paul commanded that his non-inspired writings be read in the churches along side his inspired Scripture (see 1 Cor 5:9). That the Catholic Church excluded some of "what has been written" from the New Testament proves that she, and not Scripture, is the final authority on matters of Scripture.

Even assuming Paul was referring to Scripture, in those same Scriptures Paul commands us to follow the oral Tradition and teaching authority of the Church.

---

[203] See 1 Cor 5:9; Col 4:16; Phil 3:1; 2 Cor 10:9-10.

That means not going "beyond what is written" necessarily includes obedience to Tradition and the Church. We see this even in Paul's first letter to the Corinthians. For example, ten verses after 1 Corinthians 4:6, Paul says, "I urge you, then, be imitators of me" (v.16). Here, Paul is exhorting the Corinthians to follow his example, which would mean "going beyond what is written" and thus contradicting his instructions in verse 6. Paul commands the same thing later in the letter: "Be imitators of me, as I am of Christ" (1 Cor 11:1). After giving instructions on the Eucharist, Paul says, "About the other things I will give directions when I come" (11:34). Again, if Paul were really teaching the Corinthians not to go beyond Scripture for instruction, then it would make no sense for Paul provide additional oral instructions to which he commanded equal obedience.

Of course, Paul's repeated appeals to oral Tradition and the Church, which he calls the "pinnacle and foundation of the truth,"[204] further demonstrate Paul's belief in the formal *insufficiency* of Scripture as the complete rule of faith. That, coupled with Paul's description of Scripture as "profitable" but never "sufficient," as well as the sheer ambiguity of 1 Corinthians 4:6, demonstrates that this isolated verse does not teach *sola Scriptura*.

Acts 17:11

Many Protestants use Luke's description of the Bereans in Acts 17 as another "proof-text" for *sola Scriptura*. Luke writes:

> Now these Jews were more noble
> than those in Thessalonica, for they

---

[204] See 1 Tim 3:15.

received the word with all eagerness,
examining the scriptures daily to see if
these things were so (Acts 17:11).

In this short passage, the Protestant sees that the
Berean Jews are called "noble," and then sees that they
examined the Old Testament Scriptures "daily." Based
on these brief facts, the Protestant concludes without
reservation that the Bible (which didn't exist at the
time Luke wrote Acts 17:11) is the only infallible
authority for Christians. Even though Paul was not
teaching about the nature or use of Scripture,
Protestants see their Scripture-alone theology explicit
in the verse. Even though the passage does not say the
Bereans "examined the Scriptures *alone*," Protestants
would have us believe they did. This is another
example of how Protestants read their bias into the
sacred text. Let us examine the passage in its proper
context.

Acts 17 begins with Paul's visit to a synagogue of
different Jews in Thessalonica: "And Paul went in, as
was his custom, and for three weeks he argued with
them from the scriptures, explaining and proving that
it was necessary for the Christ to suffer and to rise from
the dead, and saying, 'This Jesus, whom I proclaim to
you, is the Christ'" (Acts 17:2-3). Obviously, the
Thessalonian Jews were just as familiar with Scripture
as the Berean Jews. Paul would not have argued with
them for three weeks using Scripture if the
Thessalonians had no familiarity with Scripture. The
Bereans, the Thessalonians and *all* devout Jews were
well-acquainted with Scripture because they used it
daily in their synagogues.

This means the Bereans' use of Scripture is *not* the
reason why Luke describes them as "more noble"
(v.11). The Thessalonians used Scripture as well, but
were *less* noble than the Bereans. The Bereans were

"more noble" than the Thessalonians because they received Paul's oral teaching as the Word of God and humbly submitted to Paul's authority. Luke says "they received the word with all eagerness," in reference to the oral Tradition Paul handed on to them (v.11). In other words, the Bereans were more noble than the Thessalonians for the very thing Protestants denounce: the acceptance of oral Tradition and Church authority.

The Bereans used the Old Testament Scriptures as an *additional* witness to the oral truths they had eagerly received from Paul, but *not* as their exclusive and definitive authority. Both served as witnesses to the truth that Paul was communicating to them: The Messiah of the Old Testament was Jesus Christ of the New Testament.[205] Through a synthesis of both the oral and written Word, and under the guidance of the Apostle Paul, the noble Bereans concluded that Jesus was the long-awaited Messiah who had to die and rise again. Thus, we see in the case of the Bereans the triune pattern of Scripture, Tradition, and apostolic authority leading people to faith in Jesus Christ. As Luke says, "*Many* of them therefore believed" (v.12).

The Thessalonian Jews, on the other hand, were not as favorably disposed to Paul's authority and instruction. After Paul spent three weeks with the Thessalonians handing on to them the oral Word of God,[206] only "*some* of them were persuaded" (v.4). In fact, Luke describes the Thessalonian Jews as "jealous" and recounts how they rioted in the city and caused an uproar over Paul's teaching (vv.5-7). After the Thessalonians rejected the oral Tradition that Paul

---

[205] Robert Sungenis meticulously proves this point in *Not By Scripture Alone*, pp.132-138. See also Keating, *Catholicism and Fundamentalism*, p.140.
[206] See 1 Thess 2:13.

handed on to them, they ran Paul and his cohorts out of the city (vv.9-10).

The distinction between the Bereans and the Thessalonians teaches us that *sola Scriptura* is a false and unworkable doctrine. Both the Bereans and the Thessalonians examined the Scriptures to understand the Word of God, *but they came to different conclusions.* It took Paul, an authority *outside* of Scripture, to teach them the true meaning of Scripture. This account demonstrates quite clearly how the Scriptures are formally insufficient to resolve doctrinal questions without divine authority. The account also shows how Catholics emulate the Bereans and are led to the truth while Protestants imitate the Thessalonians and are led to error.[207]

Without Paul's apostolic authority, the Jews would have never understood their Messiah would have to die for their sins. Without Paul, the Jews would have continued to believe their Messiah would be an earthly ruler and not a heavenly king. Without the Church, the Jews would have never known about the Messiah's divinity and humanity, His two wills, His intellect, His beatific vision while on earth, or any other theological matter regarding His being. While Scripture presented many facts about the Messiah, these facts had to be interpreted by someone with divine authority. Scripture serves as a witness to the truths of the faith, but the Church is the judge and jury.

Matthew 4:1-11

Protestants also appeal to Matthew's account of Jesus' temptation in the desert when trying to convince

---

[207] For a great article on this issue, see *Why the Bereans Rejected Sola Scriptura*, Steve Ray, (*This Rock*, Vol. 8, No. 3, March 1997).

their detractors of *sola Scriptura*. Because Jesus appealed to Scripture in the face of His temptation in Matthew 4, many Protestants conclude that Jesus believed in *sola Scriptura*. They maintain this conclusion notwithstanding the fact that Jesus never commanded His apostles to write Scripture, and referred to the Church, not the Scripture, as the final authority for Christians.[208] Here is the entire passage in question:

> Then Jesus was led up by the Spirit into the wilderness to be tempted by the devil. And he fasted forty days and forty nights, and afterward he was hungry. And the tempter came and said to him, 'If you are the Son of God, command these stones to become loaves of bread.' But he answered, 'It is written,' 'Man shall not live by bread alone, but by every word that proceeds from the mouth of God.'' Then the devil took him to the holy city, and set him on the pinnacle of the temple, and said to him, 'If you are the Son of God, throw yourself down; for it is written,' 'He will give his angels charge of you,' and 'On their hands they will bear you up, lest you strike your foot against a stone.'' Jesus said to him, 'Again it is written,' 'You shall not tempt the Lord your God.'' Again, the devil took him to a very high mountain, and showed him all the kingdoms of the world and the glory of them; and he said to him, 'All these I will give you, if you will fall down and worship me.' Then Jesus said

---

[208] Mt 16:18-19; 18:17-18.

to him, 'Begone, Satan! for it is written,'
'You shall worship the Lord your God
and him only shall you serve (Mt 4:1-
11).

As with all passages of Scripture, we must examine
the passage in its proper context. Most obviously, in
this account, Jesus is not providing a dogmatic
teaching on the formal sufficiency of Scripture. He is
resisting temptation in a desert. Unlike 2 Timothy 3:16,
where Paul makes a general statement about
"Scripture" (calling it "useful"), Jesus in Matthew 4
makes no such statement about Scripture. Jesus does
not describe Scripture or explain its usefulness,
sufficiency or lack of sufficiency. He simply appeals to
Scripture as an authority. For Protestants to conclude
anything beyond that simple point is reading into the
text what does not exist.

We also note that Jesus in Matthew 4 appeals to the
Old Testament Scriptures alone (Deuteronomy 8:3, 6:16
and 6:13 respectively). If Jesus were really making a
statement about Scripture in Matthew 4 (which He is
not), then that statement should be limited to the Old
Testament or even only to the verses He quotes. As we
can see, concluding from the account in Matthew 4 that
Scripture is the *only* authority (and not just *an*
authority) for Christians is question-begging at its best.
That Jesus doesn't *always* appeal to Scripture when
preaching the gospel also undermines the Protestant
argument. Instead of using Scripture, Jesus often
appeals to His divinity as a witness to the truth.[209]
Other times Jesus appeals to His miracles.[210] Jesus uses
"two or three witnesses" to confirm the Word of

---

[209] See, for example, Jn 7:16,28,33; 8:16,18-19,23-24,28-29,38,42,54,58;
10:30.
[210] See, for example, Jn 5:36; 6:32-33; 10:25,37-38; 14:11-12.

God.[211] Jesus never appeals to Scripture alone or teaches that Scripture is the ultimate authority for Christians.

To the contrary, in Matthew 18 Jesus says, "But if he does not listen, take one or two others along with you, that every word may be confirmed by the evidence of two or three witnesses. If he refuses to listen to them, tell it to the church; and if he refuses to listen even to the church, let him be to you as a Gentile and a tax collector" (vv.16-17). Scripture is one of the "two or three witnesses" that Jesus speaks of, but the infallible voice of the Church is the *final judge*. As applied to Matthew 4, the Old Testament Scriptures serve as a witness to the truth, but Jesus is their infallible interpreter. The devil also had an interpretation of Scripture when he declared to Jesus, "He will give his angels charge of you" (Ps 91:11) but it was an erroneous one. This further proves that one must have divine guidance when interpreting Scripture lest he be led into grave error.

We also note that, out of all the possible Old Testament Scriptures Jesus could have used to rebuke the devil, He appeals first to Deuteronomy 8:3 which says: "man does not live by bread alone, but that man lives by everything that proceeds out of the mouth of the LORD." As we have seen, "everything that proceeds out of the mouth of the Lord" is His inspired Word *whether in Scripture or Tradition*. Deuteronomy 8:3 certainly has nothing to do with "Scripture alone." Like the rest of the verses Protestants summon to their defense, Matthew 4:1-11 implicitly *denies* the doctrine of *sola Scriptura*.

---

[211] Mt 18:16; 2 Cor 13:1; 1 Tim 5:19; Heb 10:28.

John 5:39

Protestants also find several "proof-texts" for *sola Scriptura* in St. John's gospel. The first one is found in chapter 5. The chapter begins with Jesus curing a man who had been ill for thirty-eight years. Because Jesus cured the man on the Sabbath, the Jews persecuted Jesus for allegedly violating the Third Commandment (v.16). Jesus rebukes the unbelieving Jews by declaring that He was the Son of God who came to give eternal life to the world (vv.17-21). In His rebuke, Jesus tells the Jews:

> You search the scriptures, because
> you think that in them you have eternal
> life; and it is they that bear witness to
> me (Jn 5:39).

It is unclear whether Jesus' statement "You search the scriptures" (Greek, *ereunao ho graphe*) is in the imperative or indicative tense.[212] Protestants argue it is in the imperative tense which means Jesus would be commanding the Jews to "search the Scriptures." However, it is more likely to be in the indicative tense because the phrase is followed by a relative clause which explains *why* the Jews "search the Scriptures" – because in doing so they think they have life eternal. Nevertheless, even if Jesus is commanding the Jews to search the Scriptures, the verse does not prove *sola Scriptura*. In fact, as we will see, the verse denies the Protestant doctrine.

First, Jesus doesn't say "search the Scriptures *alone*." Modifying the word "Scripture" with the qualifier "alone" is an unconscious, knee-jerk reaction

---

[212] Robert Sungenis points out this distinction in *Not By Scripture Alone*, pp.234-235.

that Protestants make whenever they see Jesus or the apostles referring to Holy Writ. We saw this with Matthew 4:1-11 and Acts 17:11. We also saw how Protestants make a similar error when they automatically equate the phrase "Word of God" with "Scripture."

Second, only Jesus, an authority *outside* of Scripture, was able to teach the Jews the true meaning of the Scriptures they searched. The Jews of John 5 knew Scripture, for they accused Jesus of breaking a Scriptural mandate (the Third Commandment). But the Scriptures were formally insufficient to teach them the real meaning of keeping holy the Sabbath. More importantly, using Scripture alone, the Jews were unable to discern that Jesus was the Messiah. While Jesus came to give them life, their erroneous interpretations of Scripture were leading them to eternal death.

Third, Jesus brackets His presumed instruction to "search the Scriptures" with an explanation on the necessity of having "two or three witnesses" to discern truth (similar to Matthew 18:16). Jesus says, "If I bear witness to myself, my testimony is not true; there is another who bears witness to me, and I know that the testimony which he bears to me is true" (vv.31-32). Jesus then says "You sent to John, and he has borne witness to the truth" (v.33). In other words, God the Father and John the Baptist are the necessary second and third witnesses to the truth that Jesus is the Messiah.

After Jesus says "search the Scriptures, He says "it is Moses who accuses you, on whom you set your hope. If you believed Moses, you would believe me, for he wrote of me. But if you do not believe his writings, how will you believe my words?" (vv.45-47). Moses serves as yet another witness to the truth of Jesus

Christ. Thus, Jesus emphasizes that Scripture *must be supplemented with additional witnesses* to discern the truths of salvation. Far from proving *sola Scriptura*, John 5:39 actually disproves it.

John 10:34-36

The next popular verse from St. John's gospel used by Protestants comes from chapter 10. The chapter opens with Jesus teaching the Jews that He is the only way to eternal life and the Jews, as usual, respond with obstinacy (vv.9-10). In fact, in this account, the Jews accuse Jesus of being possessed by a demon (v.20). In response, Jesus not only reiterates that He is the way to eternal life, He proclaims His divinity by declaring, "I and the Father are one" (v.30).

At this point, the Jews take up stones to stone Jesus because they think He has committed blasphemy (v.31). In response, Jesus first appeals to His miracles which testify that He is the Christ (v.32). Jesus then asks the Jews for which miracle do they seek to stone Him. The Jews answer that they seek to stone him not for his good works but for making Himself equal to God (v.33). Jesus then appeals to His second witness, Scripture, and says:

> Is it not written in your law, 'I said, you are gods'? If he called them gods to whom the word of God came (and scripture cannot be broken), do you say of him whom the Father consecrated and sent into the world, `You are blaspheming,' because I said, 'I am the Son of God'?

Before examining the passage, we note one interesting fact. St. John points out that Jesus is speaking on "the feast of the Dedication at Jerusalem" (v.22). The only time this feast is mentioned in Scripture is in 1 Maccabees 4:59 when Judas and his brothers determined that the "dedication of the altar" should be observed for eight days. Thus, John is inspired by God to rely upon a deuterocanonical book and oral Tradition in recording the feast of Dedication (Hanukkah). In fact, Jesus also recognizes the feast by analogizing the Hanukkah consecration of the sanctuary in 1 Maccabees 4:36 to His consecration to the Father in John 10:36. This is further support that Jesus and the apostles viewed the deuterocanon as inspired Scripture.

Now, back to the passage at hand. As with John 5:39 and Acts 17:11, because Jesus appeals to Old Testament Scripture, Protestants conclude that the Bible is our only infallible authority. Protestants believe their case is especially strong because Jesus says "scripture cannot be broken" (v.35). What do Catholics say in response? More of the same.

First, we see Jesus once again using the "two or three witnesses" theme when specifically mentioning "Scripture." In John 5:39, Jesus used God the Father, John the Baptist and Moses as additional witnesses to Scripture. In John 10, Jesus appeals to His miracles to supplement the witness of Scripture (vv.32,38). In fact, after Jesus left to go across the Jordan, the Jews appealed to John's oral testimony as another witness to the truths Jesus preached. Based on John's supplemental testimony, "many believed in him there" (v.42). Even though Jesus appealed to Scripture, He did not appeal to Scripture alone. Moreover, the Jews did not use Scripture alone to come to faith in Jesus (they used the oral testimony of Jesus and John as well).

Second, the passage demonstrates the absolute insufficiency of Scripture as the only source of divine truth. The Jews that Jesus addressed were very familiar with Scripture. Jesus acknowledges this when He refers the Jews to their Scriptures by asking them, "Is it not written in your law?" (v.34). Although the Jews knew Scripture, they did not know the true meaning of Scripture until a source *outside* of Scripture (Jesus and John) illuminated them. It was only *after* the Jews verified the testimony of Jesus and Scripture with the oral Tradition of John that they came to believe in Jesus.

Third, Jesus' statement "Scripture cannot be broken" (v.35) certainly doesn't mean "Scripture is our exclusive authority." Just because Scripture cannot be "broken" doesn't mean it is the *only* thing that cannot be broken. Of course, the Word of God cannot be broken and that Word includes both Scripture and Tradition. Jesus' statement about the inability to "break" Scripture is about Scripture's reliability and verifiability, not its exclusivity.

Moreover, when we view Jesus' statement in its proper context, we realize that Jesus wasn't making a doctrinal statement about Scripture *per se*. Rather, Jesus was seeking to condemn the Jews for their unbelief by using an authority (the Psalms) that they recognized. Jesus was referring to Psalm 82:5-7 which says:

> They have neither knowledge nor understanding, they walk about in darkness; all the foundations of the earth are shaken. I say, 'You are gods, sons of the Most High, all of you; nevertheless, you shall die like men, and fall like any prince.'

In short, Jesus was using this Psalm to indict the Jews for their ignorance of the very Scriptures they tried to use against Jesus. Jesus essentially asks the Jews, "if God called His people "gods" in the Psalm, then why can't I call Myself the "Son of God"? Jesus was pointing out to the Jews that their rejection of Him as God's Son was inconsistent with the plain meaning of the Psalm. More importantly, however, Jesus was revealing to the Jews that they were the "gods" of the Psalm who lacked "knowledge and understanding," who "walk in darkness" and "shall die like men" because they lacked faith in the "Son of God" who came to them. The "Scripture could not be broken" because Jesus rendered an infallible interpretation of it which indicted the Jews and from which they had no escape.

John 20:30-31

The last passage Protestants pick out from John's gospel comes from chapter 20. This time, the statement comes from the Apostle John and not Jesus. John writes:

> Now Jesus did many other signs in the presence of the disciples, which are not written in this book; but these are written that you may believe that Jesus is the Christ, the Son of God, and that believing you may have life in his name.

As you might guess, because St. John explains that he wrote his gospel so that people may believe Jesus is the Son of God, Protestants conclude that Scripture must be the Christian's only infallible authority. As usual, it is difficult to comprehend how Protestants can make such an exegetical leap. Yes, John wrote so that we can believe, but John never says Scripture is the only way one can come to believe. In fact, John never even says Scripture is *necessary* to come to faith in Christ. Certainly, many of the people to whom John preached decades before he wrote his gospel came to faith in Christ without Scripture.[213]

If the Protestant wants to argue that John is declaring the formal sufficiency of Scripture, then he should admit that John is referring *to his gospel only*. John says that many things were not written "in this book," but "*these* are written" so that we may believe. "These" refer to the things that John wrote "in *this* book," that is, his gospel. If John is making a case for formal sufficiency, then he would be declaring his gospel to be the sole rule of faith. Does John's gospel answer every question that is necessary for salvation (e.g., whether abortion, surrogate motherhood, stem cell research or polygamy is a mortal sin)? Of course not, as Protestants would even agree.

Further, John's reference to the "many other signs that were not written" in his gospel is not a rejection of those things. After all, John is speaking about the words and actions of Jesus Christ, the Eternal Word of God made flesh. As we have learned, these "other signs" of Jesus are not irrelevant and dispensable, but also part of the Deposit of Faith as preserved in oral Tradition. John even concludes his gospel by reminding us that Jesus did so many things that "the world itself could not contain the books that would be written" (Jn 21:25). John reveals that the apostles were simply not capable of recording everything Jesus taught and did, but that doesn't make them less important. In fact, according to John, we might even conclude that Scripture records only a *fraction* of God's salvific revelation. Such an argument could be used against even the material sufficiency of Scripture.

---

[213] See also Keating, *Catholicism and Fundamentalism*, p.135.

At the conclusion of John's gospel, he writes: "This is the disciple who is bearing witness to these things, and who has written these things; and we know that his testimony is true" (Jn 21:24). Like Jesus, John also calls upon the "two or three witnesses" to verify the truths of the gospel. John tells his audience that he bears witness orally (Tradition) and in writing (Scripture), and that both of these witnesses, when taken together, provide truthful testimony. Thus, John completes his written testimony by denying the formal sufficiency of it. For these reasons, neither Jesus nor John ever teaches the false doctrine of *sola Scriptura*. Instead, they explicitly reject it.

III.

The Bible and
the Church Fathers

Chapter 9

Introduction to the Fathers

In the first two sections of the book, we learned how the totality of the Word of God is found in Scripture and Tradition as interpreted by the Catholic Church. We also learned that the oral Tradition has been preserved in the Church through apostolic succession while the written Tradition has been preserved in the copies of the Scriptures. We will now look at some of the teachings of the successors to the apostles to whom the Tradition has been entrusted. We call these men the "Church Fathers" because they are our spiritual fathers in the faith. We learn what they believed about Scripture, Tradition and the authority of the Church.

Many of the Church Fathers were taught directly by the apostles (Ignatius of Antioch, Polycarp) or immediate successors to them (Justin Martyr, Irenaeus, Tertullian). These men received and passed on the very teachings of Jesus Christ and His apostles. They presided over the earliest Church councils, formulated the major dogmas of the faith, crushed the first and most threatening heresies against the faith, wrote the first commentaries on Sacred Scripture, and laid the foundation for the Church's theology for future generations. Because they were closest to Jesus and the apostles, these men provide invaluable insights into the faith of the early Church.

Most Protestants who read the Fathers are shocked to discover their explicit beliefs in such Catholic doctrines as infant baptism, oral confession, transubstantiation, the priesthood, the primacy of the Roman church and purgatory. This forces them to make a choice: they have to either conclude the entire early Church was apostate or call their nearest Catholic parish and begin RCIA classes.[214] Those who truly desire to know the Christian faith of all time must become familiar with the Fathers, for the Fathers believed and taught what Jesus taught.

In a recent debate with a Protestant about the Eucharist, I asked my opponent how he definitively knew his symbolic interpretation of John 6 was correct. He couldn't argue the plain meaning of the text supported his interpretation because it doesn't. He couldn't argue the text itself provided the correct interpretation because it doesn't. He couldn't argue other Scriptures supported a symbolic interpretation because they don't. He couldn't argue that the Eucharist is contrary to reason because it isn't (not any more than the Incarnation is contrary to reason). And he surely couldn't argue the early Church agreed with him because it didn't. My opponent could argue only that he was convicted of his own private interpretation of the text.

This is where the witness of the Fathers is most helpful. I asked my opponent whether he thought it would be helpful (theoretically, of course) to speak with the Apostle John to understand what he meant when he wrote John 6. He admitted that such a scenario would be most helpful. After acknowledging

---

[214] RCIA stands for "Rite of Christian Initiation for Adults." This is the program of preparatory classes all adults who seek to enter the Catholic Church are required to take before entering into communion with the Church.

this would be impossible, I asked him whether studying what a disciple of the Apostle John said about John 6 would be helpful. He said that it would be the next best thing to actually speaking with John.

I then rattled off four quotes from Ignatius of Antioch who was the auditor of the Apostle John. In these quotes, Ignatius interprets John 6 literally by saying that the "Eucharist" is the "flesh of Christ" and the "medicine of immortality." I followed these quotes with others from Clement, Justin Martyr, Irenaeus, Tertullian, Hippolytus, Clement of Alexandria, Origen and Cyprian. These men, who received their catechesis from the successors of the apostles during the first, second and third centuries, all agreed with Ignatius' literal interpretation of John 6.

My Protestant friend could respond only by arguing that the writings of the Fathers have no authority because they are not Scripture. Never mind that Ignatius received his literal interpretation of John 6 *from the very apostle who wrote John 6*. My Protestant opponent valued his personal opinion over that of a disciple of John (not to mention everyone else in the early Church), and all in the name of *sola Scriptura*. This, of course, is not only a rejection of apostolic Tradition, but an utter disregard for Scripture itself. It is the exaltation of private judgment over objective truth as contained in the Deposit of Faith and preserved, expounded and transmitted by the Church. Thus, we can see that pride is the root cause of *sola Scriptura*, just as it is with every other sin.

Adherence to the Fathers' common interpretation of Scripture is no small matter. While the Fathers didn't agree with each other on every doctrine, they were unanimous in their beliefs in the major doctrines of the Catholic faith (e.g., the pope, authority, the seven sacraments, purgatory). They all declared membership in the One, Holy, Catholic and Apostolic Church. Because the Fathers came from different centuries, geographies and backgrounds, their unanimity in major doctrines indicates that they received their understanding from the apostles. In other words, the doctrines with which they agree are part of the apostolic Tradition. For this reason, as we have mentioned, the Catholic Church dogmatically teaches that we are not to depart from the Fathers' interpretation of Scripture when they are unanimous.[215]

---

[215] Council of Trent, *Decree Concerning the Canonical Scriptures*, Session 4 (April 8, 1546); First Vatican Council, Session 3, Chapter 2, *On Revelation* (April 24, 1870), No. 5.

Chapter 10

Material versus Formal Sufficiency

As we will see, many of the early Church Fathers believed in the material sufficiency of Scripture. We introduced this theological concept in the first section of the book. By material sufficiency, theologians generally mean that Scripture contains all the information necessary to formulate doctrine. In other words, all of the "building blocks" for doctrine are found in Scripture, however remote, but Tradition and the Magisterium are necessary to "connect the blocks" to make the doctrine clear and understandable.

On the other hand, Protestants who believe in *sola Scriptura* believe in the formal sufficiency of Scripture. This position holds that the doctrines found in Scripture are already so clear and understandable that nothing else (i.e., Tradition and the Church) is needed to know their true meaning. In other words, the "building blocks" are already connected to form the doctrine and no other assistance from either Tradition or the Church is necessary. We have already demonstrated the error of the Protestant position.

Some Protestant apologists try to pit the concept of material sufficiency against the doctrine of Tradition. They argue that if Scripture is materially sufficient, then there is no need for Tradition. In other words,

Tradition cannot be a separate body of knowledge outside of Scripture if Scripture already contains all of the building blocks for doctrine. Thus, the Protestant thinks he is bolstering his *sola Scriptura* position by catching the Catholic in a seeming contradiction. This is a rather naïve argument for a number of reasons.

First, the Catholic Church who speaks with authority on these matters has never defined "material sufficiency" of Scripture. "Material sufficiency" is nothing more than a debated theological opinion that may or may not be accepted by Catholics. Not all Catholic theologians and exegetes agree on the meaning of the term. Tradition, on the other hand, has been defined by the Church and must be believed with divine and Catholic faith. Pitting material sufficiency against Scripture is using a theory to contradict a fact. This is an invalid argument.

The reason why "material sufficiency" is only a theory is because what is materially sufficient for one person may not be materially sufficient for another. For example, take the Immaculate Conception of Mary. Person A may argue there is an absence of biblical verses to support the dogma. No where does Scripture explicitly say "Mary was conceived without sin." Since the Immaculate Conception is a dogma of the faith, Person A may logically reject the material sufficiency of Scripture.

However, Person B may point to the Annunciation where the angel Gabriel called Mary "full of grace" (Lk 1:28). The Greek word for "full of grace" (*kecharitomene*) is a perfect, passive participle. This means Mary received a superabundance of grace in the past by a completed action whose results continue in the present. Further, the word is titular, meaning that it could be translated as "Fully-graced one." With the use of *kecharitomene*, Person B may see a "building block" for the dogma of the Immaculate Conception. Person B may conclude that Mary received her perfection of grace while in the womb of her mother Anne.

Person B may also see a connection between Mary with the Ark of the Old Covenant. For the Jews, the Ark of the Covenant was the holiest article of religious worship because it contained the Word of God on stone tablets. Because the Ark was so holy, when Uzzah touched it to prevent it from tipping over on a journey, God killed him on the spot.[216] God would never let anything defiled touch the undefiled Ark of His Word.

Mary, on the other hand, contained the Word of God not on stone tablets but made flesh in her womb. When Mary asked the angel Gabriel how she would conceive the child Jesus because she had made a life-long vow of virginity, the angel said: "The Holy Spirit will overcome you, and the power of the Most High will *overshadow* you" (Luke 1:35). The Greek word for overshadow (*episkiazo*) is the same word the sacred authors used to describe God's glory cloud overshadowing the Ark of the Old Covenant which we read in the books of Exodus, Kings and Job. Just like God's *shekinah* glory cloud overshadowed the Holy of Holies of the Old Covenant, Mary, at the Annunciation, was overshadowed by the glory of the Holy Spirit and became the "Holy of Holies" of the New Covenant.

Luke makes some other striking comparisons between the two. For example, David leapt for joy before the old Ark while John the Baptist leapt for joy before Mary;[217] David questions how the Ark could

---

[216] 2 Sam 6:7; 1 Chron 13:9-10.
[217] 2 Sam 6:16; Lk 1:41.

come to him and Elizabeth asks the same thing;[218] the old Ark remains in the house for three months and so does Mary.[219] While the old Ark of the Covenant was holy, it cannot compare to the holiness and purity of the Blessed Virgin Mary. Once again, based on a synthesis of the relevant passages, Person B may see the Immaculate Conception implicitly in Scripture and hold to Scripture's material sufficiency. Neither Person A nor Person B is wrong. Both maintain legitimate positions based upon their different perspectives.

Second, one *can* believe in both the material sufficiency of Scripture and the necessity of Tradition at the same time. Why? Because doctrine can be found both *implicitly* in Scripture (material sufficiency) and *explicitly* in Tradition. Take, for example, the most fundamental dogma of the Christian faith: *The Trinity*. There are many verses in Scripture which point to both the divinity of Christ[220] and the divinity of the Holy Spirit.[221] There are also many verses that demonstrate the Holy Ghost is a Person.[222] These verses support – yet only implicitly – the Trinitarian dogmas that were defined by the Church at her first ecumenical councils.

This is how Tertullian, in A.D. 213, could say the Father, Son and Holy Ghost are "inseparable from each other," and yet "are distinct from each other" as well.[223] This is also how Justin Martyr, Polycarp, Irenaeus, Theophilus of Antioch, Origen, Gregory the

---

[218] 2 Sam 6:9; Lk 1:43.
[219] 2 Sam 6:11; 1 Chron 13:14; Lk 1:43.
[220] Mt 4:7; 9:2; 12:8; 21:3; 28:20; Mk 2:5,28; 14:36,62; Lk 4:12; 5:20; 6:5,46; 7:48; 8:39; 17:18; 19:31,34; 22:70; Jn 5:18,21-23; 6:38; 8:12,19,23,58; 10:18,30,36,38; 12:45; 13:13; 14:6,10; 16:15,28; 17:5,24; 20:17.
[221] Mt 12:31; Lk 12:10; Jn 4:24; 14:16,26; 15:26; 16:7.
[222] Lk 12:12; Jn 14:17,26; 15:26; 16:7-8; 13-14.
[223] *Against Praxeas*, 9.

Wonderworker, and Methodius could make similar statements before the Council of Nicea was convened. Scripture provided these men implicit information about the Trinity, and Tradition provided them explicit information. The Councils at Nicea and Constantinople synthesized *all* of this information, both implicit and explicit, in bringing about their dogmatic pronouncements on the Trinity. Once again, the Scriptures were not formally sufficient for dogmatic formulation; Tradition and the Magisterium were necessary.

Chapter 11

What did the Fathers Say?

Because the teachings of the Fathers are so damaging to Protestant theology, Protestant apologists have recognized the need to deal with them. In so doing, they have discovered they can hoodwink ignorant Catholics by cherry-picking passages from the Fathers which appear, in isolation, to support *sola Scriptura*. This is called the fallacy of "special pleading": a person uses only those passages which appear to support his case while ignoring those passages which hurt his case. Many Catholics unfamiliar with the Fathers can be easily persuaded. It is a dishonest approach, and we expose it in this chapter.

For example, Protestants will quote from Antony of Egypt who said, "The Scriptures are enough for instruction."[224] Based on this quote from Antony, Protestants have no problem arguing for formal sufficiency. They fail point out that Antony also commanded us to "observe the traditions of the fathers, and chiefly the holy faith in our Lord Jesus Christ."[225] Antony, like most Fathers, believed in Scripture's material sufficiency, but never in its formal sufficiency. As we will see, all of the Fathers believed

---

[224] *Athanasius' Life of Antony, 16 (c.A.D. 360).*
[225] Ibid., *89 (c.A.D. 360).*

Scripture must be interpreted in light of the Tradition of the Catholic Church.

We also point out that any Protestant appeal to the Church Fathers to demonstrate *sola Scriptura* negates the entire theory. Why? Because any writing of a Church Father is an authority *outside of Scripture*. If Scripture is formally sufficient to explain doctrine, then the Protestant should need nothing more to prove his case. A Protestant's need to cite the Fathers demonstrates Scripture's formal insufficiency to explain doctrine. It highlights that Scripture is not self-interpreting and perspicuous. For the Protestant, leaning on the Fathers is a self-defeating exercise.

We now examine the teachings of the Fathers. I have chosen the Fathers most commonly cited by Protestant apologists in their defense of *sola Scriptura* based upon their favorable statements about Scripture. I then follow their statements about Scripture with their teachings about Tradition, the Church, apostolic succession, the sacraments (Baptism, Confession, Eucharist, Confirmation, Anointing of the Sick), the Virgin Mary, the Saints and purgatory. If the Protestant wishes to argue that Scripture is the sole rule of faith, then all of the Fathers extracted these Catholic doctrines from those very Scriptures! This creates an insurmountable contradiction for the Protestant apologist.

I hesitated to write this chapter because so much more information could be provided. For every single statement from the Fathers about Tradition or the sacraments, many more could be provided. But the reader will get the point: the Fathers were Catholics who believed in both Scripture and Tradition as interpreted by the Church. I pray that this section provides the reader a catalyst for further study of the Fathers and the history of the Catholic Church. I am also confident that the following material will convince any honest Protestant seeking the truth to re-examine his faith. As John Cardinal Henry Newman said, "to be deep in history is to cease to be Protestant."

Ambrose

Scripture: "For how can we adopt those things which we do not find in the holy Scriptures?" *Duties of the Clergy, I, 23:102 (A.D. 391).*

Tradition: "But if they will not believe the doctrines of the priests, let them believe Christ's oracles, let them believe the admonitions of angels who say, 'For with God nothing is impossible.' Let them believe the apostles' creed which the Roman church has always kept undefiled." *To Sircius, Epistle 42:5 (A.D. 391).*

The Church: "Ambrose...declares union with the Roman See to be union with the Catholic Church. Speaking of his brother Satyrus, who had arrived, after shipwreck, in a place of doubtful orthodoxy, he says: "He called the Bishop to him, and not accounting any grace true which was not of the true faith, he inquired of him whether he agreed with the Catholic Bishops, that is, with the Roman Church." *De Excessa Frat. n. 46 (A.D. 385).*

Apostolic Succession: "For they [Novatians] have not the succession of Peter, who hold not the chair of Peter, which they rend by wicked schism; and this, too, they do, wickedly denying that sins can be forgiven even in the Church, whereas it was said to Peter: 'I will give you the keys of the kingdom of heaven, and whatsoever you shall bind on earth shall be bound also in heaven, and whatsoever you shall loose on earth shall be loosed also in heaven.'"*Concerning Repentance, 7:33 (A.D. 384).*

Baptism: "And that the writer was speaking of baptism is evident from the very words in which it is stated that it is impossible to renew unto repentance those who were fallen, inasmuch as we are renewed by means of the laver of baptism, whereby we are born again, as Paul says himself: 'For we are buried with Him through baptism into death, that, like as Christ rose from the dead through the glory of the Father, so we, too, should walk in newness of life.'" *Concerning Repentance, 2:8 (A.D. 390).*

Confession: "Consider, too, the point that he who has received the Holy Ghost has also received the power of forgiving and of retaining sin. For thus it is written: 'Receive the Holy Spirit: whosoever sins ye forgive, they are forgiven unto them, and whosoever sins ye retain, they are retained.' So, then, he who has not received power to forgive sins has not received the Holy Spirit. The office of the priest is a gift of the Holy Spirit, and His right it is specially to forgive and to retain sins. How, then, can they claim His gift who distrust His power and His right?" *Concerning Repentance, 1:7-8 (A.D. 388).*

The Eucharist: "You perhaps say: 'My bread is usual.' But the bread is bread before the words of the sacrament. When consecration has been added, from bread it becomes the flesh of Christ. So let us confirm this, how it is possible that what is bread is the body of Christ. By what words, then, is the consecration and by whose expressions? By those of the Lord Jesus. For all the rest that are said in the preceding are said by the priest." *The Sacraments, (c.A.D. 390).*

Confirmation: "And then remember that you received the seal of the Spirit; the spirit of wisdom and understanding, the spirit of counsel and strength, the spirit of knowledge and godliness, and the spirit of holy fear, and preserved what you received. God the

Father sealed you, Christ the Lord strengthened you, and gave the earnest of the Spirit in your heart, as you have learned in the lesson from the Apostle." *On the Mysteries, 7:42 (A.D. 391).*

Anointing of the Sick: "Why, then, do you lay on hands, and believe it to be the effect of the blessing, if perchance some sick person recovers? Why do you assume that any can be cleansed by you from the pollution of the devil? Why do you baptize if sins cannot be remitted by man? If baptism is certainly the remission of all sins, what difference does it make whether priests claim that this power is given to them in penance or at the font? In each the mystery is one." *Penance, 1, 8:36 (A.D. 390).*

The Virgin Mary: "Mary, a Virgin not only undefiled but a Virgin whom grace has made inviolate, free of every stain of sin." *Sermon 22:30 (A.D. 388).*

Purgatory: "Give, Oh Lord, rest to your servant Theodosius, that rest you have prepared for your saints...I love him, therefore will I follow him to the land of the living; I will not leave him till by my prayers and lamentations he shall be admitted unto the holy mount of the Lord, to which his deserts call him." *De obitu Theodosii, (A.D. 395).*

Athanasius

Scripture: "For although the sacred and inspired Scriptures are sufficient to declare the truth...still, as we have not at present in our hands the compositions of our teachers, we must communicate in writing to you what we learned from them." *Against the Heathen, 1:3 (c.A.D. 318).*

Tradition: "...let us look at the very tradition, teaching, and faith of the Catholic Church from the beginning was preached by the apostles and preserved by the Fathers. On this the Church was founded; and if anyone departs from this, he neither is nor any longer ought to be called a Christian." *Ad Serapion 1:28 (A.D. 359-360).*

The Church: "The confession arrived at Nicea was, we say more, sufficient and enough by itself for the subversion of all irreligious heresy and for the security and furtherance of the doctrine of the Church." *Ad Afros Epistola Synodica, 1 (A.D. 372).*

Apostolic Succession: "…these from the Presbyters and Deacons of the Mareotis, a home of the Catholic Church which is under the most Reverend Bishop Athanasius, we address this testimony by those whose names are underwritten:--Whereas Theognius, Maris, Macedonius, Theodorus, Ursacius, and Valens, as if sent by all the Bishops who assembled at Tyre, came into our Diocese alleging that they had received orders to investigate certain ecclesiastical affairs, among which they spoke of the breaking of a cup of the Lord, of which information was given them by Ischyras, whom they brought with them, and who says that he is a Presbyter, although he is not, for he was ordained by the Presbyter Colluthus who pretended to the Episcopate… For neither is he a Presbyter of the Catholic Church nor does he possess a church, nor has a cup ever been broken, but the whole story is false and an invention." *Discourse Against the Arians, 76 (A.D. 347).*

Baptism: "And with reason; for as we are all from earth and die in Adam, so being regenerated from above of water and Spirit, in the Christ we are all quickened." *Discourse Against the Arians, III:33 (A.D. 347).*

The Eucharist: "You shall see the Levites bringing loaves and a cup of wine, and placing them on the table. So long as the prayers of supplication and entreaties have not been made, there is only bread and wine. But after the great and wonderful prayers have been completed, then the bread is become the Body, and the wine the Blood, of our Lord Jesus Christ." *Fragment of Sermon to the Newly Baptized, 26 (ante A.D. 373).*

The Virgin Mary: "O noble Virgin, truly you are greater than any other greatness. For who is your equal in greatness, O dwelling place of God the Word? To whom among all creatures shall I compare you, O Virgin? You are greater than them all O Covenant, clothed with purity instead of gold! You are the Ark in which is found the golden vessel containing the true manna, that is, the flesh in which divinity resides." *Homily of the Papyrus of Turin, 71:216 (ante AD 373).*

Augustine

Scripture: "If you produce from the divine scriptures something that we all share, we shall have to listen. But those words which are not found in the scriptures are under no circumstances accepted by us, especially since the Lord warns us, saying, 'In vain they worship me, teaching human commandments and precepts'" (Mt 5:19). *Debate with Maximus, 1 (c.A.D. 428).*

Tradition: "As to those other things which we hold on the authority, not of Scripture, but of tradition, and which are observed throughout the whole world, it may be understood that they are held as approved and instituted either by the apostles themselves, or by plenary Councils, whose authority in the Church is most useful…" *To Januarius, Epistle 5:41 (inter A.D. 400-416).*

The Church: "It is obvious; the faith allows it; the Catholic Church approves; it is true." *Sermons 117:6 (inter A.D. 391-430).*

Apostolic Succession: "I am held in the communion of the Catholic Church by...the succession of priests from the very Chair of the Apostle Peter, to whom the Lord, after his resurrection, committed his sheep to be fed, even to the present Episcopate." *Against the Epistle of Manichaeus, 4:5,5:6 (A.D 397).*

Baptism: "It is this one Spirit who makes it possible for an infant to be regenerated through the agency of another's will when that infant is brought to Baptism; and it is through this one Spirit that the infant so presented is reborn...'Unless a man be born again of water and the Holy Spirit.' The water, therefore, manifesting exteriorly the sacrament of grace, and the Spirit effecting interiorly the benefit of grace, both regenerate in one Christ that man who was in one Adam." *To Boniface, Epistle 98:2 (A.D. 408).*

Confession: "All mortal sins are to be submitted to the keys of the Church and all can be forgiven; but recourse to these keys is the only, the necessary, and the certain way to forgiveness. Unless those who are guilty of grievous sin have recourse to the power of the keys, they cannot hope for eternal salvation. Open your lips, them, and confess your sins to the priest. Confession alone is the true gate to Heaven." *Christian Combat (A.D. 397).*

The Eucharist: "For He received earth from earth; because flesh is from the earth, and He took flesh from the flesh of Mary. He walked here in the same flesh, and gave us the same flesh to be eaten unto salvation. But no one eats that flesh unless first he adores it; and thus it is discovered how such a footstool of the Lord's feet is adored; and not only do we not sin by adoring, we do sin by not adoring." *On the Psalms, 98, 9 (ante A.D. 397)*.

Confirmation: "Why, therefore, is the Head itself, whence that ointment of unity descended, that is, the spiritual fragrance of brotherly love,--why, I say, is the Head itself exposed to your resistance, while it testifies and declares that 'repentance and remission of sins should be preached in His name among all nations, beginning at Jerusalem?' And by this ointment you wish the sacrament of chrism to be understood, which is indeed holy as among the class of visible signs, like baptism itself..." *Letters of Petilian the Donatist, 2,104:239 (A.D. 403)*.

The Virgin Mary: "We must except the holy Virgin Mary, concerning whom I wish to raise no question when it touches the subject of sins, out of honor to the Lord; for from Him we know what abundance of grace for overcoming sin in every particular was conferred upon her who had the merit to conceive and bear Him who undoubtedly had no sin." *Nature and Grace, 36:42 (A.D. 415)*.

The Saints: "It is true that Christians pay religious honor to the memory of the martyrs, both to excite us to imitate them and to obtain a share in their merits, and the assistance of their prayers. But we build altars not to any martyr, but to the God of martyrs, although it is to the memory of the martyrs. No one officiating at the altar in the saints' burying-place ever says, We bring an offering to thee, O Peter! or O Paul! or O Cyprian! The offering is made to God, who gave the crown of martyrdom, while it is in memory of those thus crowned…We regard the martyrs with the same affectionate intimacy that we feel towards holy men of God in this life, when we know that their hearts are prepared to endure the same suffering for the truth of the gospel. There is more devotion in our feeling towards the martyrs, because we know that their conflict is over; and we can speak with greater confidence in praise of those already victors in heaven, than of those still combating here." *Against Faustus, 20:21 (A.D. 400).*

Purgatory: "But temporary punishments are suffered by some in this life only, by others after death, by others both now and then; but all of them before that last and strictest judgment. But of those who suffer temporary punishments after death, all are not doomed to those everlasting pains which are to follow that judgment; for to some, as we have already said, what is not remitted in this world is remitted in the next, that is, they are not punished with the eternal punishment of the world to come." *City of God, 21:13 (A.D. 426).*

Basil

Scripture: "Therefore, let God-breathed Scripture decide between us; and on whichever side be found doctrines in harmony with the Word of God, in favor of that side will be cast the vote of truth." *Epistle ad Eustathius (c.A.D. 373).*

Tradition: "Of the beliefs and practices whether generally accepted or enjoined which are preserved in the Church, some we possess derived from written teaching; others we have delivered to us in a mystery by the apostles by the tradition of the apostles; and both of these in relation to true religion have the same force." *On the Holy Spirit, 27:66 (A.D. 375).*

The Church: "To refuse to follow the Fathers [at the Catholic council of Nicea], not holding their declaration of more authority than one's own opinion, is conduct worthy of blame, as being brimful of self-sufficiency." *Epistle to the Canonicae, 52:1 (A.D. 370).*

Apostolic Succession:: "The first separatists had received their ordination from the Fathers, and possessed the spiritual gift by the laying on of their hands. But they who were broken off had become laymen, and, because they are no longer able to confer on others that grace of the Holy Spirit from which they themselves are fallen away, they had no authority either to baptize or to ordain. And therefore those who were from time to time baptized by them, were ordered, as though baptized by laymen, to come to the church to be purified by the Church's true baptism." *To Amphilochius, Epistle 188:1 (A.D. 347).*

Baptism: "And in what way are we saved? Plainly because we were regenerate through the grace given in our baptism." *On the Holy Spirit, 10:26 (A.D. 375).*

Confession: "It is necessary to confess our sins to those whom the dispensation of God's mysteries is entrusted." *Rule Briefly Treated, 288 (A.D. 374).*

The Eucharist: "To communicate each day and to partake of the holy Body and Blood of Christ is good and beneficial; for He says quite plainly: 'He that eats My Flesh and drinks My Blood has eternal life.' Who can doubt that to share continually in life is the same thing as having life abundantly? We ourselves communicate four times each week, on Sunday, Wednesday, Friday and Saturday; and on other days if there is a commemoration of any saint." *Letter to a Patrician Lady, 93 (c.A.D. 375).*

The Virgin Mary: "The friends of Christ do not tolerate hearing that the Mother of God ever ceased to be a virgin." *Homily In Sanctum Christi generationem, 5 (ante A.D. 379).*

The Saints: "These relics do you receive with a joy equivalent to the distress with which their custodians have parted with them and sent them to you. Let none dispute; let none doubt. Here you have that unconquered athlete. These bones, which shared in the conflict with the blessed soul, are known to the Lord. These bones He will crown, together with that soul, in the righteous day of His requital, as it is written, 'we must stand before the judgment seat of Christ, that each may give an account of the deeds he has done in the body.'" *To Ambrose bishop of Milan, Epistle 197 (A.D. 375).*

Purgatory: "I think that the noble athletes of God, who have wrestled all their lives with the invisible enemies, after they have escaped all of their persecutions and have come to the end of life, are examined by the prince of this world; and if they are found to have any wounds from their wrestling, any stains or effects of sin, they are detained. If, however they are found unwounded and without stain, they are, as unconquered, brought by Christ into their rest." *Homilies on the Psalms, 7:2 (ante A.D. 370).*

Clement of Alexandria

Scripture: "But those who are ready to toil in the most excellent pursuits, will not desist from the search after truth, till they get the demonstration from the Scriptures themselves." *Stromata 7:16 (post A.D. 202).*

Tradition: "Well, they preserving the tradition of the blessed doctrine derived directly from the holy apostles, Peter, James, and Paul, the sons receiving it from the father (but few were like the fathers), came by God's will to us also to deposit those ancestral and apostolic seeds. And well I know that they will exult; I do not mean delighted with this tribute, but solely on account of the preservation of the truth, according as they delivered it." *Stromata, 1:1 (post A.D. 202).*

The Church: "There being demonstration, then, it is necessary to condescend to questions, and to ascertain by way of demonstration by the Scriptures themselves how heresies failed, and how in the truth alone and in the ancient Church is both the exactest knowledge, and the truly best set of principles." *Stromata 7:15 (post A.D. 202).*

Apostolic Succession: "And that you may still be more confident, that repenting thus truly there remains for you a sure hope of salvation, listen to a tale? Which is not a tale but a narrative, handed down and committed to the custody of memory, about the Apostle John. For when, on the tyrant's death, he returned to Ephesus from the isle of Patmos, he went away, being invited, to the contiguous territories of the nations, here to appoint bishops, there to set in order whole Churches, there to ordain such as were marked out by the Spirit." *Who is the rich man that shall be saved?, 42 (A.D. 210).*

The Eucharist: "For the blood of the grape--that is, the Word--desired to be mixed with water, as His blood is mingled with salvation. And the blood of the Lord is twofold. For there is the blood of His flesh, by which we are redeemed from corruption; and the spiritual, that by which we are anointed. And to drink the blood of Jesus, is to become partaker of the Lord's immortality; the Spirit being the energetic principle of the Word, as blood is of flesh. Accordingly, as wine is blended with water, so is the Spirit with man. And the one, the mixture of wine and water, nourishes to faith; while the other, the Spirit, conducts to immortality. And the mixture of both--of the water and of the Word--is called Eucharist, renowned and glorious grace; and they who by faith partake of it are sanctified both in body and soul." *The Instructor, 2 (ante A.D. 202).*

The Virgin Mary: "But the Lord Christ, the fruit of the Virgin, did not pronounce the breasts of women blessed, nor selected them to give nourishment; but when the kind and loving Father had rained down the Word, Himself became spiritual nourishment to the good. O mystic marvel! The universal Father is one, and one the universal Word; and the Holy Spirit is one and the same everywhere, and one is the only virgin mother. I love to call her the Church. This mother, when alone, had not milk, because alone she was not a woman. But she is once virgin and mother--pure as a virgin, loving as a mother. And calling her children to her, she nurses them with holy milk, viz., with the Word for childhood. Therefore she had not milk; for the milk was this child fair and comely, the body of Christ, which nourishes by the Word the young brood, which the Lord Himself brought forth in throes of the flesh, which the Lord Himself swathed in His precious blood." *The Instructor, I:6 (A.D.202).*

Purgatory: "Accordingly the believer, through great discipline, divesting himself of the passions, passes to the mansion which is better than the former one, viz., to the greatest torment, taking with him the characteristic of repentance from the sins he has committed after baptism. He is tortured then still more--not yet or not quite attaining what he sees others to have acquired. Besides, he is also ashamed of his transgressions. The greatest torments, indeed, are assigned to the believer. For God's righteousness is good, and His goodness is righteous. And though the punishments cease in the course of the completion of the expiation and purification of each one, yet those have very great and permanent grief who are found worthy of the other fold, on account of not being along with those that have been glorified through righteousness." *Stromata, 6:14 (post A.D. 202).*

Clement of Rome

Scripture: "And thus preaching through countries and cities, they appointed the first fruits [of their labors], having first proved them by the Spirit, to be bishops and deacons of those who should afterwards believe. Nor was this any new thing, since indeed many ages before it was written concerning bishops and deacons. For thus saith the Scripture in a certain place, 'I will appoint their bishops in righteousness, and their deacons in faith.'" *1ˢᵗ Epistle to the Corinthians, 42 (c.A.D. 96).*

Tradition: "We are writing this in vein, dear friends, not only to admonish you but also to remind ourselves. For we are in the same arena and involved in the same struggle. Hence we should give up empty and futile concerns and turn to the glorious and holy rule of our tradition." *1ˢᵗ Epistle to the Corinthians, 7:2 (c.A.D. 96).*

The Church: "The church of God which sojourns at Rome to the church of God which sojourns at Corinth ... But if any disobey the words spoken by him through us, let them know that they will involve themselves in transgression and in no small danger." *1st Epistle to the Corinthians, 1,59:1 (c. A.D. 96).*

Apostolic succession: "Our apostles also knew, through our Lord Jesus Christ, and there would be strife on account of the office of the episcopate. For this reason, therefore, inasmuch as they had obtained a perfect fore-knowledge of this, they appointed those [ministers] already mentioned, and afterwards gave instructions, that when these should fall asleep, other approved men should succeed them in their ministry...For our sin will not be small, if we eject from the episcopate those who have blamelessly and holily fulfilled its duties." *1st Epistle to Corinthians, 42, 44 (A.D. 98).*

Cyprian

Scripture: "Reading and observing this, we certainly think that no one is to be restrained from the fruit of satisfaction, and the hope of peace, since we know, according to the faith of the divine Scriptures, God Himself being their author, and exhorting in them, both that sinners are brought back to repentance, and that pardon and mercy are not denied to penitents." *To Antonianus, Epistle 51[55]:27 (A.D. 252).*

Tradition: "And this it behooves the priests of God to do now, if they would keep the divine precepts, that if in any respect the truth have wavered and vacillated, we should return to our original and Lord, and to the evangelical and apostolical tradition; and thence may arise the ground of our action, whence has taken rise both our order and our origin." *Epistle to Pompey, 73 (74:9-10) (A.D. 256).*

The Church: "For we, who furnish every person who sails hence with a plan that they may sail without any offense, know that we have exhorted them to acknowledge and hold the root and matrix of the Catholic Church." *Epistle to Pope Cornelius, 44 (48):3 (A.D. 251).*

Apostolic Succession: "Our Lord, whose precepts and admonitions we ought to observe, describing the honor of a bishop and the order of His Church, speaks in the Gospel, and says to Peter: 'I say to you, That you are Peter, and upon this rock will I build my Church; and the gates of hell shall not prevail against it. And I will give you the keys of the kingdom of heaven: and whatsoever you shall bind on earth shall be bound in heaven: and whatsoever you shall loose on earth shall be loosed in heaven.' Thence, through the changes of times and successions, the ordering of bishops and the plan of the Church flow onwards; so that the Church is founded upon the bishops, and every act of the Church is controlled by these same rulers." *To the Lapsed, 1 (A.D. 250).*

Baptism: "But in respect of the case of the infants, which you say ought not to be baptized within the second or third day after their birth, and that the law of ancient circumcision should be regarded, so that you think one who is just born should not be baptized and sanctified within the eighth day...And therefore, dearest brother, this was our opinion in council, that by us no one ought to be hindered from baptism...we think is to be even more observed in respect of infants and newly-born persons..." *To Fidus, Epistle 58(64):2, 6 (A.D. 251).*

Confession: "Moreover, how much are they both greater in faith and better in their fear, who, although bound by no crime of sacrifice to idols or of certificate, yet, since they have even thought of such things, with grief and simplicity confess this very thing to God's priests, and make the conscientious avowal, put off from them the load of their minds, and seek out the salutary medicine even for slight and moderate wounds, knowing that it is written, 'God is not mocked.' God cannot be mocked, nor deceived, nor deluded by any deceptive cunning. Yea, he sins the more, who, thinking that God is like man, believes that he evades the penalty of his crime if he has not openly admitted his crime...I entreat you, beloved brethren, that each one should confess his own sin, while he who has sinned is still in this world, while his confession may be received, while the satisfaction and remission made by the priests are pleasing to the Lord?" *To the Lapsed, 28-29 (A.D. 251).*

The Eucharist: "And we ask that this bread should be given to us daily, that we who are in Christ, and daily receive the Eucharist for the food of salvation, may not, by the interposition of some heinous sin, by being prevented...from partaking of the heavenly bread, be separated from Christ's body as He Himself predicts, and warns, 'I am the bread of life which came down from heaven. If any man eat of my bread, he shall live for ever; and the bread which I will give is my flesh, for the life of the world.'" *The Treatises of Cyprian, 1, 8;(ante A.D. 250).*

Confirmation: "It is also necessary that he should be anointed who is baptized; so that, having received the chrism, that is, the anointing, he may be anointed of God, and have in him the grace of Christ. Further, it is the Eucharist whence the baptized are anointed with the oil sanctified on the altar. But he cannot sanctify the creature of oil, who has neither an altar nor a church; whence also there can be no spiritual anointing among heretics, since it is manifest that the oil cannot be sanctified nor the Eucharist celebrated at all among them. But we ought to know and remember that it is written, 'Let not the oil of a sinner anoint my head,' which the Holy Spirit before forewarned in the Psalms, lest any one going out of the way and wandering from the path of truth should be anointed by heretics and adversaries of Christ." *To Januarius, Epistle 70/69:2 (A.D. 255).*

The Saints: "We always offer sacrifices for them [deceased Celerinus, Celerina, Laurentius and Egnatius], as you remember, as often as we celebrate the passions and days of the martyrs in the annual commemoration. Nor could he, therefore, be degenerate and inferior whom this family dignity and a generous nobility provoked, by domestic examples of virtue and faith. But if in a worldly family it is a matter of heraldry and of praise to be a patrician, of bow much greater praise and honor is it to become of noble rank in the celestial heraldry! I cannot tell whom I should call more blessed,--whether those ancestors, for a posterity so illustrious, or him, for an origin so glorious. So equally between them does the divine condescension flow, and pass to and fro, that, just as the dignity of their offspring brightens their crown, so the sublimity of his ancestry illuminates his glory." *To Clergy and People, Epistle 33(39):3 (A.D. 250).*

Purgatory: "For to adulterers even a time of repentance is granted by us, and peace is given. Yet virginity is not therefore deficient in the Church, nor does the glorious design of continence languish through the sins of others. The Church, crowned with so many virgins, flourishes; and chastity and modesty preserve the tenor of their glory. Nor is the vigor of continence broken down because repentance and pardon are facilitated to the adulterer. It is one thing to stand for pardon, another thing to attain to glory: it is one thing, when cast into prison, not to go out thence until one has paid the uttermost farthing; another thing at once to receive the wages of faith and courage. It is one thing, tortured by long suffering for sins, to be cleansed and long purged by fire; another to have purged all sins by suffering. It is one thing, in fine, to be in suspense till the sentence of God at the day of judgment; another to be at once crowned by the Lord." *To Antonianus, Epistle 51 (55):20 (A.D. 253).*

Cyril of Alexandria

Scripture: "Not all that the Lord did was written down, but only what was deemed sufficient, either from the point of view of morals, or from the point of view of dogmas…" *In Joan. XII (ante A.D. 429).*

Tradition: "[W]e give thanks to God, the Savior of the world, rejoicing with one another that our Churches, both ours and yours, hold a faith in accordance with the divinely inspired Scriptures and with the tradition of our holy fathers." *Epistle to John of Antioch, 39 (A.D. 433)*.

The Church: "He suffers him no longer to be called Simon, exercising authority and rule over him already as having become His own. But by a title suitable to the thing, He changed his name into Peter, from the word *petra* (rock); for on him He was afterwards to found His Church." *In Joan. XII (ante A.D. 429)*.

Baptism: "Do you believe this?...When a newborn child is brought forward to receive the anointing of initiation, or rather of consummation through holy baptism." *Commentary on John, 7 (A.D. 428)*.

The Eucharist: "Christ said indicating (the bread and wine): 'This is My Body,' and 'This is My Blood,' in order that you might not judge what you see to be a mere figure. The offerings, by the hidden power of God Almighty, are changed into Christ's Body and Blood, and by receiving these we come to share in the life-giving and sanctifying efficacy of Christ." *Commentary on Matthew, 26, 27 (ante A.D. 425)*.

Confirmation: "The living water of holy Baptism is given to us as if in rain, and the Bread of Life as if in wheat, and the Blood as if in wine. In addition to this there is also the use of oil, reckoned as perfecting those who have been justified in Christ through holy baptism." *Commentary on the Minor Prophets, 32 (A.D. 429)*.

Anointing of the Sick: "[I]f some part of your body is suffering...recall also the saying in the divinely inspired Scripture: 'Is anyone among you ill? Let him call the presbyters of the Church and let them pray over him, anointing him with oil in the name of the Lord. And the prayer of faith will save the sick man, and the Lord will raise him up, and if he be in sins they shall be forgiven (James 5:14-15).'" *Worship and Adoration, 6 (A.D. 412).*

The Virgin Mary: "Hail to thee Mary, Mother of God, to whom in towns and villages and in island were founded churches of true believers." *Homily 11 (ante A.D. 444).*

The Saints: "Even if we make images of pious men it is not that we may adore them as gods but that when we see them we might be prompted to imitate them." *On Psalms 113 (115) (ante A.D. 444).*

Cyril of Jerusalem

Scripture: "In regard to the divine and holy mysteries of faith, not the least part may be handed on without the Holy Scriptures. Do not be led astray by winning words and clever arguments. Even to me, who tell you these things, do not give ready belief, unless you receive them from the Holy Scriptures the proof of the things which I announce. The salvation which we believe is not proved from clever reasoning, but from the Holy Scriptures." *Catechetical Lectures*, 4:17 (A.D. 350).

Tradition: "Hold fast these traditions undefiled and, keep yourselves free from offense. Sever not yourselves from the Communion; deprive not yourselves, through the pollution of sins, of these Holy and Spiritual Mysteries [the Eucharist]." *Catechetical Lectures, Mystagogical Catechesis 2:8 (A.D. 350).*

The Church: "[T]he Catholic Church. For this is the peculiar name of this Holy Church, the mother of us all, which is the spouse of our Lord Jesus Christ, the Only-begotten Son of God (for it is written, As Christ also loved the Church and gave Himself for it, and all the rest), and is a figure and copy of Jerusalem which is above, which is free, and the mother of us all; which before was barren, but now has many children." *Catechetical Lectures, 18:26 (A.D. 350).*

Baptism: "After these things, you were led to the holy pool of Divine Baptism, as Christ was carried from the Cross to the Sepulchre which is before our eyes And each of you was asked, whether he believed in the name of the Father, and of the Son, and of the Holy Ghost, and you made that saving confession, and descended three times into the water, and ascended again; here also hinting by a symbol at the three days burial of Christ...And at the self-same moment you were both dying and being born; and that Water of salvation was at once your grave and your mother. And what Solomon spoke of others will suit you also; for he said, in that case, There is a time to bear and a time to die; but to you, in the reverse order, there was a time to die and a time to be born; and one and the same time effected both of these, and your birth went hand in hand with your death." *Catechetical Lectures, 20:4 (A.D. 350).*

The Eucharist: "We have been instructed in these matters and filled with an unshakable faith, that that which seems to be bread, is not bread, though it tastes like it, but the Body of Christ, and that which seems to be wine, is not wine, though it too tastes as such, but the Blood of Christ...draw inner strength by receiving this bread as spiritual food and your soul will rejoice." *Catechetical Lectures, On the Mysteries, 22, 9 (A.D. 350).*

Confirmation: "But beware of supposing this to be plainointment. For as the Bread of the Eucharist, after the invocation of the Holy Ghost, is mere bread no longer, but the Body of Christ, so also this holy ointment is no more simple ointment, nor so to say common, after invocation, but it is Christ's gift of grace, and, by the advent of the Holy Ghost, is made fit to impart His Divine Nature. Which ointment is symbolically applied to thy forehead and thy other senses; and while thy body is anointed with the visible ointment, thy soul is sanctified by the Holy and life-giving Spirit." *Catechetical Lectures (On Chrism), 21:3 (A.D. 350).*

<u>The Virgin Mary:</u> "Many, my beloved, are the true testimonies concerning Christ. The Father bears witness from heaven of His Son: the Holy Ghost bears witness, descending bodily in likeness of a dove: the Archangel Gabriel bears witness, bringing good tidings to Mary: the Virgin Mother of God [Theotokos] bears witness: the blessed place of the manger bears witness." *Catechetical Lectures, 10:19 (A.D. 350).*

<u>The Saints:</u> "Then we commemorate also those who have fallen asleep before us, first Patriarchs, Prophets, Apostles, Martyrs, that at their prayers and intercessions God would receive our petition." *Catechetical Lectures, 23:9,10 (c. A.D. 350).*

<u>Purgatory:</u> "...all who in past years have fallen asleep among us, believing that it will be a very great benefit to the souls, for whom the supplication is put up, while that holy and most awful sacrifice [of the Eucharist] is set forth...For I know that many say, what is a soul profited, which departs from this world either with sins, or without sins, if it be commemorated in the prayer? For if a king were to banish certain who had given him of-fence, and then those who belong to them should weave a crown and offer it to him on behalf of those under punishment, would he not grant a remission of their penalties? In the same way we, when we offer to Him our supplications for those who have fallen asleep, though they be sinners, weave no crown, but offer up Christ sacrificed for our sins, propitiating our merciful God for them as well as for ourselves." *Catechetical Lectures, 23:9,10 (c. A.D. 350).*

Ephraem

Scripture: "While (the sects) mutually refute and condemn each other, it has happened to truth as to Gideon; that is, while they fight against each other, and fall under wounds mutually inflicted, they crown her. All the heretics acknowledge that there is a true Scripture. Had they all falsely believed that none existed, some one might reply that such Scripture was unknown to them. But now that have themselves taken away the force of such plea, from the fact that they have mutilated the very Scriptures. For they have corrupted the sacred copies; and words which ought to have but one interpretation, they have wrested to strange significations." *Adv. Haers. (ante A.D. 373).*

Tradition: "Be firmly persuaded of this, not as an opinion, but as truth, that whatsoever has been transmitted, whether in writing only or by word of mouth – and by consequence the divine names and appellations – is directed to this end, that we may have life, and may have it more abundantly." *Adv. Scrutat. (ante A.D. 373).*

The Church: "It is the church which perfect truth perfects. The church of believers is great, and its bosom most ample; it embraces the fullness of the two Testaments." *Adv. Haers. (ante A.D. 373).*

Apostolic Succession: "Lo! In these three successions, as in a mystery and a figure ... Under the three pastors,--there were manifold shepherds." *Nisbene Hymns, (A.D. 350).*

Baptism: "The baptized when they come up are sanctified;--the sealed when they go down are pardoned.---They who come up have put on glory;--they who go down have cast off sin." *Hymns for the Feast of the Epiphany, 6:9 (ante A.D. 373).*

Confirmation: "'And your floors shall be filled with wheat, and the presses shall overflow equally with wine and oil...' This has been fulfilled mystically by Christ, who gave to the people whom He had redeemed, that is, to His Church, wheat and wine and oil in a mystic manner...the oil is the sweet unguent with which those who are baptized are signed, being clothed in the armaments of the Holy Spirit." *On Joel 2:24 (ante A.D. 373).*

Anointing of the Sick: "They pray over thee; one blows on thee, another seals thee." *Homily 46 (ante A.D. 373).*

The Virgin Mary: "Thou alone and thy Mother are in all things fair, there is no flaw in thee and no stain in thy Mother." *Nisibene Hymns, 27:8 (A.D. 370).*

Purgatory: "Lay me not with sweet spices: for this honor avails me not; Nor yet incense and perfumes: for the honor benefits me not. Burn sweet spices in the Holy Place: and me, even me, conduct to the grave with prayer. Give ye incense to God: and over me send up hymns. Instead of perfumes of spices: in prayer make remembrance of me." *His Testament (ante A.D. 373).*

Epiphanius

Scripture: "And nothing of discrepancy will be found in Sacred Scripture, nor will there be found any statement in opposition to any other statement." *Panarion, 70:7 (A.D. 377).*

Tradition: "Apostolic traditions, holy scriptures and successions of teachers have been made our boundaries and foundations for the upholding of our faith, and God's truth has been protected in every way.

No one need be deceived by worthless stories."
Panarion, 55 (A.D. 377).

The Church: "The Scripture is in every way true. But there needs wisdom to know God, to believe him and his words, and what he has vouchsafed unto us…For every heresy is a deceiver, not having received the Holy Ghost, according to the tradition of the fathers in the holy Catholic church of God." *The Well-Anchored Man, 63 (A.D. 374).*

Apostolic Succession: "[D]uring the days of that Anicetus, bishop of Rome, who succeeded Pius and his predecessors, For, in Rome, Peter and Paul were the first both apostles and bishops; then came Linus, then Cletus ... However the succession of the bishops in Rome was in the following order. Peter and Paul, and Cletus, Clement..." *Panarion, 27:6 (A.D. 377).*

The Eucharist: "We see that the Savior took [something] in His hands, as it is in the Gospel, when He was reclining at the supper; and He took this, and giving thanks, He said: 'This is really Me.' And He gave to His disciples and said: 'This is really Me.' And we see that It is not equal or similar, not to the incarnate image, not to the invisible divinity, not to the outline of His limbs. For It is round of shape, and devoid of feeling. As to Its power, He means to say even of Its grace, 'This is really Me.'; and none disbelieves His word. For anyone who does not believe the truth in what He says is deprived of grace and of a Savior." *The Well-Anchored Man, 57 (A.D. 374).*

The Virgin Mary: "If the Holy Virgin had died and was buried, her falling asleep would have been surrounded with honor, death would have found her pure, and her crown would have been a virginal one...Had she been martyred according to what is written: 'Thine own soul a sword shall pierce', then she would shine gloriously among the martyrs, and her holy body would have been declared blessed; for by her, did light come to the world." *Panarion, 78:23 (A.D. 377)*.

The Saints: "Furthermore, as to mentioning the names of the dead, how is there anything very useful in that? What is more timely or more excellent than that those who are still here should believe that the departed do live, and that they have not retreated into nothingness, but that they exist and are alive with the Master...Useful too is the prayer fashioned on their behalf...For we make commemoration of the just and of sinners: of sinners, begging God's mercy for them; of the just and the Fathers and Patriarchs and Prophets and Apostles and Evangelists and martyrs and confessors, and of bishops and solitaries, and of the whole list of them..." *Panarion, 75:8 (A.D. 377)*.

Purgatory: "Useful too is the prayer fashioned on their behalf [of the dead], even if it does not force back the whole of guilty charges laid to them. And it is useful also, because in this world we often stumble either voluntarily or involuntarily, and thus it is a reminder to do better." *Panarion, 75:8 (A.D. 377)*.

Gregory of Nazianzus

Scripture: "We however, who extend the accuracy of the Spirit to the merest stroke and tittle, will never admit the impious assertion that even the smallest matters were dealt with haphazard by those who have recorded them." *Oration 2:105 (A.D. 362)*.

Tradition: "May we, to the last breath of life confess with great confidence that excellent deposit of the holy fathers who were nearest to Christ, and the primitive faith; that confession which we imbibed from our infancy; which we first uttered and with which may we depart this life." *Oration 6 (ante A.D. 389).*

The Church: "Seest thou that of the disciples of Christ, all of whom were great and deserving of choice, one is called a Rock and is entrusted with the Foundations of the Church." *Miscellaneous Letters (A.D. 370).*

Apostolic Succession: "He [St. Athanasius] is led up to the throne of St. Mark, to succeed him in piety, no less than in office; in the latter indeed at a great distance from him, in the former, which is the genuine right of succession, following him closely. For unity in doctrine deserves unity in office; and a rival teacher sets up a rival throne; the one is a successor in reality, the other but in name. For it is not the intruder, but he whose rights are intruded upon, who is the successor, not the lawbreaker, but the lawfully appointed, not the man of contrary opinions, but the man of the same faith; if this is not what we mean by successor, he succeeds in the same sense as disease to health, darkness to light, storm to calm, and frenzy to sound sense." *Oration 21:8 (A.D. 380).*

Baptism: "Be it so, some will say, in the case of those who ask for Baptism; what have you to say about those who are still children, and conscious neither of the loss nor of the grace? Are we to baptize them too? Certainly, if any danger presses. For it is better that they should be unconsciously sanctified than that they should depart unsealed and uninitiated." *Oration on Holy Baptism, 40:28 (A.D. 381).*

The Eucharist: "Cease not to pray and plead for me when you draw down the Word by your word, when in an unbloody manner cutting you cut the Body and Blood of the Lord, using your voice for a sword." *Letter to Amphilochius, (ante A.D. 370).*

The Virgin Mary: "If anyone does not believe that Holy Mary is the Mother of God, he is severed from the Godhead." *To Cledonius, 101 (A.D. 382).*

Gregory of Nyssa

Scripture: "Let the inspired Scripture, then, be our umpire, and the vote of truth will surely be given to those whose dogmas are found to agree with the Divine words." *On the Holy Spirit* (c.A.D. 375).

Tradition: "[I]f our reasoning be found unequal to the problem, we must keep for ever, firm and unmoved the tradition which we received by succession from the fathers." *That there are not three Gods (A.D. 375).*

The Church: "I say, that the Church teaches this in plain language; that the Only-begotten is essentially God, very God of the essence of the very God, how ought one who opposes her decisions to overthrow the preconceived opinion?" *Against Eunomius, 4:6 (inter A.D. 380-384).*

Apostolic Succession: "The bread again is at first common bread, but when the sacramental action consecrates it, it is called, and becomes, the Body of Christ. So with the sacramental oil; so with the wine: though before the benediction they are of little value, each of them, after the sanctification bestowed by the Spirit, has its several operations. The same power of the word, again, also makes the priest venerable and honorable, separated, by the new blessing bestowed upon him, from his community with the mass of men. While but yesterday he was one of the mass, one of the people, he is suddenly rendered a guide, a president, a teacher of righteousness, an instructor in hidden mysteries; and this he does without being at all changed in body or in form; but, while continuing to be in all appearance the man he was before, being, by some unseen power and grace, transformed in respect of his unseen soul to the higher condition." *On the Baptism of Christ (ante A.D. 394).*

Baptism: "[T]he birth by water and the Spirit, Himself led the way in this birth, drawing down upon the water, by His own baptism, the Holy Spirit; so that in all things He became the first-born of those who are spiritually born again, and gave the name of brethren to those who partook in a birth like to His own by water and the Spirit." *Against Eunomius, 2:8 (A.D. 382).*

The Eucharist: "He offered Himself for us, Victim and Sacrifice, and Priest as well, and 'Lamb of God who takes away the sin of the world.' When did He do this? When He made His own Body food and His own Blood drink for His disciples; for this much is clear enough to anyone, that a sheep cannot be eaten by a man unless its being eaten be preceded by its being slaughtered. This giving of His own Body to His disciples for eating clearly indicates that the Sacrifice of the Lamb has now been completed." *Orations and Sermons (ante A.D. 383).*

Confirmation: "For the Son is King, and His living, realized, and personified Kingship is found in the Holy Spirit, Who anoints the Only-begotten, and so makes Him the Anointed, and the King of all things that exist. If, then, the Father is King, and the Only-begotten is King, and the Holy Ghost is the Kingship, one and the same definition of Kingship must prevail throughout this Trinity, and the thought of 'unction' conveys the hidden meaning that there is no interval of separation between the Son and the Holy Spirit. For as between the body's surface and the liquid of the oil nothing intervening can be detected, either in reason or in perception, so inseparable is the union of the Spirit with the Son; and the result is that whosoever is to touch the Son by faith must needs first encounter the oil in the very act of touching; there is not a part of Him devoid of the Holy Spirit." *On the Holy Spirit, 16 (ante A.D. 394).*

The Virgin Mary: "It was, to divulge by the manner of His Incarnation this great secret; that purity is the only complete indication of the presence of God and of His coming, and that no one can in reality secure this for himself, unless he has altogether estranged himself from the passions of the flesh. What happened in the stainless Mary when the fullness of the Godhead which was in Christ shone out through her, that happens in every soul that leads by rule the virgin life." *On Virginity, 2 (A.D. 371).*

The Saints: "Only may that power come upon us which strengthens weakness, through the prayers of him [St. Paul] who made his own strength perfect in bodily weakness." *Against Eunomius, 1:1 (A.D. 380).*

Purgatory: "When he has quitted his body and the difference between virtue and vice is known he cannot approach God till the purging fire shall have cleansed the stains with which his soul was infested. That same fire in others will cancel the corruption of matter, and the propensity to evil." *Sermon on the Dead, (ante A.D. 394).*

Hilary of Poitiers

Scripture: "Yet it is certainly by these same words of God [Scripture] that we must come to understand the things of God." *The Trinity, 4:14 (c.A.D. 356).*

Tradition/Apostolic Succession: "…we shall not depart from the faith which we have received, through the prophets, from God the Father, through Christ our Lord, thanks to the teaching of the Holy Spirit, in the

Gospels as well as in the writings of the Apostles; the faith established by the Tradition of the Fathers, following succession of the apostles…" *Ex Oper. Hist. Fragment, 7:3 (inter A.D. 353-368).*

The Church: "The reason why the Lord sat in the ship, and the crowds stood without, is derived from the subject-matter. For he was about to speak in parables; and by this kind of action he signifies that they who are placed without the church, cannot attain to any understanding of the divine word. For the ship exhibits a type of the church, the word of life placed and preached within which, they who are without, and lie near like barren and useless sands, cannot understand." *Commentary on Matthew, 13 (c.A.D. 353-355).*

Baptism: "We are circumcised not with a fleshly circumcision but with the circumcision of Christ, that is, we are born again into a new man; for, being buried with Him in His baptism, we must die to the old man, because the regeneration of baptism has the force of resurrection." *The Trinity, 9:9 (A.D. 359).*

The Eucharist: "When we speak of the reality of Christ's nature being in us, we would be speaking foolishly and impiously – had we not learned it from Him. For He Himself says: 'My Flesh is truly Food, and My Blood is truly Drink. He that eats My Flesh and drinks My Blood will remain in Me and I in him.' As to the reality of His Flesh and Blood, there is no room left for doubt, because now, both by the declaration of the Lord Himself and by our own faith, it is truly the Flesh and it is truly Blood. And These Elements bring it about, when taken and consumed, that we are in Christ and Christ is in us. Is this not true? Let those who deny that Jesus Christ is true God be free to find these things untrue. But He Himself is in us through the flesh and we are in Him, while that which we are with Him is in God." *The Trinity, 8, 14 (A.D. 359).*

The Virgin Mary: "The Virgin, the birth, the Body, then the Cross, the death, the visit to the lower world; these things are our salvation. For the sake of mankind the Son of God was born of the Virgin and of the Holy Ghost. In this process He ministered to Himself; by His own power--the power of God--which overshadowed her He sowed the beginning of His Body, and entered on the first stage of His life in the flesh. He did it that by His Incarnation He might take to Himself from the Virgin the fleshly nature, and that through this commingling there might come into being a hallowed Body of all humanity; that so through that Body which He was pleased to assume all mankind might be hid in Him, and He in return, through His unseen existence, be reproduced in all." *The Trinity 2:24-25 (A.D. 359).*

Hippolytus

Scripture: "There is, brethren, one God, the knowledge of whom we gain from the Holy Scriptures and no other source." *Against the Heresy of One Noetus, 9 (inter A.D. 200-210).*

Tradition: "It is not by drawing on the Holy Scriptures nor by guarding the tradition of some holy person that the heretics have formulated these doctrines." *Refutation of All Heresies 1, Preface (c. A.D. 230).*

The Church: "By this Spirit Peter spoke that blessed word, 'You are the Christ, the Son of the living God.' By this Spirit the rock of the Church was established." *Discourse on the Holy Theophany, 9 (inter A.D. 217-235).*

Baptism: "The Father of immortality sent the immortal Son and Word into the world, who came to man in order to wash him with water and the Spirit; and He, begetting us again to incorruption of soul and body, breathed into us the breath (spirit) of life, and endued us with an incorruptible panoply. If, therefore, man has become immortal, he will also be God. And if he is made God by water and the Holy Spirit after the regeneration of the laver he is found to be also joint-heir with Christ after the resurrection from the dead. Wherefore I preach to this effect: Come, all you kindreds of the nations, to the immortality of the baptism." *Discourse on the Holy Theophany, 8 (inter A.D. 217-235)*

Confession: "Father, who knows the hearts of all, grant upon this your servant whom you have chosen for the episcopate to feed your holy flock and serve as your high priest, that he may minister blamelessly by night and day, that he may unceasingly behold and appropriate your countenance and offer to you the gifts of Thy holy Church. And that by the high priestly Spirit he may have authority to forgive sins..." *Apostolic Tradition, 3 (A.D. 215).*

The Eucharist: "And she [wisdom] has furnished her table…refers to His honored and undefiled body and blood, which day by day are administered and offered sacrificially at the spiritual divine table, as a memorial of that first and ever-memorable table of the spiritual divine supper." *Fragment from Commentary on Proverbs (inter A.D. 215-235).*

Confirmation: "And she said to her maids, 'Bring me oil.' For faith and love prepare oil and unguents to those who are washed. But what were these unguents, but the commandments of the holy Word? And what was the oil, but the power of the Holy Spirit, with which believers are anointed as with ointment after the laver of washing? All these things were figuratively represented in the blessed Susannah, for our sakes, that we who now believe on God might not regard the things that are done now in the Church as strange, but believe them all to have been set forth in figure by the patriarchs of old, as the apostle also says: 'Now these things happened to them for ensamples: and they were written for our instruction, on whom the ends of the world are come.'" *Commentary on Daniel, 6;18 (A.D. 204).*

Anointing of the Sick: "O God who sanctifies this oil as Thou dost grant unto all who are anointed and receive of it the hallowing wherewith Thou didst anoint kings and priests and prophets, so grant that it may give strength to all that taste of it and health to all that use it." *Apostolic Tradition, 5:2 (c. A.D. 215).*

The Virgin Mary: "He was the ark formed of incorruptible wood. For by this is signified that His tabernacle was exempt from putridity and corruption." *Orations Inillud, Dominus pascit me (ante A.D. 235).*

The Saints: "[Appealing to the three companions of Daniel] Think of me, I beseech you, so that I may achieve with you the same fate of martyrdom." *On Daniel, 11:30 (A.D. 204).*

Ignatius of Antioch

Scripture: "If I do not find it in the ancient Scriptures, I will not believe the Gospel; on my saying to them, It is written, they answered me, That remains to be proved. But to me Jesus Christ is in the place of all that is ancient: His cross, and death and resurrection, and the faith which is by Him are undefiled monuments of antiquity..." *Epistle to the Philadelphians 8,2 (c. A.D. 110).*

Tradition/The Church: "Follow the bishop, all of you, as Jesus Christ follows his Father, and the presbyterium as the Apostles. As for the deacons, respect them as the Law of God. Let no one do anything with reference to the Church without the bishop. Only that Eucharist may be regarded as legitimate which is celebrated with the bishop or his delegate presiding. Where the bishop is, there let the community be, just as where Jesus Christ is, there is the Catholic Church." *Epistle to the Smyrnaeans 8 (c. A.D. 110).*

Apostolic Succession: "Since therefore I have, in the persons before mentioned, beheld the whole multitude of you in faith and love, I exhort you to study to do all things with a divine harmony, while your bishop presides in the place of God, and your presbyters in the place of the assembly of the apostles, along with your deacons, who are most dear to me, and are entrusted with the ministry of Jesus Christ, who was with the Father before the beginning of time, and in the end was revealed…Let nothing exist among you that may divide you ; but be united with your bishop, and those that preside over you, as a type and evidence of your immortality." *Epistle to the Magnesians, 6 (c. A.D. 110).*

Confession: "Moreover, it is in accordance with reason that we should return to soberness [of conduct], and, while yet we have opportunity, exercise repentance towards God. It is well to reverence both God and the bishop." *Epistle to the Smyrnaeans, 9 (c. A.D. 110).*

The Eucharist: "They abstain from the Eucharist and from prayer, because they confess not the Eucharist to be the flesh of our Saviour Jesus Christ, which suffered for our sins, and which the Father, of His goodness, raised up again." *Epistle to Smyrnaeans, 7,1 (c. A.D. 110).*

The Virgin Mary: "There is one Physician who is possessed both of flesh and spirit; both made and not made; God existing in flesh; true life in death; both of Mary and of God; first possible and then impossible, even Jesus Christ our Lord." *To the Ephesians, 7 (c. A.D. 110).*

Irenaeus

Scripture: "[B]eing most properly assured that the Scriptures are indeed perfect, since they were spoken by the Word of God and His Spirit…" *Against Heresies, 2, 28:2 (inter A.D. 180-199).*

Tradition: "But, again, when we refer them to that tradition which originates from the apostles, which is preserved by means of the succession of presbyters in the Churches, they object to tradition, saying that they themselves are wiser not merely than the presbyters, but even than the apostles, because they have discovered the unadulterated truth…It comes to this, therefore, that these men do now consent neither to Scripture nor to tradition." *Against Heresies, 5, 20:1(inter A.D. 180-199).*

The Church: "…by indicating that tradition derived from the apostles, of the very great, the very ancient, and universally known Church founded and organized at Rome by the two most glorious apostles Peter and Paul; as also the faith preached to men…For it is a matter of necessity that every Church should agree with this Church, on account of its preeminent authority, that is, the faithful everywhere, inasmuch as the apostolic tradition has been preserved continuously by those who exist everywhere." *Against Heresies, 3, 3:2 (inter A.D. 180-199).*

Apostolic Succession: "True knowledge is [that which consists in] the doctrine of the apostles, and the ancient constitution of the Church throughout all the world, and the distinctive manifestation of the body of

Christ according to the successions of the bishops, by which they have handed down that Church which exists in every place, and has come even unto us, being guarded and preserved without any forging of Scriptures, by a very complete system of doctrine, and neither receiving addition nor [suffering] curtailment [in the truths which she believes]." *Against Heresies, 4:33:8 (A.D. 180-199).*

Baptism: "'And dipped himself,' says [the Scripture], 'seven times in Jordan.' It was not for nothing that Naaman of old, when suffering from leprosy, was purified upon his being baptized, but it served as an indication to us. For as we are lepers in sin, we are made clean, by means of the sacred water and the invocation of the Lord, from our old transgressions; being spiritually regenerated as new-born babes, even as the Lord has declared: 'Except a man be born again through water and the Spirit, he shall not enter into the kingdom of heaven.'" *Fragment, 34 (A.D. 190).*

The Eucharist: "So then, if the mixed cup and the manufactured bread receive the Word of God and become the Eucharist, that is to say, the Blood and Body of Christ, which fortify and build up the substance of our flesh, how can these people claim that the flesh is incapable of receiving God's gift of eternal life, when it is nourished by Christ's Blood and Body and is His member?" *Against Heresies, 5, 2, 2-3 (inter A.D. 180-199).*

The Virgin Mary: "For as Eve was seduced by the word of an angel to flee from God, having rebelled against His Word, so Mary by the word of an angel received the glad tidings that she would bear God by obeying his Word. The former was seduced to disobey God, but the latter was persuaded to obey God, so that the Virgin Mary might become the advocate of the virgin Eve. As the human race was subjected to death through [the act of] a virgin, so it was saved by a virgin." *Against Heresies, V:19,1 (inter A.D. 180-199).*

Jerome

Scripture: "Ignorance of the Scriptures is ignorance of Christ." *Commentary on Isaiah (inter A.D. 408-410).*

Tradition: "And let them not flatter you themselves if they think they have Scripture authority for their assertions, since the devil himself has quoted Scripture texts, and the essence of the Scriptures is not the letter, but the meaning. Otherwise, if we follow the letter, we too can concoct a new dogma and assert that such persons as wear shoes and have two coats must not be received into the Church." *Dialogue against the Luciferians, 28 (A.D. 379/382).*

The Church: "My resolution is, to read the ancients, to try everything, to hold fast what is good, and not to recede from the faith of the Catholic Church." *To Minervius and Alexander, Epistle 119 (A.D. 406).*

Apostolic Succession: "And to Timothy he says: 'Neglect not the gift that is in thee, which was given thee by prophecy, with the laying on of the hands of the presbytery...' For even at Alexandria from the time of Mark the Evangelist until the episcopates of Heraclas and Dionysius the presbyters always named as bishop one of their own number chosen by themselves and set in a more exalted position, just as an army elects a general, or as deacons appoint one of themselves whom they know to be diligent and call him archdeacon. For what function excepting ordination, belongs to a bishop that does not also belong to a presbyter?...Wherever there is a bishop, whether it be at Rome or at Engubium, whether it be at Constantinople or at Rhegium, whether it be at

Alexandria or at Zoan, his dignity is one and his priesthood is one. Neither the command of wealth nor the lowliness of poverty makes him more a bishop or less a bishop. All alike are successors of the apostles." *To Evangelus, Epistle 146:1 (ante A.D. 420).*

Baptism: "While the son is a child and thinks as a child and until he comes to years of discretion to choose between the two roads to which the letter of Pythagoras points, his parents are responsible for his actions whether these be good or bad. But perhaps you imagine that, if they are not baptized, the children of Christians are liable for their own sins; and that no guilt attaches to parents who withhold from baptism those who by reason of their tender age can offer no objection to it. The truth is that, as baptism ensures the salvation of the child, this in turn brings advantage to the parents. Whether you would offer your child or not lay within your choice, but now that you have offered her, you neglect her at your peril." *To Laeta, Epistle 107:6 (A.D. 403).*

Confession: "Just as in the Old Testament the priest makes the leper clean or unclean, so in the New Testament the bishop and presbyter binds or looses not those who are innocent or guilty, but by reason of their office, when they have heard various kinds of sins, they know who is to be bound and who loosed." *Commentary on Matthew, 3:16,19 (A.D. 398).*

The Eucharist: "After the type had been fulfilled by the Passover celebration and He had eaten the flesh of the lamb with His Apostles, He takes bread which strengthens the heart of man, and goes on to the true Sacrament of the Passover, so that just as Melchizedek, the priest of the Most High God, in prefiguring Him, made bread and wine an offering, He too makes Himself manifest in the reality of His own Body and Blood." *Commentary on Matthew, 4:26, 26 (A.D. 398).*

Confirmation: "Don't you know that the laying on of hands after baptism and then the invocation of the Holy Spirit is a custom of the Churches? Do you demand Scripture proof? You may find it in the Acts of the Apostles. And even if it did not rest on the authority of Scripture the consensus of the whole world in this respect would have the force of a command. For many other observances of the Churches, which are due to tradition, have acquired the authority of the written law, as for instance the practice of dipping the head three times in the laver, and then, after leaving the water, of tasting mingled milk and honey in representation of infancy; and, again, the practices of standing up in worship on the Lord's day, and ceasing from fasting every Pentecost; and there are many other unwritten practices which have won their place through reason and custom. So you see we follow the practice of the Church, although it may be clear that a person was baptized before the Spirit was invoked." _Against the Luciferians, 8 (A.D. 379)._

The Virgin Mary: "'There shall come forth a rod out of the stem of Jesse, and a flower shall grow out of his roots.' The rod is the mother of the Lord--simple, pure, unsullied; drawing no germ of life from without but fruitful in singleness like God Himself...Set before you the blessed Mary, whose surpassing purity made her meet to be the mother of the Lord." _To Eustochium, Epistle 22:19,38 (A.D. 384)._

The Saints: "If Apostles and martyrs while still in the body can pray for others, when they ought still to be anxious for themselves, how much more must they do so when once they have won their crowns, overcome, and triumphed? A single man, Moses, often wins pardon from God for six hundred thousand armed men; and Stephen, the follower of his Lord and the first Christian martyr, entreats pardon for his persecutors; and when once they have entered on their life with Christ, shall they have less power than before? The Apostle Paul says that two hundred and seventy-six souls were given to him in the ship; and when, after his dissolution, he has begun to be with Christ, must he shut his mouth, and be unable to say a word for those who throughout the whole world have believed in his Gospel? Shall Vigilantius the live dog be better than Paul the dead lion?" *Against Vigilantius, 6 (A.D. 406).*

Purgatory: "Other husbands scatter on the graves of their wives violets, roses, lilies, and purple flowers; and assuage the grief of their hearts by fulfilling this tender duty. Our dear Pammachius also waters the holy ashes and the revered bones of Paulina, but it is with the balm of almsgiving." *To Pammachius, Epistle 66:5 (A.D. 397).*

John Cassian

Scripture: "If you were an assertor of the Arian or Sabellian heresy, and did not use your own creed, I would still confute you by the authority of the holy Scriptures; I would confute you by the words of the law itself." *Incarnation of the Lord, 6:5 (c.A.D. 429/430).*

Tradition: "I would say that, even if you were void of sense and understanding, yet still you ought at least to follow universal consent: and not make more of the perverse view of a few wicked men than of the faith of all the Churches: which as it was established by Christ, and handed down by the apostles ought to be regarded as nothing but the voice of the authority of God, which is certainly in possession of the voice and mind of God." *Incarnation of the Lord, 6:5 (c.A.D. 429/430).*

The Church: "As you have been brought up in the Catholic faith, do that which you would do for a wrong belief. Hold fast to the teaching of your parents. Hold fast the faith of the Church." *Incarnation of the Lord, 6:5 (c.A.D. 429/430).*

Baptism: "hold fast the truth of the Creed: hold fast the salvation of baptism." *Incarnation of the Lord, 6:5 (c.A.D. 429/430).*

John Chrysostom

Scripture: "Wherefore I exhort and entreat you all, disregard what this and that man thinks about these things, and inquire from the Scriptures all these things; and having learned what are the true riches, let us pursue after them that we may obtain also eternal good things…" *On 2nd Corinthians, Homily 13 (A.D. 392).*

Tradition: "So then, brethren, stand fast, and hold to the traditions which you were taught, whether by word, or by Epistle of ours.' Hence it is manifest, that they did not deliver all things by Epistle, but many things also unwritten, and in like manner both the one and the other are worthy of credit. Therefore let us think the tradition of the Church also worthy of credit. It is a tradition, seek no farther." *On 2nd Thessalonians, Homily 4:2 (inter A.D. 398-404).*

The Church: "Do not hold aloof from the Church; for nothing is stronger than the Church. The Church is your hope, your salvation, your refuge. It is higher than the heaven, it is wider than the earth. It never waxes old, but is always in full vigor." *Eutropius,2:6 (A.D. 399).*

Apostolic Succession: "To the fellow-Bishops and Deacons." What is this? Were there several Bishops of one city? Certainly not; but he called the Presbyters so. For then they still interchanged the titles, and the Bishop was called a Deacon. For this cause in writing to Timothy, he said, 'Fulfill thy ministry,' when he was a Bishop. For that he was a Bishop appears by his saying to him, 'Lay hands hastily on no man.' (1 Tim. v. 22.) And again, 'Which was given thee with the laying on of the hands of the Presbytery.' (1 Tim. iv. 14.) Yet Presbyters would not have laid hands on a Bishop. And again, in writing to Titus, he says, 'For this cause I left thee in Crete, that thou shouldest appoint elders in every city, as I gave thee charge. If any man is blameless, the husband of one wife' (Tit. i. 5, 6); which he says of the Bishop. And after saying this, he adds immediately, 'For the Bishop must be blameless, as God's steward, not self willed (Tit. i. 7).'" *Homilies on Phillipians, 1:1 (A.D. 404).*

Baptism: "For if no one can enter into the kingdom of Heaven except he be regenerate through water and the Spirit, and he who does not eat the flesh of the Lord and drink His blood is excluded from eternal life, and if all these things are accomplished only by means of those holy hands, I mean the hands of the priest, how will any one, without these, be able to escape the fire of hell, or to win those crowns which are reserved for the victorious? These verily are they who are entrusted with the pangs of spiritual travail and the birth which comes through baptism: by their means we put on Christ, and are buried with the Son of God, and become members of that blessed Head." *On the Priesthood, 3:5-6 (A.D. 387).*

Confession: "For if any one will consider how great a thing it is for one, being a man, and compassed with flesh and blood, to be enabled to draw nigh to that blessed and pure nature, he will then clearly see what great honor the grace of the Spirit has vouchsafed to priests...For they who inhabit the earth and make their abode there are entrusted with the administration of things which are in Heaven, and have received an authority which God has not given to angels or archangels...what priests do here below God ratifies above, and the Master confirms the sentence of his servants. For indeed what is it but all manner of heavenly authority which He has given them when He says, 'Whose sins you remit they are remitted, and whose sins you retain they are retained?' What authority could be greater than this? 'The Father has committed all judgment to the Son?' But I see it all put into the hands of these men by the Son." *The Priesthood, 3:5 (A.D. 387).*

The Eucharist: "Wherefore the consecrated priest ought to be as pure as if he were standing in the heavens themselves in the midst of this power...For when you see the Lord sacrificed, and laid upon the altar, and the priest standing and praying over the victim, and all the worshipers empurpled with that precious blood, can you then think that you are still among men and standing upon earth? Are you not, on the contrary, straightway translated into Heaven...He who sits on high with the Father is at that hour held in the hands of all." *On the Priesthood (A.D. 387).*

Anointing of the Sick: "For not only at the time of regeneration, but afterwards also, they have authority to forgive sins. 'Is any sick among you?' it is said, 'let him call for the elders of the Church and let them pray over him, anointing him with oil in the name of the Lord. And the prayer of faith shall save the sick, and the Lord will raise him up: and if he have committed sins they shall be forgiven him.'" *On the Priesthood, 3:6 (A.D. 386).*

The Virgin Mary: "And when he had taken her, 'he knew her not, till she had brought forth her first-born Son. He has here used the word 'till,' not that you should suspect that afterwards he did know her, but to inform you that before the birth the Virgin was wholly untouched by man." *Homily on Matthew, 5:5 (A.D. 370).*

The Saints: "Aye, I am well assured that his intercession [Chrysostom's deceased father] is of more avail now than was his instruction in former days, since he is closer to God, now that he has shaken off his bodily fetters, and freed his mind from the clay which obscured it, and holds intercourse naked with the nakedness of the prime and purest Mind; being promoted, if it be not rash to say so, to the rank and confidence of an angel." *On the Death of his Father, Oration 18:4 (A.D. 374).*

Purgatory: "Weep for the unbelievers; weep for those who differ in nowise from them, those who depart hence without the illumination, without the seal! They indeed deserve our wailing, they deserve our groans; they are outside the Palace, with the culprits, with the condemned: for, "Verily I say unto you, Except a man be born of water and the Spirit, he shall not enter into the kingdom of Heaven"...Let us weep for these; let us assist them according to our power; let us think of some assistance for them, small though it be, yet still let us assist them. How and in what way? By praying and entreating others to make prayers for them, by continually giving to the poor on their behalf." *Homily on Phillipians, 3 (ante A.D. 404).*

Justin Martyr

Scripture: "But when you hear the utterances of the prophets spoken as it were personally, you must not suppose that they are spoken by the inspired themselves, but by the Divine Word who moves them." *First Apology, 36 (inter A.D. 148-155).*

Tradition: "And that it was foreknown that these infamous things should be uttered against those who confessed Christ...and said that it was well to preserve the ancient customs, should be miserable, hear what was briefly said by Isaiah; it is this: 'Woe unto them that call sweet bitter, and bitter sweet.'" *First Apology, 49 (inter A.D. 148-155).*

<u>The Church:</u> "Such a thing as you may witness in the body: although the members are enumerated as many, all are called one, and are a body. For, indeed, a commonwealth and a church, though many individuals in number, are in fact as one, called and addressed by one appellation." *Dialogue with Trypho, 42 (A.D. 155).*

<u>Baptism:</u> "Since at our birth we were born without our own knowledge or choice, by our parents coming together, and were brought up in bad habits and wicked training; in order that we may not remain the children of necessity and of ignorance, but may become the children of choice and knowledge, and may obtain in the water the remission of sins formerly committed, there is pronounced over him who chooses to be born again, and has repented of his sins, the name of God the Father and Lord of the universe; he who leads to the laver the person that is to be washed calling him by this name alone...And this washing is called illumination, because they who learn these things are illuminated in their understandings. And in the name of Jesus Christ, who was crucified under Pontius Pilate, and in the name of the Holy Ghost, who through the prophets foretold all things about Jesus, he who is illuminated is washed." *First Apology, 61 (inter A.D. 148-155).*

<u>The Eucharist:</u> "This food we call the Eucharist, of which no one is allowed to partake except one who believes that the things we teach are true, and has received The Washing for forgiveness of sins and for rebirth, and who lives as Christ handed down to us. For we do not receive these things as common bread or common drink; but as Jesus Christ our Savior being incarnate by God's Word took Flesh and Blood for our

salvation, so also we have been taught that the food Consecrated by the Word of prayer which comes from Him, from which our flesh and blood are nourished by transformation, is the Flesh and Blood of that incarnate Jesus." *First Apology, 66 (inter A.D. 148-155).*

The Virgin Mary: "He became man by the Virgin, in order that the disobedience which proceeded from the serpent might receive its destruction in the same manner in which it derived its origin. For Eve, who was a virgin and undefiled, having conceived the word of the serpent, brought forth disobedience and death. But the Virgin Mary received faith and joy, when the angel Gabriel announced the good tidings to her that the Spirit of the Lord would come upon her, and the power of the Highest would overshadow her: wherefore also the Holy Thing begotten of her is the Son of God; and she replied, 'Be it unto me according to thy word.' And by her has He been born, to whom we have proved so many Scriptures refer, and by whom God destroys both the serpent and those angels and men who are like him; but works deliverance from death to those who repent of their wickedness and believe upon Him." *Dialogue with Trypho, 100 (A.D. 155).*

Lactantius

Scripture: "While some there have been, not learned enough in the heavenly writings, who, unable to reply to their opponents, when they objected that is was both impossible and unbecoming that God should be enclosed within a woman's womb...have been perverted from the right path, and have corrupted the heavenly writings, so far as to fashion for themselves a new doctrine without any root or firmness." *Divine Institutions, 4:30 (inter A.D. 304-310).*

Tradition/TheChurch: "The Catholic church is therefore the only one that retains the true worship. This is the source of truth; this is the dwelling-place of faith; this is the temple of God, which whosoever enters not, or from which whosoever departs, he is an alien from the hope of life, and eternal salvation." *Divine Institutions, 4:30 (inter A.D. 304-310).*

Baptism: "But you will perhaps say, What does the baptism of water contribute towards the worship of God? In the first place, because that which has pleased God is fulfilled. In the second place, because, when you are regenerated and born again of water and of God, the frailty of your former birth, which you have through men, is cut off, and so at length you shall be able to attain salvation; hut otherwise it is impossible. For thus has the true prophet testified to it with an oath: 'Verily I say to you, That unless a man is born again of water, he shall not enter into the kingdom of heaven.' Therefore make haste; for there is in these waters a certain power of mercy which was borne upon them at the beginning, and acknowledges those who are baptized under the name of the threefold sacrament, and rescues them from future punishments, presenting as a gift to God the souls that are consecrated by baptism." *Divine Institutions, 5:19 (inter A.D. 304-310).*

Purgatory: "The same divine fire, therefore, with one and the same force and power, will both burn the wicked and will form them again, and will replace as much as it shall consume of their bodies, and will supply itself with eternal nourishment: which the poets transferred to the vulture of Tityus. Thus, without any wasting of bodies, which regain their substance, it will only burn and affect them with a sense of pain. But when He shall have judged the righteous, He will also try them with fire. Then they whose sins shall exceed either in weight or in number, shall be scorched by the fire and burnt: but they whom full justice and maturity of virtue has imbued will not perceive that fire; for they have something of God in themselves which repels and rejects the violence of the flame." *Divine Institutions, 7:21 (inter A.D. 304-310).*

Origen

Scripture: "For he knows that all Scripture is the one perfect and harmonized instrument of God, which from different sounds gives forth one saving voice to those willing to learn." *Commentary on Matthew, 2 (post A.D. 244).*

Tradition: "... so, seeing there are many who think... they hold the opinions of Christ, and yet some of these think differently, from their predecessors, yet as the teaching of the Church, transmitted in orderly succession from the apostles, and remaining in the Churches to the present day, is still preserved, that alone is to be accepted as truth which differs in no respect from ecclesiastical and apostolic tradition." *On First Principles, 1 (c.A.D. 230).*

The Church: "And Peter, on whom the Church of Christ is built, against which the gates of hell shall not prevail..." *Commentary on John, 5:3 (A.D. 232).*

Apostolic Succession: "We are not to credit these men, nor go out from the first and the ecclesiastical tradition; nor to believe otherwise than as the churches of God have by succession transmitted to us." *Commentary on Matthew (post A.D. 244).*

Baptism: "The Church received from the Apostles the tradition of giving Baptism even to infants. For the Apostles, to whom were committed the secrets of divine mysteries, knew that there is in everyone the innate stains of sins, which must be washed away

through water and the Spirit." *Commentary on Romans,
5:9 (A.D. 244).*

Confession: "In addition to these there is also a
seventh [sacrament], albeit hard and laborious: the
remission of sins through penance...when he does not
shrink from declaring his sin to a priest of the Lord."
Homilies on Leviticus, 2:4 (A.D. 248).

The Eucharist: "Unless you eat the flesh of the Son
of Man, and drink His blood, you have no life in
you...' – then the flesh thus spoken of is that of the
Lamb that takes away the sin of the world...Again, we
eat the flesh of the Lamb, with bitter herbs, and
unleavened bread, when we repent of our sins and
grieve with sorrow which is according to God..."
Commentary on John, 10, 13 (A.D. 232).

Anointing of the Sick: "In this way [the sacrament]
there is fulfilled that too, which the Apostle James says:
'If then, there is anyone sick, let him call the presbyters
of the Church, and let them impose hands upon him,
anointing him with oil in the name of the Lord; and the
prayer of faith will save the sick man, and if he be in
sins, they shall be forgiven him.'" *Homily on Leviticus,
2:4 (A.D. 244)* .

The Virgin Mary: "This Virgin Mother of the Only-
begotten of God, is called Mary, worthy of God,
immaculate of the immaculate, one of the one." *Homily
1 (A.D. 244).*

Purgatory: "For if on the foundation of Christ you
have built not only gold and silver and precious stones
(1 Cor.,3); but also wood and hay and stubble, what do
you expect when the soul shall be separated from the
body? Would you enter into heaven with your wood
and hay and stubble and thus defile the kingdom of
God; or on account of these hindrances would you

remain without and receive no reward for your gold and silver and precious stones; neither is this just. It remains then that you be committed to the fire which will burn the light materials; for our God to those who can comprehend heavenly things is called a cleansing fire. But this fire consumes not the creature, but what the creature has himself built, wood, and hay and stubble. It is manifest that the fire destroys the wood of our transgressions and then returns to us the reward of our great works." *Homilies on Jeremiah (A.D. 244).*

Polycarp

Scripture/Tradition: "Let us then serve Him in fear, and with all reverence, even as He Himself has commanded us, and as the apostles, who preached the gospel unto us, and the prophets who proclaimed beforehand the coming of the Lord [have alike taught us]...Wherefore, forsaking the vanity of many, and their false doctrines, let us return to the word which has been handed down to us from the beginning." *Epistle to the Philippians, 6-7 (c.A.D. 135).*

The Church: "[A]ll the people wondered that there should be such a difference between the unbelievers and the elect, of whom this most admirable Polycarp was one, having in our own times been an apostolic and prophetic teacher, and bishop of the Catholic Church which is in Smyrna. For every word that went out of his mouth either has been or shall yet be accomplished." *Martyrdom of Polycarp, 16:2 (A.D. 155).*

Apostolic Succession: "Wherefore, it is needful to abstain from all these things, being subject to the presbyters and deacons, as unto God and Christ. The virgins must also walk in a blameless and pure conscience." *Epistle to the Philippians, 5 (c.A.D. 135).*

Baptism: "Polycarp declared, 'Eighty and six years have I served Him [from infancy], and He never did me injury: how then can I blaspheme my King and Savior?'" *Martyrdom of Polycarp, 9 (A.D. 155).*

The Saints: "For Him indeed, as being the Son of God, we adore; but the martyrs, as disciples and followers of the Lord, we worthily love on account of their extraordinary affection towards their own King and Master, of whom may we also be made companions and fellow disciples! The centurion then, seeing the strife excited by the Jews, placed the body in the midst of the fire, and consumed it. Accordingly, we afterwards took up his bones, as being more precious than the most exquisite jewels, and more purified than gold, and deposited them in a fitting place, whither, being gathered together, as opportunity is allowed us, with joy and rejoicing, the Lord shall grant us to celebrate the anniversary of his martyrdom, both in memory of those who have already finished their course, and for the exercising and preparation of those yet to walk in their steps." *Martyrdom of Polycarp 17,18 (A.D. 155).*

Tertullian

Scripture: "If it is nowhere written, then let it fear the woe which impends on all who add to or take away from the written word." *Against Hermogenes, 22* (inter A.D. 200-206).

Tradition: "It remains, then, that we demonstrate whether this doctrine of ours, of which we have now given the rule, has its origin in the Tradition of the apostles, and whether all other doctrines do not ipso facto proceed from falsehood. We hold communion with the apostolic churches because our doctrine is in no respect different from theirs. This is our witness of truth." *Against Heresies, 21 (c.A.D. 200).*

The Church: "the Catholic Church possesses one and the same faith throughout the whole world, as we have already said." *Against Heresies, 1:10,3 (A.D. 180).*

Apostolic Succession: "But if there be any (heresies) which are bold enough to plant themselves in the midst Of the apostolic age, that they may thereby seem to have been handed down by the apostles, because they existed in the time of the apostles, we can say: Let them produce the original records of their churches; let them unfold the roll of their bishops, running down in due succession from the beginning in such a manner, that bishop shall be able to show for his ordainer and predecessor some one of the apostles or of apostolic men,--a man, moreover, who continued steadfast with the apostles. ... Then let all the heresies, when challenged to these two tests by our apostolic church, offer their proof of how they deem themselves to be apostolic." *Against Heresies, 33 (A.D. 200).*

Baptism: "When, however, the prescript is laid down that 'without baptism, salvation is attainable by none' (chiefly on the ground of that declaration of the Lord, who says, 'Unless one be born of water, he hath not life')." *On Baptism, 12:1 (A.D. 203).*

Confession: "The Pontifex Maximus--that is, the bishop of bishops--issues an edict: 'I remit, to such as have discharged (the requirements of) repentance, the sins both of adultery and of fornication.'" *On Modesty, 1 (A.D. 220).*

The Eucharist: "These two baptisms He sent out from the wound in His pierced side, in order that they who believed in His blood might be bathed with the water; they who had been bathed in the water might likewise drink the blood." *On Baptism, xvi (A.D. 203).*

Confirmation: "After this, when we have issued from the font, we are thoroughly anointed with a blessed unction,--a practice derived from the old discipline, wherein on entering the priesthood, then were wont to be anointed with oil from a horn, ever since Aaron was anointed by Moses. Whence Aaron is called 'Christ,' from the 'chrism,' which is 'the unction'; which, when made spiritual, furnished an appropriate name to the Lord, because He was 'anointed' with the Spirit by God the Father; as written in the Acts:

'For truly they were gathered together in this city against Thy Holy Son whom Thou hast anointed.' Thus, too, in our case, the unction runs cornally, (on the body,) but profits spiritually; in the same way as the act of baptism itself too is carnal, in that we are plunged in water, but the effect spiritual, in that we are freed from sins." *On Baptism, 7 (A.D. 206).*

Anointing of the Sick: "For they are bold enough to teach, to dispute, to enact exorcisms, to undertake cures--it may be even to baptize." *Against Heresies,, 49 (A.D. 200).*

The Virgin Mary: "And indeed it was a virgin, about to marry once for all after her delivery, who gave birth to Christ, in order that each title of sanctity might be fulfilled in Christ's parentage, by means of a mother who was both virgin, and wife of one husband." *On Monogamy, 8 (A.D. 213).*

The Saints: "As often as the anniversary comes round, we make offerings for the dead as birthday honors." *The Crown, 3 (A.D. 211).*

Purgatory: "All souls, therefore; are shut up within Hades: do you admit this? It is true, whether you say yes or no: moreover, there are already experienced there punishments and consolations; and there you have a poor man and a rich...In short, inasmuch as we understand 'the prison' pointed out in the Gospel to be Hades, and as we also interpret 'the uttermost farthing' to mean the very smallest offence which has to be recompensed there before the resurrection, no one will hesitate to believe that the soul undergoes in Hades some compensatory discipline, without prejudice to the full process of the resurrection, when the recompense will be administered through the flesh besides." *A Treatise on the Soul, 58 (A.D. 210).*

Theodoret of Cyrus

Scripture: "By the grace of the spirit they dived into the depths of God-inspired scripture and both themselves perceived its mind, and made it plain to all that are willing to learn." *To the Monks, Epistle 151 (A.D. 431).*

Tradition: "So have I learned not only from the apostles and prophets but also from the interpreters of their writings, Ignatius, Eustathius, Athanasius, Basil, Gregory, John, and the rest of the lights of the world; and before these from the holy Fathers in council at Nicea, whose confession of the faith I preserve in its integrity, like an ancestral inheritance, styling corrupt and enemies of the truth all who dare to transgress its decrees." *To Florentius, Epistle 89 (A.D. 449).*

The Church: "I hope then that your piety will deign, if there really are any, though I cannot believe it, who disobey the apostolic doctrines to close their mouths, to rebuke them as the laws of the Church require, and teach them to follow the footsteps of the holy Fathers and preserve undefiled the faith laid down at Nicea in Bithynia by the holy and blessed Fathers, as summing up the teaching of Evangelists and Apostles." *To the Bishops of Cicilia, Epistle 84 (ante A.D. 446).*

The Eucharist: "Eran.--You have opportunely introduced the subject of the divine mysteries for from it I shall be able to show you the change of the Lord's body into another nature. Answer now to my questions.
Orth.--I will answer.
Eran.--What do you call the gift which is offered before the priestly invocation?
Orth.--It were wrong to say openly; perhaps some uninitiated are present.
Eran.--Let your answer be put enigmatically.
Orth.--Food of grain of such a sort.
Eran.--And how name we the other symbol?
Orth.--This name too is common, signifying species of drink.
Eran.--And after the consecration how do you name these?
Orth.--Christ's body and Christ's blood.
Eran.--And do yon believe that you partake of Christ's body and blood?
Orth.--I do." *Eranistes, 2 (A.D. 451).*

The Saints: "The noble souls of the triumphant are sauntering around heaven, dancing in the choruses of the bodiless; and not one tomb for each conceals their bodies, but cities and villages divide them up and call them healers and preservers of souls and bodies, and venerate them a guardians and protectors of cities; and when they intervene as ambassadors before the Master of the universe the divine gifts are obtained through them; and though the body has been divided, its grace has continued undivided. And that little particle and smallest relic has the same power as the absolutely and utterly undivided martyr." *The Cure of Pagan Maladies, 8:54 (A.D. 449).*

Theophilus of Antioch

Scripture: "It would be acting according to demonic inspiration to follow the thinking of the human mind and to think there could be anything divine apart from the authority of the Scriptures." *Pascal Letter of 401 (A.D. 181).*

Tradition/The Church: "And as in the sea there are islands, some of the habitable, and well-watered, and fruitful, with havens and harbors in which the storm-tossed may find refuge – so God has given to the world which is driven and tempest-tossed by sins, assembles – we mean holy churches – in which survive the doctrines of the truth, as in the island-habors of good anchorage; and into these run those who desire to be saved, being lovers of the truth, and wishing to escape the wrath and judgment of God." *To Autolycus, 2:14 (c.A.D. 181).*

Baptism: "Moreover, the things proceeding from the waters were blessed by God, that this also might be a sign of men's being destined to receive repentance and remission of sins, through the water and laver of regeneration,--as many as come to the truth, and are born again, and receive blessing from God." *To Autolycus, 2:16 (A.D. 181).*

Confirmation: "And about your laughing at me and calling me 'Christian,' you know not what you are saying. First, because that which is anointed is sweet and serviceable, and far from contemptible. For what ship can be serviceable and seaworthy, unless it be first caulked [anointed]? Or what castle or house is beautiful and serviceable when it has not been anointed? And what man, when he enters into this life or into the gymnasium, is not anointed with oil? And what work has either ornament or beauty unless it be anointed and burnished? Then the air and all that is under heaven is in a certain sort anointed by light and spirit; and are you unwilling to be anointed with the oil of God? Wherefore we are called Christians on this account, because we are anointed with the oil of God." *To Autolycus, I:12 (A.D. 181)*

Vincent of Lerins

Scripture: "Since the canon of Scripture is complete, and sufficient of itself for everything, and more than sufficient, what need is there to join with it the authority of the Church's interpretation..." *Commonitory, 2:5 (c.A.D. 434).*

Tradition: "Therefore, it is very necessary, on account of so great intricacies of such various error, that the rule for the right understanding of the prophets and apostles should be framed in accordance with the standard of Ecclesiastical and Catholic interpretation." *Commonitory, 2:5 (c.A.D. 434).*

The Church: "This, I say, is what the Catholic Church, with the authority of a General Council: and, secondly, if some new question should arise on which no decision has been given, they should then have recourse to the opinions of the holy Fathers...this ought to be accounted the true and Catholic doctrine of the Church, without any doubt or scruple." *Commonitory, 29:77 (c.A.D. 434).*

Apostolic Succession: "Examples there are without number: but to be brief, we will take one, and that, in preference to others, from the Apostolic See, so that it may be clearer than day to every one with how great energy, with how great zeal, with how great earnestness, the blessed successors of the blessed apostles have constantly defended the integrity of the religion which they have once received." *Commonitory, 6:15 (A.D. 434).*

The Virgin Mary: "For by the singular gift of Him who is our Lord and God, and withal, her own son, she is to be confessed most truly and most blessedly--The mother of God 'Theotokos,'...because in her sacred womb was wrought that most sacred mystery whereby, on account of the singular and unique unity of Person, as the Word in flesh is flesh, so Man in God is God." *Commonitory, 15 (c.A.D. 434).*[226]

---

[226] The foregoing material was taken from the following resources: Pusey, Keble, and Newman, eds., Library of the Fathers of the Holy Catholic Church, (Oxford, 1838-1888); Migne, J.P., ed., Patrologia Latina Cursus Completus, 221 vols., (Paris: Vives, 1844-1855); Berington, Jos., Rev. and Kirk, John, Rev., The Faith of Catholics, 3 vols., (London: Dolman, 1846); Migne, J.P., ed., Patrologia Graeca Cursus Completus, 161 vols., (Paris: Vives, 1857-1866); Roberts, Alexander and Donaldson, James, eds., The Ante-Nicene Christian Library: Translations of the Fathers down to A.D. 325, (Edinburgh, 1866-72); Lindsay, Colin, The Evidence for the Papacy, (London: Longmans, 1870); Allnatt, Charles F. B. ed., Cathedra Petri – The Titles and Prerogatives of St. Peter, (London: Burns & Oates, 1879); Coxe, Cleveland A., ed., The Ante-Nicene Fathers: The Writings of the Fathers down to A.D. 325 (a reprint of the Edinburgh Series), (Buffalo and New York, 1884-86); Schaff, Philip and Wace, Henry, eds., A Select Library of Nicene and Post-Nicene Fathers of the Church, 14 vols., Series 1 and 2, (Buffalo and New York, 1886-1900); Hefele, Joseph Charles, History of the Councils of the Church, 5 vols., (Edinburgh: T&T Clark, 1896); Cayre, Fulbert, Manual of Patrology and History of Theology, 2 vols. (Paris: Society of St. John, 1936-1940), trans. by H. Howitt; Quasten, J. and Plumpe, J.C., eds., Ancient Christian Writers, (New York: Paulist, 1946 -); Schopp Ludwig and Defarri Roy J.,eds., The Fathers of the Church (Washington D.C.: CUAP:, 1948-); Quasten, Johannes, Patrology, 4 vols. (Westminster: Christian Classics, 1950-86); Tixeront, Joseph, A Handbook of Patrology (St. Louis: Herder, 1951), trans. by Raemers, S.A.; Corpus Christianorum, Series Latina, (Turnholti: Typographi Brepols Editores Pontificii, 1953 -); Bettenson, Henry, The Early Christian Fathers, (Oxford: OUP, 1956); Denzinger, Henry, The Sources of Catholic Dogma, (St. Louis: Herder, 1957), trans. by Deferrari Roy J.; Altaner, Berthold, Patrology (Freiburg: Herder, 1960), trans. by Graef, Hilda C.; Willis, John R., The Teachings of the Church, (Montreal: Palm, 1966);

Bettenson, Henry, Documents of the Christian Church, (Oxford: OUP, 1967); Hamell, Patrick, Handbook of Patrology (Staten Island: Alba House, 1968); Bettenson, Henry, The Later Christian Fathers, (Oxford: OUP, 1970); Jurgens, William A., The Faith of the Early Fathers, 3 vols. (Collegeville: Liturgical, 1970-1979); Pelikan, Jaroslav, The Emergence of Catholic Tradition (100 – 600), (Chicago: UCP, 1971); Jesuit Fathers of St. Mary's College, The Church Teaches (Rockford: TAN, 1973); Wiles, Maurice and Santer, Mark, Documents in the Early Christian Thought (Cambridge: CUP, 1975); Corpus Christianorum, Series Graeca (Turnholti: Typographi Brepols Editores Pontificii, 1977 -); Kelly, J.N.D., Early Christian Doctrines, (San Francisco: Harper, 1978); Danielou, Jean and Marou, Henri, The Christian Centuries – The First Six Hundred Years, vol. 1, (London: Paulist, 1964); Carroll, Warren H., The Founding of Christendom, (Front Royal: CCP, 1985); Barry, Coleman J., Readings in Church History, (Westminster: Christian Classics, 1985); Barrios, George A., The Fathers Speak (Crestwood: VSP, 1986); The Building of Christendom, (Front Royal: CCP, 1987); Stevenson, James, ed., A New Eusebius: Documents illustrating the history of the Church to AD 337, (London: SPCK, 1987); Stevenson, James, ed., Creeds, Councils and Controversies: Documents illustrating the history of the Church AD 337-461, (London: SPCK, 1989); Ferguson, Everett, Encyclopedia of Early Christianity (New York: Garland, 1990); Di Berardino, Angelo, Encyclopedia of the Early Church, vols. 1-2 (New York: Oxford UP, 1992); Harrison, Carol ed., Early Church Fathers, (London: Routledge, 1996 -); Rotelle, John E. ed., The Works of Augustine (A Translation for the 21st Century), (Hyde Park: New City Press, 1996 -).

Chapter 12

Summation

As we said in the Preface, the ultimate dividing line between Catholics and Protestants is authority. All of the other doctrinal, moral and disciplinary issues that divide Catholics and Protestants flow from this singular question. Did Jesus appoint one supreme shepherd (Peter and his successors) over His people, or many different shepherds? Did Jesus will us to be governed by a living teaching authority (the Church) or by a book (the Bible)? Did Jesus establish a visible Church with a hierarchy made up of a pope, bishops, priests and deacons, or is the Church simply an invisible body of believers loosely connected by their faith in the Scripture alone?

The gravity of the question of authority cannot be overemphasized. Why? Because the issue of authority is not just a quibble about words. It is not just a trivial disagreement between two camps of faithful Christians on different but parallel roads to salvation. It is not simply something about which Christians "can agree to disagree." Far from it. Rather, answers to these questions bear upon our eternal destiny. The right answer leads to eternal salvation, and the wrong answer leads to eternal damnation. St. Peter warns us that interpreting Scripture incorrectly leads to eternal destruction (2 Pet 3:16). Our Lord also says in no uncertain terms, "he that believeth not shall be condemned" (Mk 16:16). Hence, if *sola Scriptura* is a false doctrine, then those who follow it are on the road to condemnation.

The Scriptures prove this truth over and over again. One example previously alluded to suffices. In John's Gospel, chapter 6, Jesus emphatically declares: "Truly, truly, I say to you, unless you eat the flesh of the Son of man and drink his blood, you have no life in you" (Jn 6:53). For 2,000 years, the Catholic Church has interpreted these words literally, which form the basis of the Church's doctrine of the Eucharist (that the bread of the Holy Mass becomes the flesh of Jesus Christ through the miracle of transubstantiation). If the Catholic Church is wrong (and thus the Holy Ghost did not guide her for 20 millennia), then Catholics are committing idolatry by worshiping mere bread and are condemned. However, if the followers of *sola Scriptura* are wrong, then they "have no life" in them because they reject "the bread of life," and are condemned. There is no middle ground.

In today's age of ecumenism and interreligious dialogue, such "black-and-white" thinking is not popular. It is much more politically correct to say that Catholics and Protestants are common "brothers in Christ" and that Protestants only lack the "fullness of truth" which is found in the Catholic Church. Such erroneous ideas render the necessity of believing in the "One, Holy, Catholic and Apostolic Church" quite superfluous and unnecessary. It is also an egregious insult to God the Father who established the Church "with the blood of His own Son" (Acts 20:28). If Jesus Christ is the Savior of His Body (Eph 5:23), the Church, then one must be a member of the Church to be saved. It is that simple.

When a person is baptized, he becomes a member of the Catholic Church, the Mystical Body of Christ. As St. Paul teaches, there is only "one baptism" (Eph 4:4).

However, once that person reaches the age of reason, he must submit his intellect to the truths that God has revealed "through the Church" (see Eph 3:10). If the person willfully rejects a doctrine of the Church, that person sins against the Faith and severs himself from the Body of Christ.[227] Those who reject any part of the Catholic Faith reject the entire Faith and can no longer be called "Christian."[228] As Jesus said, if one refuses to listen even to the Church, he is outside of God's covenant family (see Mt 18:18). This is why the Church has faithfully proclaimed throughout the ages the dogma *extra ecclesiam nulla salus est* (outside the Church there is no salvation).[229] Whoever is saved, is saved by Jesus Christ through the Catholic Church.

---

[227] Such willful rejection of the Faith would not include those people who are invincibly ignorant of the necessity of being Catholic to save their souls. While it appears that most practicing Protestants and Orthodox willfully choose to remain outside the true Church (if not for doctrinal reasons, then because the Faith is too "demanding"), only God is the judge of invincible ignorance. This also does not mean all Catholics will be saved. If Catholics do not persevere in grace to their death, they too will be damned, and more harshly than those who did not know the truth (Lk 12:48; Heb 10:29; 2Pet 2:20).

[228] We might even say that Protestants and the Orthodox worship a false Christ because their "Christ" did not establish the Catholic Church which is the only ark of salvation.

[229] Athanasian Creed (c.400); Pope Pelagius, *Quod ad dilectionum ad episcopos schismaticos* (c.585); Pope St. Gregory the Great, *Moralia in Iob* (c.590); Pope Innocent III, *Apostolicae Sedis Primatus ad Iohannem* (1199); Fourth Lateran Council (1215); Pope Boniface VIII, *Unam Sanctam* (1302); Pope Eugene IV, *Cantate Domino* (1441); Pope Leo XII, *Ubi Primum* (1825); Pope Pius VIII, *Traditi Humilitati Nostrae* (1829); Pope Gregory XVI, *Summo Iugiter Studio* (1832); Bl. Pope Pius IX, *Singulari Quadam* (1854); *Quanto Conficiamur Moerore* (1863); and *Syllabus of Errors* (1864); Pope Leo XIII, *Annum Ingressi Sumus* (1902); Pope St. Pius X, *Jucunda Sane* (1904); *Catechism of Pope St. Pius X* (1903-1914); Pope Benedict XV, *Ad Beatissimi Apostolorum* (1914); Pope Pius XI, *Moralium Animos* (1928); Second Vatican Council, *Lumen Gentium* (1964).

In 1517, Luther ignited the Protestant revolt by accepting God and Jesus Christ, but rejecting the Church. In 1717, Freemasonry accepted God, but rejected Jesus Christ and the Church. In 1917, the year Our Lady came to Fatima, atheism (the chief error of Russia) rejected God, Jesus Christ and the Church. *Nota bene*: This progression of error was borne from sinful man's exaltation of his own private judgment over the authority of God's Holy Catholic Church. Hence, these errors can be traced *directly to the Protestant "Reformation" and sola Scriptura.* Ironically, that means Protestant "Christianity" was the catalyst for the eventual *rejection* of Jesus Christ and the origin of the pervasive apostasy that plagues the world today. While Luther declared that destroying the Mass would destroy the Church, he didn't realize that removing the Church would ultimately result in the removal from society of Jesus Christ Himself.

All people are obliged to embrace the truth once they have been presented with it, no matter what the cost. In this book, we have presented the truth about Scripture and Tradition. We have demonstrated that neither Jesus, nor the apostles, nor the early Church Fathers taught *sola Scriptura*. We have seen how Scripture itself teaches us to follow Tradition and the Church and not Scripture alone. We have examined the historical facts, and used our own God-given reason and logic. For example, we learned how an effect can never be greater than its cause, which means if the canon of Scripture is infallible (effect), the Church who determined it must also be infallible (cause). This also demonstrates the falsity of *sola Scriptura*, because the canon is an infallible truth that is necessary for our salvation but was determined by an authority *outside* of Scripture. Even Luther admitted that this authority is the Roman Catholic Church. Based on the evidence presented in this book, we have proven that *sola Scriptura* is a false doctrine.

Of course, the goal of this book is not to win arguments, but rather to win souls for Jesus Christ by bringing them into His Church. The primary way to do that is through deeds and not words. However, for those who believe that "being a good person" is all we need to do to be saved, remember what St. Paul teaches: we can give away all our goods to the poor, and even deliver our bodies to be burned, but if we have not charity, it profits us nothing (1Cor 13:3). Charity – along with faith and hope – is graciously infused into our souls by God through the sacrament of baptism, and maintained and increased through the other six sacraments of the Catholic Church (see Rom 5:5; Titus 3:5-7). Hence, salvation is not simply attained by "living a good life" and "believing on Jesus," as many Protestants profess. It is about living and dying in a state of grace. The reality is that we cannot have true, supernatural faith in Christ or perform good works worthy of salvation without this infused grace. God grants us this grace through Christ's Mystical Body, the Catholic Church.

Many converts have "read" themselves into the Catholic Church by studying apologetical and historical arguments during their investigative journey (moved, of course, by God's grace). I hope this simple book can be such an instrument, providing information worthy of the reader's consideration and further investigation. If through this book only one soul is moved to embrace the Church, it was infinitely worth writing. If that is you, please share this book with others. If that is not you, don't stop here, but continue your research. God calls all men to the knowledge of His truth (1Tim 2:4), and since the truth is one, the Church is one. Only the Catholic Church both claims and proves to be the one true Church of Christ. Grace be with you all (Titus 3:15).

Selected Bibliography

Barrett, David B., Kurian, George T. and Johnson, Todd M. *The World Christian Encyclopedia*. Oxford University Press 2001 edition.

Catechism of the Catholic Church. United States Catholic Conference, Libera Editrice Vaticana, 1994.

Clark, Francis. *Eucharistic Sacrifice and the Reformation* Westminster, MD: Newman Press, 1960.

Codex Iuris Canonici (1983 Code of Canon Law), Latin-English Edition. Washington: Canon Law Society of America, 1999

Collins, Raymond F. *Introduction to the New Testament*. Garden City, NY: Doubleday & Company, Inc, 1983.

Graham, Henry G. *Where We Got the Bible*. San Diego, CA: Catholic Answers, 1997; original edition St. Louis, Mo: B. Herder Book Company, 1911.

Grisar, Hartmann. *Martin Luther: His Life and Work*. Westminster, MD: Newman Press, 1961.

Holy Bible, Douay-Rheims Version. Rockford, IL: TAN Books and Publishers, Inc., 2000.

Holy Bible, Revised Standard Version – Catholic Edition. San Francisco, CA: Ignatius Press, 1994.

Keating, Karl. *Catholicism and Fundamentalism*. San Francisco, CA: Ignatius Press, 1988.

Luther, Martin. *Luther's Works*. ed. and trans. Jaroslav Pelikan, et. al. St. Louis, MO: Concordia Publishing House (vols. 1-30); Philadelphia, PA: Fortress Press (vols. 31-55), 1955-1979.

Metzger, Bruce M. *The Text of the New Testament: Its Transmission, Corruption and Restoration*. Oxford University Press, 1992.

Michuta, Gary. *Why Catholic Bibles Are Bigger*. Port Huron, MI: Grotto Press, 2007.

Newman, John Henry. *On the Inspiration of Scripture*, eds. J. Derek Holmes and Robert Murray. Washington: Corpus Books, 1967.

O'Brien, John A. *The Faith of Millions*. Huntington, IN: Our Sunday Visitor, 1963,1974).

Peters, Joel. *Sola Scriptura? 21 Reasons to Reject Sola Scriptura* (Rockford, IL: TAN Books and Publishers, 1999.

Salza, John. *The Biblical Basis for the Catholic Faith*. Huntington, IN: Our Sunday Visitor, 2005.

Salza, John. *The Biblical Basis for the Papacy*. Huntington, IN: Our Sunday Visitor, 2007.

Salza, John. *The Biblical Basis for the Eucharist*. Huntington, IN: Our Sunday Visitor, 2008.

Sungenis, Robert. *The Catholic Apologetics Study Bible, Vol. I, The Gospel According to Matthew*. Goleta, CA: Queenship Publishing, 2003.

Sungenis, Robert. *Not By Scripture Alone*. Goleta, CA: Queenship Publishing, 1997.

Vine, W.E. *Vine's Expository Dictionary of New Testament Words*. Mclean, VA: McDonald Publishing House, nd.

About the Author

John Salza is an attorney and renowned Catholic apologist, author and speaker. Mr. Salza is the creator of ScriptureCatholic.com, one of the most popular apologetics sites on the Internet. ScriptureCatholic.com is a veritable library of over 2,000 Scripture citations and over 800 quotes from the early Church Fathers that explain and defend the Catholic Faith. The site also includes a popular Q&A section and other helpful resources.

Mr. Salza is the author of the following books by Our Sunday Visitor: *The Biblical Basis for the Catholic Faith*; *The Biblical Basis for the Papacy*; *The Biblical Basis for the Eucharist*; and, *Masonry Unmasked: An Insider Reveals the Secrets of the Lodge*. He is also the author of *Why Catholics Cannot Be Masons* and *The Mystery of Predestination – According to Scripture, the Church and St. Thomas Aquinas* (TAN Books) and *The Biblical Basis for Purgatory* (St. Benedict Press) as well as the booklet *Honor Your Mother, Defend Your Queen: A Marian Treasury* (Relevant Radio). Mr. Salza is also a columnist for *The Remnant Newspaper*, *Catholic Family News*, and serves as President of Apologetics for the American Catholic Lawyers Association.

John Salza is a frequent guest and host on Catholic radio including Searching the Word, The Drew Mariani Show, Kresta in the Afternoon and The Voice of Catholic Radio. Mr. Salza has an apologetics feature on Relevant Radio called "Relevant Answers" which runs six times a day, seven days a week. He also has a daily apologetics spot on the Eternal Word Television Network's (EWTN) Global Catholic radio program called "Catholic Q&A." Mr. Salza has appeared numerous times on EWTN to discuss a variety of apologetics topics.